THIS TIME
WE WIN
REVISITING THE TET OFFENSIVE

James S. Robbins

Encounter Books ℯ New York • London

Some parts of this book were adapted in whole or part from previously published essays by the author appearing in National Review Online, including, inter alia, "Why Baghdad Fell," Apr. 14, 2003; "Baghdad Tet: How the Bad Guys Can Win," Mar. 15, 2006; "Hue, Again (and Again)," June 21, 2006; "Anchorman: The Legend of Walter Cronkite," July 27, 2006; "Civil War in Iraq?" Nov. 30, 2006; "Inventing Atrocities," Aug. 10, 2007; "Tet +40," Jan. 31, 2008.

First American edition published in 2010 by Encounter Books, an activity of Encounter for Culture and Education, Inc., a nonprofit, tax exempt corporation. Encounter Books website address: www.encounterbooks.com

Manufactured in the United States and printed on acid-free paper. The paper used in this publication meets the minimum requirements of ANSI/NISO Z39.48 1992 (R 1997) (*Permanence of Paper*).

FIRST AMERICAN EDITION

LIBRARY OF CONGRESS CATALOGING-IN-PUBLICATION DATA

Robbins, James S., 1962–
This time we win: revisiting the Tet Offensive/by James S. Robbins.
p. cm.
Includes bibliographical references and index.
ISBN-13: 978–1–59403–229–5 (hardcover: alk. paper)
ISBN-10: 1–59403–229–7 (hardcover : alk. paper) 1. Tet Offensive, 1968. I. Title.
DS557.8.T4R63 2010
959.704'342—dc22
2009049374

10 9 8 7 6 5 4 3 2 1

to

E.L.R.

CONTENTS

CONTENTS

I.

INTRODUCTION

Most of what people hear about the Tet Offensive is wrong. The 1968 battle during the Vietnam conflict is billed as the moment when public support for the war effort, already rocky, dropped out. Allied forces quickly won the battle, but news reports exaggerated the scale of the attacks and the destruction they wrought, generating a sense that the contest had ended in a draw at best. Antiwar sentiment surged, and a harried President Lyndon Johnson bowed to public pressure and chose not to run for re-election. The battle marked the dividing line between gradual progress toward an ill-defined victory and

You had to see the low walls of enemy dead stacked like cordwood outside that ring of armor to understand our bewilderment when we read that we had been defeated.

—COLONEL MICHAEL D. MAHLER, 3/5TH CAVALRY, VIETNAM 1967–68

slow descent to a humiliating defeat. At least this is the received wisdom of Tet.

It is now commonly understood that Tet was a U.S. military victory but a political defeat. Yet at the time the battle was widely considered an American defeat in both respects. The enemy attacks were seen as largely symbolic, in which success was measured not by seizing and holding square miles of territory but commanding column inches of newsprint and minutes of television air time. The fact that the enemy was swiftly defeated on the ground was immaterial; that it could mount an attack at all was considered a military triumph. This impression was promoted by the press, antiwar activists, North Vietnamese propagandists, and President Lyndon Johnson's domestic political opponents.

Many still believe that the enemy intentionally staged a symbolic attack in order to "send a message," to gain advantage in negotiations, or "to get the Americans to the bargaining table." That perspective diminishes the magnitude of the Communist defeat by defining North Vietnamese objectives down to what they achieved. But Tet was not an attempt by the North Vietnamese and Viet Cong simply to send a message. It was a last-ditch, desperation assault seeking a victory they saw slowly but surely slipping away. The North Vietnamese sought to foment a general uprising of the South Vietnamese people, to overthrow the Saigon government and force a Communist triumph. But despite frantic attacks by Viet Cong guerrillas and North Vietnamese regulars, the hoped-for popular uprising did not take place, and after a few days' fighting the majority of the Communist forces were driven off or destroyed. It was a historic, catastrophic failure.

Decades after the disastrous offensive, Tet continues to shape perceptions of American conflicts. Tet has become more than a battle; it is a legacy, a legend, a continually replicating story line. It has become a powerful symbol divorced from its reality. The Tet narrative is fixed deep in the historical memory of those old enough to remember it, of those slightly younger who experienced its echoes, and especially of the generations who received the version of events rendered by historians and reporters after the fall of

South Vietnam in 1975, when the arrival of defeat affirmed their long-standing belief in its inevitability.

Tet is kept alive by the pervasive use of analogy in public discourse, not as an analytical framework to better understand or contextualize events but as a form of shorthand used to brand those events for media consumption. Such analogies are exercises in perception management, whether or not they have anything to do with the course and conduct of the insurgency or terrorist threat in question. The Tet story line is always lurking when U.S. forces are engaged against weak, unconventional enemies that lash out under limited and exceptional circumstances and briefly capture the attention of the media. Tet is then refought in these new guises, amplified in the media/political echo chamber. The battle is a handy framework for revisiting familiar themes—intelligence failure, war crimes, terrorism, troop surges, leadership breakdown, and media bias, among others.

There is a tendency in some quarters to give an "A for effort" to any collection of terrorists, insurgents, guerrillas, or other thugs who momentarily shock public perception through sudden, unanticipated acts of violence, regardless of whether they achieve any significant objectives. Tet has become the standard an enemy has to meet in order to achieve victory, not actually winning, not prevailing on the battlefield, but seeming to, or in some cases simply trying to. It is a self-imposed asymmetric disadvantage that is difficult to overcome. More important, it is a standing invitation to our enemies to seek low-cost, dramatic, and violent means of achieving high-impact strategic effects.

America's humiliation in the Vietnam War has inspired contemporary terrorists and insurgents of many stripes. The current crop of terrorists well understands the Tet dynamic. Osama bin Laden has long known that the United States cannot be defeated in a stand-up, symmetrical, conventional struggle. In 1996 he wrote,

> due to the imbalance of power between our armed forces
> and the enemy forces, a suitable means of fighting must be

adopted, e.g. using fast-moving light forces that work under complete secrecy. In other word to initiate a guerrilla war, in which the sons of the [Muslim] nation, and not the military forces, take part. And as you know, it is wise, in the present circumstances, for the armed military forces not to be engaged in conventional fighting with the forces of the crusader enemy.[1]

Bin Laden and other terrorists have routinely mentioned Vietnam as a model for the type of victory they are seeking, a debilitating blow to the American will that results in demoralization at home and withdrawal of the troops abroad. Central to al Qaeda's assessment of the United States is that our country cannot tolerate a long-term struggle, and can be defeated by striking at the national morale. Prussian military theorist Karl von Clausewitz posited a "trinity" essential for the successful prosecution of war, requiring synchronization with three necessary elements—the fighting forces, the political leadership, and the national will.[2] The terrorists realize they cannot defeat our military or sway the political leadership directly, so they seek to strike at our critical vulnerability, our national commitment to continue to prosecute the struggle. In a February 2003 message bin Laden stated,

We can conclude that America is a superpower, with enormous military strength and vast economic power, but that all this is built on foundations of straw. So it is possible to target those foundations and focus on their weakest points which, even if you strike only one-tenth of them, then the whole edifice will totter and sway, and relinquish its unjust leadership of the world.[3]

Or as he said in a November 2001 message, as al Qaeda and the Taliban were under siege in Afghanistan, "the American people had risen against their government's war in Vietnam. They must do the same today."[4]

The terrorists believe that short, sharp engagements will puncture the American will and cause the United States to lose its determination to fight. They drew this lesson not only from Tet but also from Beirut in 1983, after the Marine barracks bombing and other terror attacks, and from Somalia in October 1993, after the downing of two U.S. MH-60 Blackhawk helicopters and the death of 18 U.S. Army Rangers. In his March 20, 1997, interview with Peter Arnett, whose 1968 reporting from Saigon and elsewhere played a critical role in shaping public perceptions of Tet, bin Laden discussed his view of the American lack of resolve in the face of armed resistance. Al Qaeda fighters, he said,

> participated with their brothers in Somalia against the
> American occupation troops and killed large numbers of
> them. . . . After a little resistance, the American troops left
> after achieving nothing. They left after claiming that they were
> the largest power on earth. They left after some resistance
> from powerless, poor, unarmed people whose only weapon is
> the belief in Allah the Almighty. . . . If the U.S. still thinks and
> brags that it still has this kind of power even after all these suc-
> cessive defeats in Vietnam, Beirut, Aden, and Somalia, then let
> them go back to those who are awaiting its return.[5]

Terrorists and insurgents view America's national will as an Achilles heel, and they seek to replicate the conditions that have allowed small, weak forces to defeat the most powerful nation in human history. Vietnam in particular has inspired a generation of terrorists. In a July 9, 2005, letter to al Qaeda in Iraq leader Abu Musab al Zarqawi, al Qaeda second in command Ayman al Zawahiri prompted him to note well "the aftermath of the collapse of American power in Vietnam—and how they ran and left their agents." In an al Jazeera interview in 2006, Hassan Nasrallah, leader of the Lebanese Hizbullah, noted the inspirational and instructive quality of the U.S. defeat in Vietnam, both to insurgent groups and to U.S. allies:

> I cannot forget the sight of the American forces leaving
> Vietnam in helicopters, which carried their officers and sol-
> diers. . . . This is the sight I anticipate in our region. . . . The
> Americans will gather their belongings and leave this

region. . . . They will leave the Middle East, and the Arab and Islamic worlds, like they left Vietnam. I advise all those who place their trust in the Americans to learn the lesson of Vietnam . . . and to know that when the Americans lose this war—and lose it they will, Allah willing—they will abandon them to their fate, just like they did to all those who placed their trust in them throughout history.[6]

The key to striking at this critical American vulnerability is to harness Tet-like narratives and replicate the conditions in the information domain that turned Tet from a North Vietnamese rout to a Communist victory. To win this way they must engage the media and U.S. domestic political opposition. Terrorists study the U.S. media and how it operates, as well as its importance to the type of war they seek to fight. Osama bin Laden wrote to Taliban leader Mullah Omar, "It is obvious that the media war in this century is one of the strongest methods; in fact, its share may reach 90 percent of the total preparation for battles."[7]

Reporters and opinion journalists, who seek to package stories using preexisting themes in order to give immediate (and potentially erroneous) context to events, are particularly susceptible to terrorist exploitation. In August 2006, Najd al Rawi of the Global Islamic Media Front published an essay entitled "The Global Media: A Work Paper for Invading the U.S. Media." Among the potential targets for terrorist information operations he lists "American forums . . . chat rooms, well-known American newspapers and magazines, American TV stations which have websites and electronic email addresses, and well-known American writers such as [Thomas] Friedman and [Francis] Fukuyama."

The terrorists understand how writers, editors, and producers generate story lines, and they seek to provide useful hooks and compelling visuals. One such attempt sought to engage the analogy of the assault on the U.S. embassy during Tet. In March 2006, Iraq's internal security forces broke up a plot to employ 421 al Qaeda fighters as guards controlling access to Baghdad's International, or "Green," Zone. In a scenario reminiscent of the Trojan Horse, the terrorists planned to storm the U.S. and British embassies, take hostages, and generally wreak havoc. They were "one bureaucrat's signature away" from implementing the plan when it was uncovered.[8]

A surprise attack by 400 fanatics inside the IZ, augmented by insurgents smuggled into the zone just prior to the assault, would have generated mayhem. Videos and photographs of the attack would have proliferated quickly over the Internet and through the traditional mass media. The coalition counterattack would have been immediate and overwhelming, and few of the enemy would have survived. Nevertheless, by the time the last of the insurgents were hunted down, the attack would have achieved its objective—not to defeat coalition forces, but to seize and hold the only ground the insurgents could hope to command, the attention of the global mass media.

One can imagine the news coverage of al Qaeda fighters in the American embassy. The story line would be irresistible—Tet Offensive, the Sequel. A surprise urban guerrilla assault on a key symbol of American power would immediately be cast as a replay of the January 31, 1968, Viet Cong attack on the U.S. embassy in Saigon. Then, 19 VC sappers penetrated the compound but failed to occupy the embassy proper. A sharp firefight ensued, and the Viet Cong forces were quickly overwhelmed. The effort was poorly planned, ineffectively executed, and quickly dispatched; however, early erroneous reports, first relayed by then Associated Press reporter Peter Arnett, among others, credited the VC with taking the first floor of the building. The story then grew in the telling. Moreover, while the attackers had been either killed or captured within hours of the assault, film of the attack ran and reran on network news programs, giving the impression of a much more significant action. Furthermore, the press and even the Administration quickly credited the enemy with having achieved a "psychological victory," even though the Communists had failed to come close to meeting their military objectives.

Even a minor direct assault on the Baghdad embassy would have been sufficient to engage the Tet analogy, particularly if the terrorists had coupled it with a media campaign that explicitly made the comparison. In 2006, given the softened public support for the war effort, an upcoming mid-term election, and a wounded White House, the political impact would have been far out of proportion to the military significance of the attack. Fortunately, the Iraqis were able to break up this plot before it was executed, but it nevertheless demonstrated that the terrorists have correctly diagnosed how to make their attacks strategically significant.

Not every such attempt succeeds even when the attack is carried out. Not all images and situations are replicable with the same impact, especially when the terrorists are being a little too obvious. For example, on April 5, 2006, the Shura Council of Mujahedin posted a Web video showing the charred remains of a U.S. helicopter pilot being dragged through some fields, in a transparent attempt to evoke similar imagery from Mogadishu in 1993 that caused disquiet in the United States and helped undercut the U.S. commitment to the ongoing Somalia mission. But the Shura Council video was not widely distributed and had no apparent impact.[9] On July 10, the same group tried again, releasing another video showing the desecrated bodies of Privates Thomas Lowell Tucker and Kristian Menchaca.[10] This video also provoked no great Western media response, and on September 22, 2006, the Shura Council released yet another video showing the same two soldiers being dragged behind a truck and then burned.[11] The video generated some press attention and was finally compared to Mogadishu, but the attempt did not have the intended impact.

The insurgent information war in Iraq was aided by the propensity of domestic critics of U.S. military efforts to invoke the Vietnam War whenever possible. It is an iron rule of politics that every conflict must be compared to Vietnam sooner or later, and anything that can prompt the analogy triggers a 1960s flashback. The size of the conflict, the global context, weapons, doctrine, force structure, domestic politics, terrain, motivation, and most other relevant points of comparison were different, but the key variable was the same—reporters, activists, and politicians looking for a story line, a hook, something to say when they have run out of substantive critiques. A "Vietnam" story is a form of analytical autopilot, a narrative that writes itself. Opponents of the Iraq war and its conduct awaited something to dub "Tet," to harness the same sense of stalemate and hopelessness. The opposition press sought the "Walter Cronkite Moment," the public epiphany by a respected opinion leader that would brand the effort as doomed to failure. These framing concepts and others shape public understanding of current events that have little to do with the Tet Offensive, but the paradigm is unavoidable, the analogy irresistible.

The Vietnamization of the Iraq war was immediate. Comparisons to Vietnam were not intended to lend clarity through examination of the two conflicts as case studies in counterinsurgency, but rather to couch the discussion in terms of inevitable defeat. Any mention of Vietnam by the Bush Administration in the context of Iraq was seized on as a tacit if not explicit admission that the conflict was unwinnable. This dynamic was frustrating to specialists seeking to understand the two conflicts as examples of unconventional warfare. Furthermore, policymakers were forced into awkward situations where they had to ignore the comparison publicly, and if they later noted that some similarities might exist, that observation alone was seized as an "admission" or "concession" that Vietnam was relevant. And because the Vietnam War is remembered by a large segment of the political class as pointless, immoral, and illegitimate, mere mention of Vietnam tends to delegitimize any conflict to which it is compared.

Policymakers and the fighting forces in Iraq were aware of the Tet analogy and the extra burdens it imposed on them. In June 2004, then Secretary of Defense Donald Rumsfeld noted that the Iraqi insurgents have "read about Tet and the fact that if they make a big enough splash—even though they get a lot of people killed and we pound them—they end up winning psychologically."[12] Over time, any dramatic acts of bloodshed in Iraq, any increase in casualties or other such events would spur talk of Vietnam in general and Tet in particular. Yet for all the Tet talk, there has not been anything remotely like it.

A series of bombings during Ramadan in October 2003 quickly engaged the media's Tet-response mechanism.[13] The impulse was fed by statements released by al Qaeda and bin Laden that invoked Vietnam. And the Vietnamization of the story line kicked into high gear when President Bush stated that the rash of attacks was a sign of desperation, which struck some as a kind of Johnson-era doublespeak.

The spring 2004 attacks in Fallujah also generated a great deal of Tet and Vietnam speculation. On March 31, Iraqi insurgents ambushed a convoy conducting food deliveries for a local contractor. Four armed American civilians were dragged from their vehicles, killed, and set afire. Their charred bodies were later suspended from a box-girder bridge over the Euphrates amid scenes of revelry. Coverage of the event shocked and angered Americans. In its scope, scale, casualties, or by any other metric, the attack bore no relation to Tet, but to some the comparison was irresistible, even those who should have known better. Arthur Schlesinger, Jr., historian and former Special Assistant to President John Kennedy, noted that "Fallujah has been compared to the Viet Cong's Tet offensive in 1968, which set in motion a process that drove President Lyndon B. Johnson from the White House."[14]

Operation Vigilant Resolve, the initial attempt to restore order to Fallujah, was hampered by this sort of negative commentary and press coverage and was halted before its objectives were reached. An analysis by the U.S. Army's National Ground Intelligence Center (NGIC) noted: "The outcome of a purely military contest in Fallujah was always a foregone conclusion—coalition victory. . . . But Fallujah was not simply a military action, it was a political and informational battle. . . . The effects of media coverage, enemy information operations and the fragility of the political environment conspired to force a halt to U.S. military operations." The report concluded that sensationalistic and slanted press accounts were "crucial to building political pressure to halt military operations."[15]

Operation Phantom Fury, the assault that reestablished control over Fallujah in November 2004, was likewise compared to Tet. "The belligerent trumpetings of the U.S. Marines bode ill for Al-Fallujah," journalist Patrick Cockburn wrote. "Sgt Major Carlton W. Kent, the senior enlisted Marine in Iraq, told troops that the battle would be no different from Iwo Jima. In an analogy the Pentagon may not relish, he recalled the Tet offensive in Vietnam in 1968 and added: 'This is another Hue city.'"[16] Sergeant Major

Kent was invoking Hue, like Iwo Jima, as a significant achievement and celebrated touchstone in Marine Corps history. But Mr. Cockburn was working from a different set of premises in which any allusion to Tet was pregnant with foreboding.

On June 24, 2004, al Qaeda detonated bombs in six Iraqi cities, killing over 100 people. The operation quickly drew the Tet tag. Commentator Morton Kondracke stated that "America's enemies are launching what they hope will be the Iraqi equivalent of the 1968 Tet offensive, hoping to undermine the June 30 handover of power to Iraqis." A French report noted that while it might not have the same scope as Tet, "like this famous precedent, it has goals that are more political than military. These simultaneous and coordinated attacks are aimed not so much at 'preventing the transfer of sovereignty' as showing, to the Iraqis above all, that what happens on 30 June will be devoid of meaning."[17] Yet the attacks did not delay the transfer of sovereignty, which took place two days early.

In June 2005, insurgents launched a massed assault on Baya'a, the largest police complex in Baghdad. The enemy attacked in human waves, supported by mortars, rocket launchers, and suicide car bombs used as a form of tactical fire support. However, in challenging the U.S. with conventional tactics, the enemy lost the advantages of guerrilla warfare, with which it was better acquainted and more adept. The attack was soundly repulsed, and many insurgents were killed. "The enemy spent weeks, maybe months planning this," Lieutenant Colonel David Funk, the U.S. infantry commander responsible for the area, noted. "They failed spectacularly." But Funk noted that even in defeat the enemy can benefit. "The media got Tet wrong and they're getting Iraq wrong. We are winning but people won't know that if all they are hearing about is death and violence."[18]

The Tet analogy took off in earnest late in the 2006 congressional campaign when President Bush seemed to give it credence. Thomas Friedman had written on October 18 in the *New York Times* that a recent uptick in violence in Iraq during Ramadan could be the "jihadist equivalent of the Tet offensive."[19] It was not a very good use of the analogy, even with the qualifier "jihadist equivalent," which is not setting the bar very high. President Bush was asked about Friedman's statement on ABC News's "This Week with George Stephanopoulos":

STEPHANOPOULOS: Tom Friedman wrote in the *New York Times* this morning that what we might be seeing now is the Iraqi equivalent of the Tet Offensive in Vietnam in 1968. Tony Snow this morning said, "He may be right."Do you agree? .

BUSH: He could be right. There's certainly a stepped-up level of violence, and we're heading into an election.

STEPHANOPOULOS: But what's your gut tell you?

BUSH: George, my gut tells me that they have all along been trying to inflict enough damage that we'd leave. And the leaders of al Qaeda have made that very clear. . . . They believe that if they can create enough chaos, the American people will grow sick and tired of the Iraqi effort and will cause our government to withdraw.[20]

Bush's analysis simply noted what the Iraqi insurgents and al Qaeda had been saying all along, that their primary means of achieving victory would be through creating a perception of success, not by actually winning. But the subsequent reaction from the press, the blogosphere, and the Democrats made it sound as though the President had declared unilateral surrender. Bush seemed to have affirmed the full validity of the Vietnam analogy, with its connotations of "quagmire" and defeat. When President Bush visited Vietnam in November 2006, the analogy was all the press seemed to want to discuss.

By that time, drawing parallels to Vietnam was hardly newsworthy, and in some respects the comparisons were apt, since most irregular or unconventional wars are to a degree similar. Nevertheless, while one can draw some parallels, in the most significant respects one cannot. There were no good Iraqi analogs to North Vietnam, China, or the Soviet Union, no thousands of uniformed enemy "regulars" with bases in-country, and no chance of general escalation to large-scale conventional—much less nuclear—warfare.[21]

Furthermore, small fluctuations in indiscriminate violence such as those that alarmed Mr. Freidman are not the equivalent

of Tet, which was a comprehensive plan to foment mass uprisings in South Vietnam leading to an overthrow of the government
as prelude to a conventional takeover. The planning and preparation for the Tet attacks took at least nine months. The offensive
was executed nearly simultaneously in cities and hamlets across
the country. The respective levels of violence are noteworthy:
there were 106 U.S. dead in Iraq in October 2006, and despite
Friedman's fears of a meltdown, the level of violence declined in
November, with 70 U.S. dead. The average number of U.S. troops
killed in Vietnam per month in 1968 was 1,382, and in February
1968, during Tet, the total was 2,255, the second highest monthly
total of the war.[22]

The insurgents in Iraq never demonstrated the operational
acumen of our enemies in Vietnam. But today's unconventional
adversaries do not need to mount comprehensive nationwide offensives to achieve strategic effects, because the North Vietnamese
already did the work for them decades ago. The most important
difference between Tet and any contemporary insurgent action
is that today's insurgents know what the North Vietnamese did
not—they do not have to win battles to achieve strategic victories.

The reaction to the President's October 2006 interview is a
case in point. The insurgents did not have to conduct a series
of coordinated major operations in order to reap substantial
rewards in the media; they needed only to create enough chaos
to harness the power of analogy and structure their violence in
such a way that its magnitude was amplified by others. As long
as there are journalists, pundits, experts, and politicians willing
to make the comparison to more significant battles of the past,
the insurgents will always have the opportunity to achieve victory
by association.

RESISTING THE ANALOGY

The Tet analogy is durable but not indestructible. It is possible
to fight back against this self-imposed asymmetric disadvantage and unlink the power of analogy from the terrorist arsenal.
Some have sought to discount the market in advance, to discuss

the phenomenon explicitly so that when the terrorists attempt to exploit it they find it is old news. For example, in February 2007 Senator John McCain stated, "A lot of us are also very concerned about the possibility of a, quote, 'Tet Offensive.' You know, some large-scale attack that could then switch American public opinion the way that the Tet Offensive did."[23] In June 2007, Frederick Kagan and William Kristol noted that "al Qaeda is clearly taking a page from the Viet Cong's book. The terrorists have been mounting a slow-motion Tet offensive of spectacular attacks on markets, bridges and mosques, knowing that the media report each such attack as an American defeat. The fact is that al Qaeda is steadily losing its grip in Iraq, and these attacks are alienating its erstwhile Iraqi supporters. But the terrorists are counting on sapping our will as the VC did, and persuading America to choose to lose a war it could win."[24] In July 2007, General David Petraeus suggested that Sunni extremists would try to "pull off a variety of sensational attacks and grab the headlines to create a 'mini-Tet,'" shortly before his high-profile testimony before Congress the following September.[25] In these cases Tet was invoked as a means of shaping perceptions before the fact, of getting ahead of the inevitable Tet-themed stories should such attacks have been launched. But the anticipated large-scale insurgent operation timed to disrupt the September 2007 testimony did not take place.

Tet continues to shape perceptions of war and standards for evaluating victory. The Tet story has been told many times, and even though it has been described well and in great detail, the myths of Tet remain a standing challenge to the conduct of America's unconventional wars. The purpose of this book is defense in depth—an answer to the myth and those who appeal to it. The book reviews the context of the Vietnam War, from both the allied (primarily U.S. and South Vietnamese) and Communist perspectives; the enemy plan, and what it hoped to achieve; U.S. perceptions of the enemy and knowledge of the coming attacks; the attacks themselves, particularly the often referenced assault on the U.S. embassy in Saigon, other attacks in Saigon and elsewhere in the country, and the battles of Hue and Khe Sanh; the story of General Nguyen Ngoc Loan and the famous photograph of him summarily executing Viet Cong assassin Bay Lop; the role of the media in shaping perceptions of the offensive; U.S. public opinion before and after Tet; and the political response to the offensive, which snatched defeat from the jaws of victory.

This book does not purport to be a comprehensive history of every aspect of the Tet Offensive, but it does explore key themes in light of the evolution of the Tet narrative in the decades since the events took place in 1968. This effort will not prevent Tet from remaining a rhetorical and symbolic tool used by the enemy or others, but it will supply some ready responses to those who seek to employ the analogy as a means of winning victories in the critical information domain. Tet remains a standing challenge to the conduct of war and is a continuing source of inspiration to our foes. America's enemies all want another Tet, but only we can give it to them. If we are not armed against the analogy, if we do not possess a clear understanding of the lessons learned from that experience, we will find ourselves reliving the Tet Offensive again and again.

II.

VIETNAM, THE LIMITED WAR

"The basic issue in Vietnam is this," John P. Roche wrote in 1968. "Can a free society fight a limited war?" Roche was a career academic, former head of Americans for Democratic Action, and self-described "old-fashioned liberal Cold Warrior" who served as special adviser to President Johnson in 1966–68.[1] Roche saw Vietnam as a test case for robust liberal internationalism in the face of Communist expansion. But he grappled with the paradox of the country fighting a war without being in a state of war; of having an enemy that desired to defeat us while we did not attempt to defeat him; of engaging in a conflict in which we did

> No country has ever profited from protracted warfare.
>
> —SUN TZU

not seek clear-cut victory but a negotiated, compromise peace. "It is very difficult to tell a young soldier," he continued, "'Go out there and fight, perhaps die, for a good bargaining position.'"[2]

The Tet Offensive can be understood only in the context of the limited war assumptions that the Johnson Administration accepted for the fight in Vietnam. The premises that pointed toward war limitation—fear of escalation, concern over Chinese intervention, casualty aversion, and cost control—were debatable, and not universally accepted, but they were basic elements in President Johnson's decision-making. And although the United States fought an explicitly limited war, the enemy did not. This introduced a fatal asymmetry in the conflict. In the long run it meant that the United States lost in Vietnam by choice; we chose not to do the things we needed to do in order to win. Tet proved the case.

THE STRATEGIC CONTEXT OF VIETNAM

The United States became involved in the Vietnam conflict gradually, responding to circumstances, not by design or as part of a long-term strategy. The simmering conflict in Indochina in the late 1950s was peripheral to larger Asian security issues, such as Taiwan, and was seen as a distraction from the primary U.S. military focus on NATO and the central front in Europe. However, over time Vietnam became a critical Cold War battlefront, and a test of President Kennedy's—and later Johnson's—Flexible Response strategy.

The military coup against South Vietnamese President Ngo Dinh Diem in November 1963 marked the beginning of the events that drew the United States ineluctably into large-scale conflict in Indochina. The Kennedy Administration had considered Diem something of a problem for some time, and the United States government, while not complicit in the coup, let the plotters know that America would not intervene to save its democratic ally. Shortly thereafter Diem was overthrown and murdered, and his elected government was dissolved. If nothing else this event placed a moral burden on the United States: we helped break South Vietnamese democracy; we were obligated to fix it.[3]

South Vietnam officially was declared a United States vital interest on August 7, 1964, in Congressional Joint Resolution 1145, "To promote the maintenance of international peace and security in southeast Asia," better known as the Tonkin Gulf Resolution. The resolution was written in the wake of attacks by North Vietnamese torpedo boats on the destroyers *U.S.S Maddox* and *U.S.S Turner Joy* in the Gulf of Tonkin on August 2.[4] Section Two stated, "The United States regards as vital to its national interest and to world peace the maintenance of international peace and security in southeast Asia," and would take "all necessary steps, including the use of armed force," to assist South Vietnam in the defense of its freedom. The resolution passed unanimously in the House and with two dissenters in the Senate. The Tonkin Gulf Resolution codified in law an interest that was sealed in blood within a year as U.S. combat forces began to arrive in South Vietnam and engage the enemy. After the commitment of American combat forces, the survival of South Vietnam became critical if for no other reason than U.S. prestige was at risk; once a country is engaged in a war, it is very important to win it.

U.S. LIMITED OBJECTIVES

Defining victory in a limited war is open to interpretation. Over time the Vietnam War became captive of several premises that, once they were accepted, directed the war's course with Euclidian precision. The United States placed restrictions on its conduct of the war—geographical, operational, and political—that prevented it from being fought in a way that would respond to Hanoi's aggression in a language the Communists would understand.

The United States had four strategic objectives in the war in Vietnam: contain the conventional threat from North Vietnam; pacify the countryside and defeat the Viet Cong; train and equip the Armed Forces of South Vietnam (AFSVN) to defend the country with minimal U.S. assistance; and promote political stability and democracy in South Vietnam.[5] Missing from this list is the objective of defeating North Vietnam or threatening the survival of the Communist regime in Hanoi. In fact, the United States explicitly and publicly ruled out regime change as a war objective, even though it was the primary focus of Hanoi's efforts in the South. This approach created an asymmetry that made successful conclusion of the conflict difficult. The U.S. conducted a limited war against an enemy with unlimited objectives.[6]

Johnson's approach was consistent with the global containment strategy, which sought to maintain the status quo in the free world until the Communist bloc sought peace, reformed from within, or imploded. In Vietnam the United States was fighting for a strategic stalemate. Washington defined victory not in terms of winning, but of not losing. Johnson stated this objective in a speech at Johns Hopkins on April 7, 1965, entitled "Peace Without Conquest." The United States, he said, sought to "convince the leaders of North Viet Nam—and all who seek to share their conquest—of a very simple fact: We will not be defeated. . . . Armed hostility is futile. Our resources are equal to any challenge. Because we fight for values and we fight for principles, rather than territory or colonies, our patience and our determination are unending." The President did not tell the North Vietnamese that they would be defeated, but that they could not win. He did not say he was seeking victory; he sought a draw. This stance gave the strategic initiative to the enemy; it would determine when the fighting ceased and it was given the opportunity to test whether American patience was as durable as the President claimed.[7]

Because the United States sought a victory that did not entail conquering the enemy or overthrowing its government, the conflict would necessarily end through negotiations. In his "Peace Without Conquest" address Johnson declared that the United States was prepared to engage in "unconditional discussions" at any time to settle the differences between the North and South. This was Johnson's policy throughout the war. The use of force in Vietnam was seen as a means of influencing the enemy's thinking, not forcing it to submit to Washington's will. As long as Hanoi was unwilling to come to the bargaining table, the U.S.

would demonstrate that there was a price to pay for continued resistance. However, resistance was itself part of Hanoi's negotiation strategy. As John Roche explained to President Johnson:

> Like an old Leninist, [Ho is] willing to negotiate whether
> you're bombing or not. . . . He wants to win. If he thought
> it would be useful to his cause he'd negotiate with you with
> bombs coming down his chimney. . . . He's waiting to throw in
> negotiations, negotiations as a weapons system. He's waiting
> to utilize it at the most vulnerable time in American politics,
> namely just before the election of 1968.[8]

The Communists did not oppose negotiations; they supported them the way rope supports a hanged man.[9] But they showed little inclination to bargain in the first years of U.S. military involvement in Vietnam. And the longer they resisted, the more impatient the United States became to see signs that they wanted to bargain. Over time the elusive objective of negotiation came to be perceived in the United States as an end in itself, rather than a means to reach a settlement of differences, or to set terms for surrender. This perception, of negotiating as an unqualified good, had a negative impact on the execution of U.S. strategy and shifted war objectives in a way that came into vivid focus in the wake of Tet.

FLEXIBLE RESPONSE

The United States pursued its limited ends in Vietnam with correspondingly limited means. President Kennedy's limited war paradigm was known as Flexible Response. It was a reaction to the Eisenhower Administration's Massive Retaliation doctrine, in which aggression of any kind anywhere was to be met with immediate, unrestrained force. This doctrine may have had the intended deterrent effect on Soviet military action against Western Europe, but over time it lost credibility and utility. It became clear that the United States was not going to use nuclear weapons to settle the many brushfire wars developing around the world in the 1950s, and the country showed little propensity for any other form of direct military intervention.

The collapse of the French and British empires after World War II prompted numerous power struggles in the newly independent countries, and the Communist bloc quickly took advantage of the upheavals. The Soviets referred to these struggles as Wars of National Liberation, and the Chinese called them People's Wars. Whatever the term, they were means whereby the Communist states could promote and underwrite revolutionary movements without courting U.S. nuclear retaliation. General Maxwell Taylor, who was skeptical of the Massive Retaliation doctrine, observed that Wars of National Liberation were "the form of aggression which the Communists in Hanoi, Peking and Moscow have all proclaimed as the favored technique of the future for the expansion of militant communism. The term 'war of national liberation' is merely Communist jargon for the use of terrorism and guerrilla warfare to subvert a non-Communist government while disguising the aggression as a civil revolt."[10]

These new challenges required new strategies and were the central national security issue for the Kennedy Administration. Kennedy's Flexible Response doctrine sought to meet Communist challenges with equivalent types and levels of force across the conflict spectrum. At the high end of the spectrum Kennedy undertook a nuclear buildup in pursuit of deterrence. At mid-level he maintained and began to modernize U.S. conventional forces, particularly in Europe. And in the realm of what came to be known as low-intensity conflict, the Kennedy Administration aggressively developed the tools and doctrine necessary to counter guerrillas and other unconventional threats. This emphasis included not only the use of Special Forces—the Green Berets became a particular favorite of the Kennedy Administration and especially of Robert Kennedy—but also development aid, the Peace Corps, USAID, political reform efforts, and intelligence support for countries threatened by Communist insurgencies. Flexible Response was a robust tool that gave the President a variety of credible options in pursuit of not only U.S. security and global stability but also the promotion of democratic development and the export of U.S. ideals. As such it was the centerpiece of liberal internationalism. John Roche observed, "Limited war was conceived of by liberals as *the liberal* alternative to massive retaliation and/or isolationism."[11]

AVOIDING NUCLEAR ESCALATION

The Flexible Response doctrine divided conflict into three neat categories—nuclear, conventional, and unconventional. The key, of course, was to be able to engage at the low end of the conflict scale without jumping up to higher ends; in other words, limited war had to stay limited. The Soviet nuclear arsenal had grown to the point where it could inflict tremendous damage on the United States, and some feared that the proxy brushfire wars in the developing world might accidentally bring about a general engagement leading to a thermonuclear exchange. The term "escalation" had taken up residence in the strategic vocabulary. Herman Kahn's 1965 work, *On Escalation,* was particularly alarming; his "escalation ladder" featured 44 steps, in which conventional warfare entered at step 12, and nuclear war was fought from step 21 upward, with 24 separate nuclear scenarios.[12]

Kahn saw escalation as a tool of statecraft that decision-makers could utilize to achieve rational wartime objectives, even while fighting limited nuclear conflict and without automatically bringing about a global thermonuclear engagement. But others viewed escalation as an unpredictable and unmanageable phenomenon, which if extended into the nuclear realm would lead to disastrous consequences. Decision-making under those circumstances would be essentially irrational and uncontrollable. President Kennedy noted, after the Cuban Missile Crisis, that "the essence of ultimate decision remains impenetrable to the observer—often, indeed, to the decider himself."[13]

The outbreak of the First World War became the subject of much study around the time of the Missile Crisis. It was the classic case of a small, relatively unimportant, peripheral crisis escalating beyond reason to become a ruinous global conflict costing millions of lives. As Bismarck had famously predicted, general war in

Europe was brought about by "some damned foolish thing in the Balkans."[14] Barbara Tuchman's Pulitzer Prize-winning account of the war's outbreak, *The Guns of August*, published earlier in 1962, became enormously popular. President Kennedy was deeply impressed by the book. He encouraged his Cabinet to read it, and it influenced his handling of the Cuban Missile Crisis. Thus somewhere in the background of the debate over the conduct of the Vietnam War loomed Austria's bombardment of Belgrade in July 1914. Those who counseled that the United States take an "all or nothing" approach in Southeast Asia, such as Army Chief of Staff Harold K. Johnson, had to come to grips with the possibility that "all" might lead the country, through some unpredictable and unwanted series of events, into a global nuclear conflagration. But there was no general agreement on this point; an opinion poll showed that by 1967 the American people were evenly divided over whether the war in Vietnam would eventually cause World War III (40%) or prevent it (41%).[15]

The strategists of the time concluded that the most effective way to prevent an escalatory spiral was to have clear, generally understood, and widely accepted firebreaks and conflict barriers, lines that would not be crossed. In the case of Vietnam, the literal line was the 17th parallel, the border between North and South marked by the ironically named "demilitarized zone," or DMZ. The United States unilaterally accepted the 17th parallel as the northward limit for military action on the ground, a limit never observed or accepted by the North vis-à-vis the South. The precedent that most influenced this decision was the Korean War.

NO MORE KOREAS

The Korean War presented a proximate historical case that strongly influenced Vietnam strategy. There was a peculiar symmetry between the two conflicts—an Asian state divided along a parallel, a Communist north bordering China and backed by the Soviet Union, and a war raging in the south against a U.S.-supported, Western-oriented developing country. Korea had been a costly and inconclusive struggle, one that the upper echelons of the U.S. military were not eager to repeat. Journalists dubbed the military leaders opposed to future limited land wars in Asia the "Never Again Club." Their thinking was very influential in the 1950s and helped prevent more vigorous moves by the United States to assist the French in their struggle against the Viet Minh, or to support the South Vietnamese government in the Diem period with anything beyond supplies and advisers.

Once the United States committed itself to fighting on the ground in Vietnam, the Korean War analogy still influenced strategic decision-making. The analogy held that if the U.S. took the war north across the DMZ, China would intervene militarily and the Korean War would be replayed. In the meantime (since October 16, 1964) China had become a nuclear power, and the Soviet nuclear arsenal was much larger and posed more of a threat than it had in the early 1950s. The U.S. would have found it difficult to threaten the use of nuclear weapons to deter China, as it had in 1953, without facing some form of response.[16] Secretary of State Dean Rusk summarized the prevailing view of China in 1967, calling the Vietnam War a test case for Asia's ability to survive with a semblance of freedom. "Within the next decade or two," he said, "there will be a billion Chinese on the mainland, armed with nuclear weapons, with no certainty about what their attitude toward the rest of Asia will be."[17] China was not to be provoked. Thus since the decision to cross the 49th parallel in the Korean War was seen as the root of Chinese intervention in 1950, in the Vietnam War the 17th parallel became sacrosanct as far as major ground operations were concerned.

The American public shared the opinion that Chinese involvement was to be expected—a Gallup poll of August 10, 1965, found that 78% of Americans thought Chinese intervention was likely should the U.S. "start winning" the war in Vietnam. But the public was willing to engage the enemy should this occur. A March 1966 survey showed that 73% supported continuing the fight if "Red China decides to send a great many troops."[18] This assumed of course that the Chinese would have been as eager to fight in Vietnam as they had been in Korea. In 1950 Mao had been encouraged by Stalin to intervene in the Korean conflict, a move he made against his best instincts. Mao believed that the best approach to unifying Korea under Communist rule was through conducting a guerrilla war in the south, not mounting a conventional conflict. But he followed Stalin's lead, and the Soviet leader rewarded him by allowing China to bear the brunt of the fighting while the Soviet Union provided only materiel and diplomatic support. The eventual armistice gave Communist China nothing more for its sacrifices than the same buffer zone they would have enjoyed had Mao's suggested long-term guerrilla war approach been undertaken. As John Roche observed, what American decision-makers did not understand was that "from the Chinese point of view the lesson [of Korea] was 'never fight a land war in Asia with the Americans' because they lost a million dead. What a debacle from [China's] point of view."[19]

Ironically, even given Chinese intervention in 1950, the Korean War was shorter than the war in Vietnam; the United States suffered only two thirds the casualties in Korea that it did in Vietnam (killed and wounded); and South Korea's freedom and independence were maintained. So, while from the perspective of 1964 replaying the Korean War in Vietnam looked like something to be avoided, by 1975 Korea stood as a model of success compared to the Vietnam tragedy.

In addition to the 17th parallel, the United States chose to limit the scope of the war by honoring the national borders of Laos and Cambodia, two countries that were officially neutral but were in fact central to the Communist war effort. Laos and Cambodia were critical sanctuaries and supply routes for the Communists, which they used throughout the war while giving lip service to the countries' neutral status under international law. The United States inexplicably accepted this fiction; as Harry Summers observed, "Neutrality was a myth we inflicted on ourselves."[20] By limiting the area in which the ground war was actively conducted, the U.S. ceded the Cambodian and Laotian sanctuaries and supply routes to the North.[21]

In effect the United States chose to fight the ground war in the South and to accept the disruptions to the South Vietnamese

26

people, government, and economy that entailed. This policy was stated explicitly in order to manage enemy and international perceptions that the war was limited. But in so doing the United States gave the North Vietnamese a geographic and psychological comfort zone. Large numbers of Communist troops were freed up for combat in the South who would have been reserved for defensive contingencies had the question of the scope of U.S. operations been in doubt.[22] General Bruce Palmer, Jr., commander of II Field Force, Vietnam, from March to July 1967 and Deputy Commander of the United States Army in Vietnam to June 1968, noted that had the U.S. even simply maintained the credible threat of amphibious landing in the North, thousands of troops would have been dedicated to coastal defense and denied to operations against Saigon. This perception could have been reinforced by maritime exercises, visible presence, and intelligence operations of the sort that kept German troops tied up around Calais in the spring of 1944 and away from the eventual site of the Overlord landings in Normandy.[23]

The United States could also have established a foothold north of the DMZ and in northeastern Laos to cut Communist supply lines and push the war zone out of the South, as Confederate General Robert E. Lee attempted to do with his invasions of the North in 1862 and 1863.[24] This would have prompted the enemy to focus its efforts on removing the lodgment, thereby giving the United States the benefits of fighting on the tactical defensive against a massed enemy, bringing to bear the full force of U.S. firepower. This strategy would have drawn North Vietnamese regulars out of their positions in the South, taking pressure off Saigon and allowing more progress in pacifying the countryside. The incursion would also have served as a standing threat of further action in the North, which itself would have forced Hanoi to tie down even greater numbers of men and resources, and would have become the enemy's chief preoccupation in terms of time and planning. The liberated zone could have been organized with a free North Vietnamese government, standing as a manifest political challenge to the Communist regime in Hanoi. Finally, seizing ground in the North would have served as a more effective bargaining chip for negotiations than simply trying to extract promises of good behavior without regime-threatening consequences.

Nevertheless, the United States chose not to bring the land war to the North, or even to allow Hanoi to wonder whether such a threat existed. Our enemy knew it was safe and acted accordingly. Commenting on the Korean War, Vice Admiral C. Turner Joy, who headed the United Nations Command delegation to the Korean Armistice Commission, noted that "the limitations imposed on allied military operations encouraged the adversary to keep fighting, weakened support for the war effort at home, and ultimately prolonged the conflict."[25] This was a lesson that had to be relearned in Vietnam, with grievous consequences.

JOHNSON, THE LIMITED LEADER

The greatest limit the United States faced in the conduct of the war in Vietnam was its Commander in Chief. President Johnson, though a successful politician, was not the type of war leader the conflict required. Johnson was skilled in the arts of deal-making and compromise, useful talents for the type of war he wanted to fight, but counterproductive faced with the enemy he was actually fighting.

In his January 8, 1964, State of the Union address President Johnson said, "It will not be a short or easy struggle, no single weapon or strategy will suffice, but we shall not rest until that war is won." He was referring to the War on Poverty. The most noted limit Johnson placed on the war was to keep Vietnam from interfering with his ambitious domestic political agenda. This included his civil rights initiatives, education reform, the War on Poverty, the new Medicare and Medicaid programs, funding for the arts, and the other Great Society programs.

A more important limit was Lyndon Johnson's lack of perspective regarding the enemy. Johnson's outlook on the nature of the conflict was reflected in the April 1965 "Peace Without Conquest" speech noted above. He offered a deal to Hanoi: if the Communists would end the conflict and allow the South to pursue its own course, the United States would embark on a billion dollar aid program to develop North Vietnam and the region generally. He promised education, medical, and food programs, a list reflecting most of the aspects of his 1965 domestic legislative agenda. For example, he noted that "the vast Mekong River can provide food and water and power on a scale to dwarf even our own TVA." Just as he would build a Great Society in the United States, he promised a Great Society for Southeast Asia. After the speech Johnson leaned over to one of his assistants and said, "Old Ho can't turn that down. Old Ho can't turn that down."[26]

But the Communist response was swift and definitive. Hanoi denounced the deal as a "bribe" that "conceals [America's] warlike acts." Radio Peking called the proposal "full of lies and deceptions." Moscow called it "noisy propaganda."[27] The Communists were unwilling to bend on their essential objective, the unification of Vietnam under Hanoi's rule. Any proposal rejecting that premise was dead on arrival.

Johnson never seemed to grasp the Communists' commitment to victory on their own terms. John Roche wrote a memo March 27, 1967, with his take on Ho's motivations. He later noted:

> I tried to explain in that memo that Ho Chi Minh was not a Mayor Daley who was waiting to be bought. Johnson didn't have an ideological bone in his body and he was convinced that everybody had a button. . . . Johnson kept saying, "What does he want? What does he want?", as if, you know, three post offices, a new municipal sewer system, or something like that would do it. I said, "He wants to win."

Ho Chi Minh was a committed revolutionary who had been fighting for a unified Communist Vietnam for almost five decades. His perspective on politics was fundamentally different from Johnson's. Ho could not be dealt with as a Chicago ward boss could be. He would never accept a deal unless it moved him closer to his ultimate and unquestioned objective. And like a good Leninist he would be willing to conclude a deal with the intention of breaking it at a more advantageous time, when the United States had shifted its attention elsewhere.

OSD VS. JCS

The United States was also limited by an institutional struggle within the Defense establishment. There was a perennial conflict between the Joint Chiefs of Staff and the Office of the Secretary of Defense over how to run the war. The latter claimed that the conflict was over the constitutionally mandated civilian control of the military; the former saw it as civilians seeking to direct and micromanage military operations in ways far beyond their expertise and the scope of constitutional mandates.[28]

The Joint Chiefs had desired from early in the conflict to move forcefully against North Vietnam. In 1965 President Johnson asked the Chiefs whether the United States could win in Vietnam. The chairman, General Earl G. "Bus" Wheeler, commissioned a staff study chaired by his assistant, Lieutenant General Andrew Goodpaster, USMA 1939, a decorated World War II veteran, adviser to President Eisenhower and Princeton Ph.D. The study recommended moving aggressively against the North with a blockade and bombing campaign and immediately building up troop strength in the South to 500,000. Goodpaster said that "the Joint Chiefs of Staff were very much in accord with the results of the study and it fit into their continued view that if we were to continue to be engaged there, we should use our forces with full effectiveness and not engage in the piecemeal and the tit for tat and other processes that didn't bring our full force to bear."[29]

But when the Chiefs briefed their plan to the President on November 10, 1965, Johnson lost his temper and in pure LBJ style unleashed a profanity-laced tirade at the senior military leaders. Marine Lieutenant General Charles G. Cooper, who at the time was a Major and aide to the Chief of Naval Operations, on hand to hold up the briefing map, related the scene. Johnson listened patiently to the briefing, then suddenly flew into a rage:

Discarding the calm, patient demeanor he had maintained throughout the meeting, [Johnson] whirled to face them and exploded. I almost dropped the map. He screamed obscenities, he cursed them personally, he ridiculed them for coming to his office with their "military advice." Noting that it was he who was carrying the weight of the free world on his shoulders, he called them filthy names He then accused them of trying to pass the buck for World War III to him. It was unnerving, degrading. He told them he was disgusted with their naïve approach toward him, that he was not going to let some military idiots talk him into World War III. It ended when he ordered them to "get the hell out of my office!"[30]

The Chiefs were humiliated, and the scene illustrates the President's intransigence about escalation. Johnson saw a direct connection between pressing the fight in Vietnam and bringing on global nuclear engagement. Ironically, Johnson eventually would raise the number of troops even above what the Chiefs had recommended based on the Goodpaster study, but he would fight the war on his terms. His fear of escalation reinforced his already strong control instincts, as illustrated by his acting as the "target officer" for air operations against the North, being unwilling to delegate even this limited authority outside of the White House.[31]

To fight the war his way, Johnson turned to Secretary of Defense Robert McNamara, one of the whiz kids, the "best and the brightest" who had come to Washington with the Kennedy Administration. McNamara had enjoyed a meteoric career rise in the 1950s at Ford Motor Company, and served as corporate president for a few months before his appointment in 1961. At age 44 he was the youngest Secretary of Defense up to that time, and he took over the department in an era when defense outlays comprised half of the total federal budget.

McNamara was famous, or infamous, for bringing modern corporate management practices and systems analysis to the Defense Department. Corporate executives may well be sound choices for peacetime management of the department, but

McNamara's systems approach proved to be inadequate for fighting a war. Management and leadership are distinct areas of expertise, requiring different knowledge and skill sets. McNamara was a skilled manager, but his leadership skills left something to be desired. The Defense Department was also populated by political appointees, intellectuals, party loyalists, or those who knew the right people, often lacking practical knowledge of military affairs. This made the conduct of war difficult both for the uniformed personnel and the civil servants who often had a much greater understanding of how to fight and win wars but who were frequently sidelined and overruled. General Thomas White, former Air Force Chief of Staff, noted in 1963, "In common with many other military men, active and retired, I am profoundly apprehensive of the pipe-smoking, tree-full-of-owls type of so-called 'defense intellectuals' who have been brought into the nation's capital."[32]

Applying systems analytical models to waging war produced a statistically driven approach to conflict that minimized human factors and glorified metrics. Game theory, which was a popular means of evaluating strategy at the nuclear level, given its limited variables and easy to discern dichotomies, was applied to all levels of warfare, regardless of their complexities. State Department official James C. Thompson, Jr. captured the abstract tone of post-Camelot war fighting:

> In quiet, air-conditioned, thick-carpeted rooms such terms as "systemic pressure," "armed reconnaissance," "targets of opportunity" and even "body count" seemed to breed a sort of games-theory detachment. . . . At a discussion of how heavy our bombing should be, and how extensive our strafing, an Assistant Secretary of State explained, "It seems to me that our orchestration should be mainly violins, but with periodic touches of brass."[33]

John Roche noted that "the problem with McNamara and Co. was that they never could distinguish between a war and a war game." . . . When you think you have absolutely mastered a war

32

game, you discover a war game is not a war; it is something quite different. It is like deciding you are going to go into buying up downtown Boston because you're an expert at Monopoly." Roche, who had been an Army Air Force Staff Sergeant in the Second World War, thought that one of the problems was that the senior civilians in the national security establishment had served as staff officers in the war, not as enlisted men or in combat. McNamara, for example, served in the Army Air Force Office of Statistical Control, where he analyzed the effectiveness of strategic bombing campaigns. Roche believed this type of experience colored his view of the nature of war. "If a guy, in say, an army unit in New Guinea, was in trouble and couldn't get an air strike," Roche said, "and managed to get out an emergency message that the radio was busted, McNamara's reply would be, 'Well, immediately order a new radio.'"[34]

General David Petraeus later wrote of this period, "The invasion of [the military's] domain in the early 1960s by what many perceived to be misguided amateurs and transient meddlers was resisted. As the decade went on, the military became increasingly frustrated by Secretary of Defense McNamara's 'obsession with getting control of the defense budget,' and by the micro-management of the war effort in general."[35] A December 1967 Harris survey showed that the public agreed with the assessment that the civilian leadership of the Department of Defense was hamstringing the military. Asked if "in Vietnam, the military has been handicapped by civilians who won't let them go all out," 65% agreed, 25% were not sure, and only 10% disagreed. And even in the heyday of public approval of the Administration's conduct of the war McNamara did not have strong public backing. In a survey in the winter of 1965–66, only 13% of the public rated his performance as a A, 14% as a B, 12% as a C, 12% as D or F, and 42% responded, "Don't know who McNamara is."[36]

GRADUALISM AND ATTRITION

The President's limits on the conduct of the war produced a two-part strategy known as "gradualism and attrition." Gradualism was the air component, in which strategic bombing was used to fine-tune the punishment meted out to the North, intended to be harsh enough to compel the regime to come to the bargaining table but not so severe as to topple it. Meanwhile, the ground strategy in the South would keep the threat manageable at low cost through attrition warfare and pacification.

The air campaign began in December 1964, when the United States initiated limited operations against the Laotian panhandle called Operation Barrel Roll. More extensive bombing soon followed. On February 6, 1965, the Viet Cong attacked a U.S. military compound at Pleiku in the Central Highlands, killing eight Americans, wounding 126, and destroying ten aircraft. This attack prompted President Johnson to launch a bombing campaign code-named Operation Rolling Thunder. Rolling Thunder was an experiment in coercive diplomacy that sought gradually to inflict greater and greater levels of punishment in an attempt to discover the enemy's breaking point. Periodic bombing pauses of different lengths were implemented to measure enemy responses. Targeting and other restrictions were put in place to prevent doing too much damage to the enemy or destabilizing the Hanoi regime. The bombing campaign was the perfect expression of McNamara's systems approach as applied to warfare, and it was no doubt rooted in his experiences as a bombing analyst in World War II. To McNamara, war was a matter of inputs and outputs. The inputs—violence—could be modulated to gauge the outputs—enemy reactions. To adherents of the McNamara school, warfare was a stimulus/response mechanism, measurable, controllable, and abstract.

The 37-day bombing pause in Operation Rolling Thunder that began on December 24, 1965, provides a case study in the conceptual limits of this approach. The pause was an attempt to show U.S. sincerity, to give the North an opportunity to reciprocate and de-escalate. This was McNamara's notion of a way to "send a message." Confident and secure in America's overwhelming power, the Pentagon's civilian leaders gave little credence to human factors, such as Hanoi's desire to win and the sacrifices the Communists would make to continue the struggle. To them the bombing

Enemy View of Pauses

pause was not seen as an act of generosity or magnanimity; it was viewed as an example of American weakness. And it had no apparent effect. North Vietnamese Prime Minister Pham Van Dong denounced the pause as a "campaign of lies."[37]

For their part, the American people were less interested in bombing used as a coercive tool to communicate Administration intentions than as a weapon for winning the war. A Gallup survey taken shortly before the December 1965 bombing pause showed that only 21% of the public supported easing the pressure; 16% wanted to continue the bombing as it had been, and 52% wanted to unleash an all-out bombing campaign until the North gave up.[38]

Between 1964 and 1968 the U.S. undertook 16 bombing pauses and proffered 70 separate peace initiatives, with no apparent influence on North Vietnamese thinking or behavior.[39] The importance of force modulation to Johnson's strategy is underlined by the fact that in his memoir, *The Vantage Point*, the President provides a list showing the dates of the bombing pauses, their duration and type, as well as a detailed chronological list of peace initiatives. It is remarkable reading, in that all of these efforts were met with the same response, outright rejection by the North Vietnamese. For a White House team eagerly looking for subtle signals in response to their sincere overtures, they missed the obvious conclusion. The North Vietnamese were not interested in our peace feelers. They were fighting a war, and they wanted to win.

If anything, the gradualist approach had the opposite effect on North Vietnamese views of the United States. Gradualism—with its failure to inflict sudden, dramatic, unlimited pain on the enemy—was viewed as weakness. While the United States saw itself as an omnipotent power choosing not to use overwhelming force as a humanitarian gesture or to avoid escalation, from the enemy's point of view it was standing up to the strongest power in human history and surviving. This bolstered, not diminished, the enemy's will to continue the fight. And because escalation was gradual (in keeping with the "scientific" application of force), it allowed the enemy to adapt. The theoretical pain threshold that U.S. strategists were seeking was dynamic; it changed over time.

35

What hurt one day was acceptable the next. As one senior Air Force officer concluded, "We taught the bastards to cope."[40]

The lessons of strategic bombing campaigns in previous wars seemed to have been ignored. The most important of these was that bombing tends to cause enemies to retrench; it creates public support for the regime and builds will to resist. This was true in the German Blitz on Britain and during the Allied raids on Germany. Bui Tin, former North Vietnamese colonel and editor of the *People's Daily*, noted that the North "stood surprisingly firm in contending with the bombers of the Rolling Thunder operations. . . . Factories collapsed, bridges were broken, roads torn to bits, schools and hospitals razed to the ground. But all this only raised the level of bitterness and hatred at being attacked so inhumanely, and conveyed new purpose to our combatants. Our traditional patriotism was strengthened. It inspired us to affirm our fundamental sense of nationhood."[41]

Meanwhile the United States faced an unexpected "exogenous variable," its declining favor in world opinion. As the war dragged on the U.S. looked increasingly like a bully. The limited bombing campaign was not portrayed as limited by the war's international critics, who compared the tonnage dropped in the North to levels used in World War II. And criticism grew as the campaign continued. A more severe but decisive air campaign would have attracted less criticism if only because it would have ended sooner.

While the gradualist bombing campaign was being carried out in the North, the stage was set for attrition warfare in the South. In February 1966 at a meeting in Honolulu with top U.S. and South Vietnamese leaders, MACV commander General William Westmoreland was issued his objectives for the year, number one objective being to "attrit, by year's end Viet Cong and North Vietnamese forces at a rate as high as their capability to put men in the field."[42] This was known colloquially as the "crossover point." To the game-theorist advocates of attrition warfare, the crossover point constituted stalemate, the point at which a rational enemy should realize the futility of his actions and stop fighting. In practice this objective institutionalized the "body count," because in

36

Body counts

order to know whether the crossover point had been reached, decision-makers had to know how many of the enemy were taken out of action. Body counts were unreliable for a number of reasons but were symptomatic of the metrics-focused mindset. But the objective of high body counts allowed implementation of "search and destroy" tactics against the enemy, which gave U.S. forces something to plan for and a means of taking the initiative. And body counts appealed to the press because, as AP reporter Malcolm Browne said, "Numbers are ideally suited to headline writing."[43]

The body-count system was also ideally suited to McNamara's overwhelming faith in numbers. Data were his means of giving the impression of knowledge and control. "McNamara was a strange bird." John Roche noted:

> I'll never forget him at a Cabinet meeting at the time when there was a railroad strike in July of 1967. The machinists were going on strike. Johnson worked himself into a frenzy about this "treason." Johnson says to McNamara who's sitting across the table next to Humphrey at the Cabinet table, "Bob, how many train loads of material for our boys in Vietnam is this going to affect?" and McNamara snaps back, "Thirteen, Mr. President." I was sitting in the back there against the wall. I sort of looked at him and meditated: "One, did he wing it, or two, does he believe it?" I'm not sure which is worse. He was this kind of bird. He had a penchant for simulated exactitude.[44]

Metrics of this sort tended to become their own rationale. Requirements for precise numbers on enemy strength and losses led to endless interagency debates about who to count and how to count them. This problem will always arise when decision-makers take what is by nature a subjective art and try to make it an objective science. Said General Westmoreland, "Intelligence is at best an imprecise science—it is not like counting beans; it is more like estimating cockroaches." In irregular warfare these issues are magnified. The Viet Cong forces were difficult to classify. Many were part-time local militia, support personnel and political cadres. Some people were coerced into helping the VC; others were more committed. Some would be pro-government during the day and pro-guerrilla at night. It was virtually impossible to agree on the numbers, location, state of readiness, combat effectiveness, or significance of VC cadres to the overall war effort.

Given these and other problems, estimates of enemy strength varied widely. Military Assistance Command Vietnam (MACV) J-2 and the Defense Intelligence Agency (DIA) came up with consistently lower figures than the CIA did. The November 1967 National Intelligence Estimate on Vietnam, the last one compiled before the Tet Offensive, was a compromise document that showed overall decreases in both North Vietnamese Army and Viet Cong strength in Vietnam over the course of that year.[45] The compromise figure illustrates the unavoidably political nature of such estimates and the unfortunate consequences when policymakers demand levels of precision the data cannot support.[46] As the truism goes, if you want intelligence really bad, you will get really bad intelligence.

At the beginning of 1967 the Communist strength in the South was estimated at 282,000, including PAVN and the Viet Cong. On November 25 MACV lowered its estimate of Communist strength in the South from 294,000 to 223,000–248,000, of which around a quarter were PAVN, a quarter Viet Cong, a third other irregular forces, and the rest support troops. CIA numbers were somewhat larger. As noted above, the count was speculative. American military and civilian intelligence agencies were being asked to determine two things that were essentially unknowable—precisely how many forces the Communists were mobilizing and how many were being rendered *hors de combat*. Manpower should not have been a problem for the North; its population was 18 million, against 12 million for the South. The CIA consistently assessed the manpower base as adequate, and continuing materiel support from the Soviet Union and China ensured that Hanoi could continue fighting at some level indefinitely. But the Joint Chiefs became so frustrated over the Administration's fixation on nailing down this issue that they considered resigning en masse in the fall of 1967.[47] A South Vietnamese assessment of the Tet Offensive concluded that the heavy emphasis on trying to measure Communist capabilities and the scant attention paid to analyzing their intentions constituted one of the principal failures of the intelligence system leading up to the battle.[48]

In fact, the crossover point was said to have arrived sometime in the spring of 1967. In April, Donald J. MacDonald, director of the U.S. Agency for International Development in Vietnam, reported to the House Foreign Affairs Committee, "We feel we are rapidly approaching—if we are not already there—the crossover point" at which Communist losses outstripped recruitment.[49] In late June a military spokesman said the crossover point had been reached the previous March.[50] In late October after a tour of South Vietnam, retired Army General Omar N. Bradley declared that the crossover point had been reached, and rejected the notion that the war was in stalemate. "I don't call it stalemate when, almost everywhere, the enemy is avoiding contact and our troops are progressively digging him out and pushing him back," he said. "I don't call it stalemate when, by every measurement, the other side is getting weaker and we are getting stronger."[51]

Meanwhile, the United States had imposed limits on its manpower. Going into 1967 there were 385,000 U.S. troops and approximately 800,000 others, including South Vietnamese and allied personnel from Australia, New Zealand, South Korea, Thailand, and the Philippines. At the March 1967 Guam Conference Westmoreland asked for an additional 200,000 troops. Johnson agreed to authorize less than half that amount and set a troop ceiling of 470,000, to be reached by increments up to June 1968. This number was later raised to 525,000. At the end of 1967 there were approximately 486,000 U.S. troops in-country, of which 331,000 were Army and 78,000 Marines. The troop ceiling became a major issue after Tet, when more troops were urgently needed, because once such limits are set it becomes harder to adapt when circumstances change. Furthermore, the post-Tet call for reinforcements over Johnson's arbitrary ceiling contributed to the perception that the war was being lost because it seemed that more men were needed than the number the White House had previously determined were needed to win. In addition, troop limits communicated the wrong message to an enemy the United States sought to influence through attrition warfare, namely that there was a limit to the American commitment.

Ultimately the order of battle debate underscored the fact that the Americans and the North Vietnamese were fighting two different types of war. The U.S. conflict was akin to a chess match, with planned moves in a defined battle space, an assumed perfect knowledge of the enemy's strength on the ground, and established rules that the Americans believed both sides understood and accepted. The enemy was playing poker, a game in which psychological factors are as important as what cards each side holds, in which bluff and luck can play a decisive role, and in which it is possible to win with a losing hand. And while the Americans were playing chess in a complex manner that sought to force a draw, the North Vietnamese wanted to end their game holding all the chips. As North Vietnamese commanding General Vo Nguyen Giap observed in 1969, the "United States has a strategy based on arithmetic. They question the computers, add and subtract, extract square roots, and then go into action. But arithmetical strategy doesn't work here. If it did, they'd have already exterminated us."[52]

III.

THE WAR AND PUBLIC OPINION

The Tet Offensive is central to the "Vietnam Syndrome."[1] Tet did not give birth to the syndrome but may be called its moment of conception. It is generally believed that the Tet Offensive was the point at which the American people finally and irrevocably turned against the Johnson Administration and its conduct of the war. The conventional wisdom is that a previously supportive public came quickly to believe, rightly or wrongly, that the United States was involved in a losing effort and the time had come to seek an expeditious exit from Vietnam. The public disillusionment was spurred by press reports that portrayed Tet as a defeat instead of a

It's silly talking about how many years we will have to stay in the jungles of Viet Nam when we could pave the whole country and still be home by Christmas.

—RONALD REAGAN

victory and by the belief that the Administration had been lying about the positive trends it had been reporting for years.

But Tet was not the point at which Johnson lost Middle America. There was no sudden collapse in public support for the war effort because of the Communist attacks. The public actually had become disillusioned with Johnson's conduct of the war over a year before Tet. By January 1968 most Americans had already broken ranks with Johnson's limited war strategy, and the majority disapproved of his conduct of the war before the first shots of the Tet Offensive were fired. And while some wanted the United States to pull out of the conflict, most Americans wanted dramatically to escalate the war and finish the job.

PUBLIC OPINION 1962–1967

Vietnam crept slowly into public consciousness as the conflict in Indochina developed, and at first it was hardly noticed. An August 28, 1962, Gallup poll showed that the American people believed the most important issues facing the country were the threat of war (15%), the threat of communism (13%), and U.S./Russian relations (12%). The Vietnam issue—linked with Laos, given the ongoing crisis with the Pathet Lao—was mentioned by less than half of a percent. By April 29, 1964, Vietnam was registering with 2% of Americans as the most important issue, a statistically insignificant rise. Race and civil rights had by then taken center stage, with 42% citing these as the most important issues. But of those Americans who were focused on Vietnam, 42% thought matters were being handled as well as could be expected, and 45% believed things were going badly.[2]

By August 1964, during the Gulf of Tonkin crisis and subsequent war authorization, Vietnam ranked as the third most important issue at 14%, behind civil rights (36%) and nuclear war (18%). Polling then showed 73% of the public satisfied with the way the issue was being dealt with, and Johnson was favored 58% to 15% as better able than Republican Presidential candidate Barry Goldwater to deal with the situation in Vietnam if things got worse.[3] But this lopsided result was a rally effect caused by the events in the Gulf of Tonkin. By election day and Johnson's landslide victory against Goldwater, the public had again soured on the President's handling of Vietnam, with Gallup reporting 37% approving and 48% disapproving.[4] Harris polls reflected the same slumping trend, bottoming out in January 1965, with 41% approving of Johnson's handling of Vietnam and 59% disapproving.

The public again rallied behind Johnson during the summer and fall of 1965 as U.S. combat forces were deployed to Vietnam and began operations against the Communists. By then Vietnam had largely surpassed civil rights as the number one issue of public concern.[5] Johnson reached his high-water mark in Gallup survey approval numbers on September 21, 1965, with 58% approving of his war policy, 22% disapproving, and 20% with no opinion. Similarly, Harris poll data showed Johnson peaking in September and December 1965, with 66% approval and 34% disapproval. President Johnson's peak support level was not as high as the approval ratings enjoyed by later Presidents when U.S. troops went into combat—for example, George H.W. Bush, who initially saw 91% support for Operation Desert Storm in 1991, and George W. Bush, who had similarly high initial numbers for the wars in Afghanistan (2001) and Iraq (2003). Even at his most popular, Johnson never had such overwhelming public support for his conduct of the Vietnam War.

Johnson's peak levels of public support coincided with the sense among Americans that the situation in Vietnam was deteriorating; for example, in July 1965 Johnson's rating was 52% approval and on the way up, while at the same time 70% believed the situation in Vietnam was getting worse, and only 6% felt it was getting better.[6] This dynamic can be explained by understanding that the American people felt there was a deepening crisis and rallied behind the President instead of abandoning him. In November 1965, no doubt buoyed by this level of public support, the Administration unleashed U.S. combat forces to engage the North Vietnamese in the Battle of Ia Drang.

Johnson's approval ratings stayed above 50% until mid-spring 1966, when he suffered his first collapse in public support. According to Gallup, by April 1966 Johnson's approval rating had dropped below 50%. From June 1966 to June 1967 the public was largely evenly divided, slightly more supportive in the first six months, slightly less so in the second six months. Public opinion reached its own crossover point in December 1966, when more disapproved of LBJ's handling of the war than approved (47/42). The numbers fluctuated narrowly for six months before turning decisively south in the summer of 1967, crossing the 50% disapproval rate in July 1967 and bottoming out August 29, 1967, at 60% disapproval to 27% approval. This was Johnson's lowest war approval rating for his entire term of office. Johnson's numbers rose somewhat before Tet—up to a tepid 39% approval in January 1968—but the "collapse" recorded in the Gallup poll the week after the battle was only four points. Thus, contrary to the assumptions of the Tet narrative, Johnson did not go into the battle with broad public support, and he could not lose what he did not have to begin with.

LBJ VS. THE HAWKS

A commonly held belief is that "hawks" were those who supported President Johnson's conduct of the Vietnam War, while "doves" were those who opposed it. In this view high disapproval ratings for Johnson's policies translated into greater support for pulling out of Vietnam. But it is a mistake to read disapproval of Administration strategy as disapproval of the war effort per se. Digging deeper into poll data one finds that, more often than not, a larger number of those who opposed Johnson's conduct of the war did so not because they wanted the United States to withdraw from Vietnam, but because they rejected the limited war paradigm. They did not want to abandon the war effort; they wanted to take the gloves off and finish the job. In the summer of 1967, at the low point of LBJ's public support in handling the war effort, only 32% of the American people wanted to pull out of South Vietnam, while 50% wanted to escalate, to seek not a tie but a win. The hawks did not support Johnson; they were the largest bloc opposed to his limited war policies, and were some of his fiercest critics.

The range of public opinion regarding war strategies was much greater than simply "stay" or "go." An April 29, 1964, Gallup poll on courses of action in Vietnam, during the adviser period before combat troops had been put in and when the public was still not focused on the war, showed that 7% wanted to keep with the adviser policy, 12% wanted more diplomatic pressure, 11% wanted to pull out, 12% wanted to escalate, and 11% wanted all or nothing—either "go all the way or pull out." The plurality response was "don't know," at 27%. Polling as the crisis escalated into 1965 continued to show a wide and mostly consistent range of public views about future courses of action in Vietnam, except for statistically significant increases in the "all out war" category (up to 19% on June 29, 1965) and "don't know" (39%).

The June 29, 1965, Gallup poll showed that those who approved of Johnson's handling of Vietnam during the initial rally period gave reasons such as he was doing the best he could, that Communism had to be contained, that the fight was vital to U.S. security, and once committed the U.S. had to finish the job. Those who disapproved for the most part expressed "dovish" concerns— too many Americans were being killed, it's none of our business, the effort is going nowhere, it could lead to escalation to broader conflict. And around a fifth of those who disapproved did so on the basis that Johnson was not aggressive enough.[7]

One of the problems with trying to interpret any of these poll numbers is the fact that not every respondent understood exactly what Johnson's strategy was. The June 29, 1965, Gallup poll showed that 52% of Americans correctly characterized Johnson's strategy as gradually stepping up the military effort until the Communists were ready to negotiate. However, 21% thought the United States was seeking "military victory" over the Communists, 6% believed we were seeking immediate negotiations, and 21% did not know what the strategy was. As to what policy we should be following, 34% wanted military victory, 30% sought escalation leading to negotiation, 14% desired some form of immediate negotiations, 9% wanted to pull out, and 14% had no opinion.[8]

PUBLIC POLARIZATION AND THE DESIRE TO ESCALATE

The opinion dynamic shifted in 1966. Americans wanted to see results after large numbers of combat troops were deployed to South Vietnam. But the Administration's measures of progress did not translate well into the indicators of victory to which Americans were accustomed. Because the war was progressing in a way that the American people did not understand, their response was instinctive—go get the job done already. Johnson's support collapsed in 1966 because the public did not buy into his limited war premise. The Vietnam honeymoon was over.

Americans grew discouraged with Johnson because he was not trying to win. Defense Secretary McNamara was pursuing an esoteric limited-war strategy intended to bring about a negotiated settlement retaining the status quo in Southeast Asia. In that sense, "victory" meant ending the war with what we started with. By the summer of 1966, with support for Johnson's policies declining, the public showed greater desire to escalate the conflict. A particularly revealing poll on courses of action in Vietnam taken in June 1966 showed that only 6% supported Johnson's strategy, 11% wanted troop drawdowns, and 18% wanted a complete pullout. However, 23% wanted to escalate the war against the North, and an impressive 42% desired to "quickly build up our forces in Vietnam to as many as one million men and make an all-out effort to defeat North Vietnam."[9] A similar poll from August 1966 showed 17% support for withdrawal, 18% support for the status quo, and 55% support for escalating the war against the North.[10] Thus very early in the conflict the public was signaling its desire for a wider war aiming for victory, not a limited war fought to a negotiated draw.

A series of Harris polls between September 1965 and June 1966 documented the various ways in which the public wanted to escalate the conflict. Support for blockading North Vietnamese ports rose from 38% to 53%. Sentiment for bombing Hanoi rose

from 20% to 34%. But the polls also showed the limits of escalatory sentiment at that time. Those who wanted to bomb the
Chinese mainland remained steady around 13%, while those
supporting the use of tactical nuclear weapons held at about that
same level.[11]

Over time the unthinkable became increasingly acceptable.
An April 1967 Gallup survey showed 26% support for the nuclear
option, which is a sizable cohort, given the serious consequences
of the use of nuclear weapons, something Secretary of State Dean
Rusk said was "generally accepted to be insane." Only 15% in the
same poll desired immediate negotiation or withdrawal.[12] How
nuclear weapons could have been utilized in a war of this nature
is open to question, but the responses at least reflect a visceral
desire to simply settle the problem once and for all. A Harris poll
taken in December 1967 on the eve of Tet showed that support
for using nuclear weapons had basically doubled since June 1966,
from 13% to 25%, and approval for actions against China tracked
right along, rising from 12% to 25%. As well, 47% advocated occupying the DMZ, and 49% supported a ground invasion of North
Vietnam. By this time the country had lost over 16,000 troops,
and the idea that that they had been sacrificed only to maintain
the status quo was growing less acceptable.

Most Americans understand war as a "win or lose" proposition, preferably "win." And in order to achieve victory the plurality
of Americans thought Johnson had to be tougher. This conclusion
was captured in a July 1967 poll conducted by the White House
that showed 42% of the public desiring escalation in Vietnam,
30% wanting some form of de-escalation, and only 19% satisfied
with the way things were going. "The nearest thing to a consensus
is a more militant position," the study noted, although "one
would not know this from reading the newspapers or watching
television."[13]

The author of the White House study concluded that the
poll showed "the value of holding the middle ground, even if it
is small," which of course was what Johnson wanted to hear. Yet
the middle ground was shrinking. The public was radicalizing at
both ends of the spectrum as the war progressed. The numbers

calling for a pullout from Vietnam were increasing along with the numbers supporting escalation, though to a lesser degree. For example, according to Gallup in April 1967 11% wanted to pull out of Vietnam, which rose to 31% by October. Yet over the same period sentiment favoring escalation rose from 37% to 53%. The biggest decline was in those with no opinion, dropping from 25% to 5% as the previously uncommitted took sides. A sense of impatience had settled in, and people wanted the war to end one way or another, either all or nothing. And it is striking that in the fall of 1967 almost as many people wanted to settle the Vietnam conflict with nuclear weapons as wanted to wash their hands of it. Furthermore, as late as May 1967 49% of Americans said they did not have a "clear idea of what the Vietnam War is all about."[14]

POLICY PRIORITIES AND VIETNAM

Another take on the public's view of the war was revealed in a Harris poll released days before Tet.[15] The survey asked people to rate the importance of the war compared with other government policies and programs. For example, asked if they believed the country could afford both war funding and antipoverty programs, 48% said yes, 39% said no. Asked if Great Society programs should be reduced because of the Vietnam War, 64% said no. But asked if it came down to a choice between "emphasis on the war or more emphasis on rebuilding city ghettos," 52% chose Vietnam as a priority against 30% for inner-city programs. If forced to make the choice, a majority would rather see Vietnam funded than a key aspect of the Great Society. When asked which specific government efforts should retain funding in the face of budget cuts, Vietnam was the plurality favorite with 23%, followed by education (20%) and fighting crime (15%). Asked which programs should be cut, only 5% cited the war in Vietnam, while the plurality (32%) would elect to cut the space program. (This was a year after the Apollo 1 accident, in which three astronauts died, and in the middle of a 23-month gap in manned space launches.) 21% would elect to cut welfare or antipoverty programs, and 13% would cut new highway construction. Thus while the public had little faith in the Johnson Administration's conduct of the war effort, Vietnam remained the number one public spending priority, even over the pillars of the Great Society.

THE PUBLIC MOOD AND POLITICS

Politics reflected the dynamic of the public divide. Democrats tended to favor Johnson's policies more than Republicans did but were not in universal agreement. Republicans often favored a get tough approach but with certain caveats. A June 1966 poll showed the general public ambivalent over which political party could better handle the situation: 26% thought the Democrats, 22% chose the Republicans, 29% thought they could handle it equally well, and 23% didn't know.[16]

Republicans

In the spring of 1964 Vietnam was mostly mentioned in polls in connection with U.S. Ambassador to South Vietnam Henry Cabot Lodge's run for the Republican presidential nomination. Lodge had been appointed to the post by John F. Kennedy, some say to remove a potential Republican challenger from the political scene. However, in the spring of 1964 Lodge had become a surprise front-runner. In February he had polled a meager 2% support, far behind Nelson Rockefeller (26%), George Romney (20%), Richard Nixon (17%), and Barry Goldwater (14%). By a March 13 poll, after a write-in victory in the New Hampshire primary, Lodge had surged into first place with 38% support, while Rockefeller's numbers had tumbled. The same survey suggested that foreign policy was Johnson's greatest vulnerability, which may explain the support for Lodge at that point in the contest. Lodge heard the New Hampshire results after returning to Saigon from an inspection tour in the field with Secretary McNamara. The ambassador insisted he was not a candidate but remained the front-runner in Gallup surveys through the early summer. A July 1964 poll showed him the third most respected prominent American, named by 38% of respondents, coming in behind Robert F. Kennedy with 47% and the most respected American, FBI Director J. Edgar Hoover, with 62%. (The two least respected public figures were George Wallace with 47% disrespect and Martin Luther King with 42%.) However, Lodge chose not to campaign actively, and the "draft Lodge" movement soon collapsed, with Goldwater eventually emerging as the nominee.

Vietnam was not a major issue in the 1964 campaign, but the conflict dogged Goldwater. In May 1963 he had stated on ABC's "Issues and Answers" that "defoliation of the forests [in South Vietnam] by low-yield atomic weapons could well be done" to help interdict the supply routes from North Vietnam to the Viet Cong. This statement played to the Democratic argument that the Arizona senator was too reckless to be given control of the nuclear arsenal. Goldwater was later the subject of the famous "Daisy" ad, showing a small girl picking petals from a flower transforming into a nuclear countdown, which became the least run/most rerun political ad in history. An October 1964 poll showed that 44% believed that the chance for nuclear war would increase under Goldwater, compared with 8% under Johnson. Goldwater's generally more bellicose stand toward North Vietnam allowed Johnson to present himself as a "peace" candidate, which later prompted charges that during the campaign he had been concealing his intention to escalate the war.[17]

The Republicans were the minority in Congress throughout the war and for the most part supported the war effort, although they were not shy about criticizing the President when the opportunity warranted. On August 8, 1967, House minority leader Gerald Ford, a frequent Johnson critic, accused the Administration of "pulling punches" in bombing while Americans died on the ground. Ford said, "I strongly felt that although I agreed with the goals of the Johnson administration in Vietnam, I vigorously criticized their prosecution of the war."[18] Ford and Senate minority leader Everett Dirksen would tag-team Johnson, although Dirksen was more willing to show public support for Johnson's policies, particularly when he began to escalate the war. However, on December 5, 1967, Ford and Dirksen charged that the Administration had not done all it could to find a negotiated settlement.

Richard Nixon was predictably hawkish, if only because the view was politically expedient, and in an August 22, 1967, interview in *The Christian Science Monitor* he called for "massive pressure" to shorten the war, though explicitly excluding nuclear weapons, no doubt mindful of Goldwater's example. Michigan governor George Romney, who in early 1967 was a favorite for the Republican nomination, effectively wrecked his candidacy on September 4, 1967, when he explained his softening stance on the Vietnam War by saying his initial support of the war effort was due to "brainwashing" by generals and diplomats.

The most noted spokesman for escalation was Ronald Reagan. Reagan believed throughout the war that it was immoral not to pursue victory by the most effective and expeditious means possible. In October 1965, while running for governor of California, he summed up this view succinctly:

> If you ask a man to lay down his life for his country, the least
> you can do is tell him that he has the right to win . . . It's
> silly talking about how many years we will have to stay in the
> jungles of Viet Nam when we could pave the whole country
> and put parking stripes on it and still be home by Christmas.
> It's ridiculous to trade bombers for bamboo bridges. If the
> President is pursuing this thing with all his might to put an
> end to it as quickly as possible than I'm behind him. But there
> are indications that he is not pursuing it with all his might.[19]

Reagan wanted to declare war on North Vietnam, mount a full blockade of the country, and do whatever it took to achieve victory. The Democrats mocked his views as naïve and simplistic. "As a hero in the movies he had two hours of film to solve everything," California Democratic Party chairman Robert Coate stated. "We do not dare let him leap from his childlike world into our adult world."[20] There was some concern that Reagan's stance might be mischaracterized, as Goldwater's had been about using nuclear weapons, and that this would hurt his campaign. But in November 1966 Reagan defeated incumbent Democrat Pat Brown and was elected governor with over 57% of the vote.

As governor, Reagan continued to speak his mind on the Vietnam issue, and a December 1967 Harris poll revealed that his views were very popular. Asked whether Reagan was "right to want to win total victory in Vietnam," 65% agreed, 12% disagreed, and 23% were not sure. But paradoxically, not everyone thought Reagan was hawkish, and in a Gallup poll in December 1967, 39% rated Reagan as a hawk, 27% a dove, and 34% don't know.[21]

Democrats

The war debate on the Democratic side was more nuanced. Democrats controlled the White House and both houses of Congress, thus being responsible for the war's strategy, policies, financing, conduct, and oversight. Johnson had won in 1964 with the largest popular vote percentage in U.S. history to date and was a skilled veteran of Washington politics. One would expect his hold on power to be firm. And while Democrats were generally more supportive of the President, the collapse of public opinion during the 1966–67 period made the Vietnam issue ripe for exploitation by his political foes.

Johnson was most wary of Senator Robert F. Kennedy, brother of the late President. Johnson had long worried about a Camelot resurgence led by RFK. "Johnson had a Kennedy phobia," John Roche said. "Not a sparrow dropped without the intervention of Bobby."

Robert Kennedy had taken an early interest in Vietnam, particularly as a test case for the Special Forces, of which he was a fervid supporter. He kept a green beret on his desk while he was attorney general, and is said by Michael Forrestal of John Kennedy's National Security Council staff to have coined the term "counterinsurgency." Robert Kennedy was instrumental in convincing Special Forces commander Lieutenant General William Yarborough to allow his Harvard classmate forty-year-old writer Robin Moore to join the Green Berets as a civilian (with the rank of "author") to train and fight with the unit. Moore spent 11 months with the Special Forces, including a deployment to Vietnam, all of which informed his best-selling novel *The Green Berets*, published in May

1965. In July 1968 the film adaptation of the novel was released, starring John Wayne, which ironically was roundly denounced as pro-war propaganda. For example, film reviewer Wayne Wilson wrote that "'The Green Berets' brings to mind those ugly little 1942 propaganda films promoting hatred and blind patriotism. It isn't as tasteless or fictitious as the epics that showed Japanese soldiers throwing babies into the air and spearing them on bayonets, but the intent, obviously, is the same."[22]

Kennedy began speaking publicly about alternative Vietnam policies in the spring of 1967, but his major break with the Johnson Administration came on November 26 that year. Kennedy gave a speech in which he stated that Johnson had shifted the war aims set by President Kennedy and undermined America's moral position globally. The speech was a political chess move. Senator Kennedy sought to distance his brother's Vietnam policies (which he played an active role in establishing) from what followed under Johnson. In this way he could detach the Kennedy legacy from Johnson and position himself to come out openly against the war. This was especially important because the Johnson team had begun to sprinkle their talking points with quotes from President Kennedy that supported intervening in Vietnam in order to shore up liberal support for the President.

Robert Kennedy was aided in reimaging the past by loyal former members of the Kennedy Administration, some of whom, like him, also served under Johnson. This effort was part of a general desertion of that part of the Democratic intelligentsia aligned with the Kennedys. John Roche termed the desertion the "revolt of the Jacobins," referring to the French Revolutionary group that had a habit of executing its own leaders. "When Arthur Schlesinger suddenly announced his repudiation of the war in Vietnam" in May 1967, Roche said, "I said—paraphrasing Acton—that if power corrupts, the absence of power corrupts absolutely, with reference specifically to Schlesinger. Dean Rusk liked that so much that he called me up at dawn when he got the Post."[23] The Kennedy loyalists could be counted on to give brother Robert whatever ideological cover he needed to repudiate his previous views of the war, and the effort was effective. By the end of

1967 54% of Americans viewed Kennedy as a dove, to 25% who considered him a hawk.[24]

Three days after Kennedy's Vietnam speech another Democrat more openly challenged Johnson. On November 29, 1967, peace candidate Eugene McCarthy announced that he would run against Johnson for the 1968 Democratic nomination for President. McCarthy sought to harness the momentum of the peace movement, which by then had garnered considerable press attention. The peace movement had shown impressive growth based on the numbers of people turning out at rallies. The April 17, 1965, SDS protest in Washington, D.C., attracted 25,000 people, at the time the largest antiwar rally ever in the capital. Three times that number gathered in Washington on October 21, 1967, during the march on the Pentagon. Nevertheless, while the peaceniks effectively seized the popular imagination, they represented a minority of public opinion, and only a small fraction of Americans actually took part in the movement. An April 1967 Gallup poll asked whether people would like to participate in a peace rally if one were organized locally, and only 9% said yes. When asked if they had actually participated in a rally, 99% said no.[25]

The peace movement promoted the idea that American youth were generally opposed to the war effort, and claimed to be the voice of its generation. Young people made up the bulk of those who turned out at rallies, and media-friendly stunts, such as Abbie Hoffman's "plan" during the October 1967 march to levitate the Pentagon through meditation, turn it orange, and drive out the evil spirits, became magnets for commentary, even though Hoffman's effort involved only a few dozen Yippies. Some observers noted that the increase in youth participation in the peace movement picked up when college-aged young men began to be drafted in large numbers in late 1967.[26]

The high visibility of the movement and the fact that it was dominated by young people left the impression that most young people in America wanted the U.S. out of Vietnam. This was not true. Many polls showed that the sentiments of young people regarding the war either tracked with the general population or were slightly more supportive of the war effort. A White House poll in July 1967 showed that 28% of younger people wanted to "get out soonest" from Vietnam, compared with a national result of 29%, but 67% wanted to "stay and reach [the] goal," higher than the national result of 60%, and over twice the number of young people who wanted to pull out.[27]

A June 1967 national poll showed "a direct correlation between youth and support for the war. The younger the group, the more who think we did *not* make a mistake in sending troops [emphasis in original]." This poll and the July White House poll also showed that support for the war was higher among those with more education and higher incomes.[28] Johnson's general approval rating was low on campus, with 38% approval and 53% disapproval, which might lead one to believe that the colleges were nests of doves.[29] But according to Gallup, in May 1967, at the onset of the Summer of Love and Flower Power, hawks outnumbered doves on college campuses 49% to 35%, and among draft-age young men the hawk edge was even greater, 56% to 30%. Among young women the doves had a four-point lead, 42% to 38%. The gender gap on college campuses was mirrored nationally. A June 1967 poll showed "a heavily hawkish position of the men of the country and a generally dovish position by the women." Men were twice as likely than women to want to go for military victory even if risking war with China (44.4% vs. 21.3%), whereas women were twice as likely to pull out the troops immediately (21.2% vs. 10.6%).[30]

The peace movement was high profile because its leaders consciously gave the media strange and compelling images, the result of strategies designed to play well on TV. However, the peace groups were not wildly popular with the American people in general, particularly in the early years of the war. A September 1965 Harris survey found that 65% of Americans thought that war protestors were harmful to American life, while only 5% thought them helpful. An October 1965 poll found that 58% of Americans thought Communists had been involved "a lot" in demonstrations, and a further 20% thought they had been somewhat involved.[31] A December 1965 Harris poll found that 74% of Americans thought the "main reason behind the demonstrations against the war in Vietnam" was either people "just demonstrating against something" (34%), being tools of the Communists (26%), or avoiding the draft (14%). Only 25% thought that the demonstrators were motivated by moral opposition to the war (14%) or feelings that the war was wrong (11%). In the same poll, 64% of Americans felt that the protestors had a right to nonviolently protest the war. When protests became more violent and disruptive, the public was quick to denounce them. For example, with respect to the 1968 Democratic convention in Chicago, which was disrupted by Vietnam War protesters, 56% of the public approved of the harsh methods used by the Chicago police to deal with the protestors, while 31% disapproved.[32]

There is no doubt that in general terms the enemy saw the peace movement as a tool to be exploited. Bui Tin, former North Vietnamese colonel and editor of the *People's Daily*, said that the antiwar movement "was essential to our strategy. Support of the war from our rear was completely secure while the American rear was vulnerable. Every day our leadership would listen to world news over the radio at 9 a.m. to follow the growth of the American antiwar movement." Visits to Hanoi by Jane Fonda and former Attorney General Ramsey Clark and various church ministers "gave us confidence that we should hold on in the face of battlefield reverses. Those people represented the conscience of America. The conscience of America was part of its war-making capability, and we were turning that power in our favor. America lost because of its democracy; through dissent and protest it lost the ability to mobilize a will to win."[33] The North Vietnamese were not unwitting beneficiaries of the peace movement; they understood that public opinion was a critical American vulnerability. It was something they openly encouraged. In the fall of 1967 North Vietnamese Premier Pham Van Dong sent a message to the peaceniks, saying that "the Vietnamese people thank their friends in America and wish them great success in their mounting movement."

However, the peace movement was not representative of the majority of Americans, or even of the majority who opposed the President's war policies. In the years leading up to Tet, America had grown dissatisfied with Johnson's limited war approach, and an all-or-nothing mood had developed in the country. Escalatory moves in the fall of 1967 seemed to rally the public to an extent. But while Johnson enjoyed a slight bump in public confidence just before Tet, he did not go into the battle with overwhelming support, and when the battle was joined and the voices favoring escalation intensified, President Johnson chose not to listen.

IV.

THE VIEW
FROM HANOI

In August 1967, word began to circulate in Viet Cong circles that a "new situation and mission" was about to emerge that would bring about the culmination of the war, which would "split the sky and shake the earth." This rumor was the first signal of a plan that had been in the works since the previous January, intended to foment a general uprising in the South and drive the Americans out. If the offensive worked as planned, it would mean the end of the war. If not, it could spell defeat of the Communist cause.

It has become a commonplace saying that as long as the guerrilla is not losing he is winning. The implication is

> If you attack cities, your strength will be exhausted.
>
> —SUN TZU

that as long as the guerrilla survives he can sustain the hope of eventually wearing down his opponent. But this cliché makes a realistic definition of victory over the guerrilla impossible, since it makes his mere survival a persistent symbol of regime defeat. Furthermore, simple survival is not the guerrilla's definition of victory, and was not the view in Hanoi.

The strategic goal of the North Vietnamese Communists was never in doubt: unification of North and South Vietnam under Hanoi's rule. This was their unwavering objective from the division of Vietnam under the Geneva agreement in 1954 to the fall of Saigon on April 30, 1975. This objective was established by North Vietnamese leader Ho Chi Minh, who had founded the Viet Minh movement in 1941 and became the head of the Democratic Republic of Vietnam after the French defeat in 1954. Ho was a lifelong Communist who had committed himself to the cause while living in France in 1919, and he was a founding member of the French Communist Party in 1921. Throughout the 1920s and 1930s he was active in the Soviet-backed Communist International and traveled throughout East Asia organizing and proselytizing for Moscow. He participated in the anti-Japanese resistance during the Second World War and was briefly the head of a self-declared provisional Vietnamese government after Japan was defeated. But the French reasserted control over Indochina, and a war commenced that lasted until the French defeat at the battle of Dien Bien Phu and the settlement reached shortly thereafter at Geneva.

Throughout the American involvement in Vietnam and to a large extent since, Ho's apologists portrayed him as a nationalist and anti-imperialist rather than a Communist. The struggle in the South was billed as an indigenous uprising or civil war that the North was uninvolved with. One practical reason for this portrayal was that it allowed Hanoi to maintain that it was staying within the letter of the Geneva agreement, which banned interference in the internal affairs of the respective states. To this end, in the spring of 1959 the North Vietnamese Politburo approved a plan to establish the Central Office for South Vietnam (COSVN) to coordinate the Viet Cong's armed struggle, and the National Liberation Front (NLF) was founded in December 1960 to serve as the political face of the struggle. "We always said there was only one party, only one army in the war to liberate the South and unify the nation," Bui Tin said. "At all times there was only one party commissar in command of the South."[1] These groups gave political cover to Hanoi, even though they took orders from the North, were supplied and sustained by the North, and North Vietnamese troops played an active role fighting in the South.

Calling the conflict in Vietnam a civil war was part of a broader Communist deception strategy. In 1950, Soviet Deputy Foreign Minister Jakob A. Malik put forth the proposition that any Communist insurgency is by its nature a civil war, hence not the business of any outside parties that might seek to intercede. The Soviet Union pressed this argument at the outbreak of the Korean War to argue against international intervention against the North Korean invaders. The Soviets asserted that since the conflict was an internal Korean affair, there was no legal or moral basis for the U.N. to get involved. When it was noted that Moscow was giving overt support to Pyongyang, this support was downplayed as "fraternal assistance."[2]

With respect to Vietnam, Communist propagandists consistently claimed that it was a single country artificially and unlawfully divided and that the final disposition of the government must be left to the Vietnamese people alone. American antiwar circles adopted this line, and when they described the conflict as a "civil war" the embedded message was "U.S. out of Vietnam." John Roche noted in 1969 that "the thrust of the propaganda attack was to convert an externally organized attack into a 'civil war.' Regrettably, it was a brilliantly successful exercise in rewriting history, one that could be used as a model of effective political warfare."[3] Lyndon Johnson was under no illusions that the Viet Cong was an independent force; he said, "They got just about as much independence as a sharecropper in Mississippi."[4] And the American people likewise understood the true nature of the struggle. A February 1965 Harris poll showed that only 7% of Americans thought the escalating violence was part of a South Vietnamese civil war.

The notion that the Viet Cong consisted of purely indigenous fighters also fed the belief that the war in South Vietnam was a purely guerrilla war. In fact, it was more complex than that. The conflict was rooted in the Maoist theory of revolutionary warfare, or people's war, in which guerrilla warfare was an important but not decisive aspect. Guerrilla warfare, like terrorism, is a weapon of the weak, a tool of the violent political extremist faced with a much stronger regime. But the guerrilla does not want to remain a guerrilla; he seeks to overthrow the regime and achieve power, which frequently requires escalation to conventional warfare.

Mao developed a three-stage insurgency model, beginning with political organization and small-scale opposition, evolving into guerrilla warfare over time as manpower increases and some areas are liberated (a phase he called "strategic stalemate"), and culminating in the third stage with conventional armed conflict with the adversary, and a decisive battle (the "strategic counteroffensive"). This was how the Viet Minh had defeated the French, and it was General Giap's model for beating the Americans. Bui Tin noted that Giap "believed that guerrilla warfare was important but not sufficient for victory. Regular military divisions with artillery and armor would be needed."[5]

The strategic counteroffensive, however, can be mounted only when the correlation of forces favors the insurgents, and the balance of power shifted in different phases of the Vietnam conflict. From 1959 to 1963 the Communist strategy was called *Khoi Nghia*, General Uprising.[6] It featured broad-based political/military activity in the countryside and the cities, seeking to indoctrinate, agitate, and create conditions of chaos that would one day culminate in a general move toward revolution. It was geared toward creating a prerevolutionary state of consciousness in the peasants and other citizens, and delegitimatizing the Diem regime. The Communists also sought to directly confront the growing U.S. presence in the country. On July 8, 1959, Viet Cong guerrillas attacked the American advisers' residence at Bien Hoa, killing Major Dale R. Buis and Master Sergeant Chester Ovnand. Theirs are the first names recorded on the Vietnam Veterans Memorial, and Hanoi regards this attack as its declaration of war against the United States in Vietnam.

After the coup against Diem and assassination of President Kennedy in November 1963, Hanoi seized the opportunity to exploit the disruption in Saigon and Washington and embarked on a phase of Revolutionary Guerrilla War, using the standard Maoist model that had worked well against the French. North Vietnamese Regulars (PAVN) invaded the South and began to move against South Vietnamese Army (ARVN) units, engaging and generally defeating them. Over the next year the crisis intensified, and South Vietnamese forces were on the verge of collapse. This was the context of the United States conventional military buildup in the South to stem the tide and give the Saigon forces a chance to regroup.

The critical turning point in this phase of the war in the South was the battle of the Ia Drang Valley in mid-November 1965. U.S. mobility and firepower proved more than a match for the larger PAVN forces, and the Ia Drang engagement ended Hanoi's belief that it would be able to win a quick conventional victory. The battle was not only a tactical victory for the Americans but also a key test of airmobile operational concepts and a strategic milestone. After Ia Drang the contest could truly be said to be joined from the American perspective.

During the period from November 1965 to the spring of 1967 the Communists experimented with various responses to the growing U.S. presence, trying to find an effective military formula. As Washington sent more forces to the South, Hanoi did likewise. The Communist world supplied ample weapons and other materiel support, and the Ho Chi Minh Trail supply line was constantly flowing. But there were limits to what resourcing could achieve. U.S. air mobility made North Vietnamese conventional or large-scale guerrilla attacks more costly because it was more difficult for the Communist forces to withdraw to safety afterward. U.S. ground strength, combined with artillery and naval and air power, was more than a match for whatever tactical innovations the PAVN could devise.

63

The North Vietnamese armed forces did not win a significant military victory after the large-scale introduction of American troops, and by the spring of 1967 the Communist leadership in Hanoi knew it had serious problems. The guerrilla war in the countryside was ongoing, but that alone would not bring victory, and conventional attacks against American forces resulted in stinging defeats. And while the Johnson Administration could accept—indeed, explicitly sought—stalemate in the South, the Communists could not win without expelling the United States and seizing Saigon. They knew they could not defeat the American forces in a head-to-head fight; thus they sought a strategy that could bring force to bear long enough to overthrow the Saigon government, deprive the Americans of their reason for being in the country, and prompt them to leave.

The conceptual framework that eventually became the Tet Offensive was discussed at the Lao Dong Party Central Committee meeting January 23–26, 1967.[7] Party leaders had gathered to review the course of the war and began their talks toward the end of Operation Cedar Falls, the largest and most effective U.S. offensive in South Vietnam up to that point. The first half of 1967 was a particularly active time for American forces. In February the U.S. launched Operation Junction City, a four-month U.S./South Vietnamese combined operation that was even more punishing than Cedar Falls. Operation Manhattan, which began in April 1967, aimed at the tunnel complexes in the Long Nguyen Secret Zone and was also effective. These operations demonstrated the combat reach of U.S. forces, including armor and mechanized infantry, into areas the VC considered to be sanctuaries. This combat reach forced the enemy to move most of its headquarters, training bases, supply centers, and concentration areas into Cambodia, although the VC continued to be active on the ground in the areas that had been targeted.[8]

To North Vietnamese military leaders Giap and Thanh, the outcome of the American operations was disastrous. Years of progress establishing infrastructure inside South Vietnam had been undone. High-level North Vietnamese delegations visited

China and the Soviet Union to ascertain the views of their backers regarding the struggle. Beijing recommended that Hanoi "persist in the military struggle to the very end," likening it to a hundred-mile walk.[9] Moscow favored a diplomatic settlement, but the North Vietnamese were completely opposed to any negotiations with the United States.

Meanwhile the situation was growing steadily worse for the Communists. The U.S. was escalating its bombing campaign and widening the number of targets. North Vietnamese planners feared that the Red River dikes would be bombed, inundating hundreds of square miles of farmland as well as Hanoi. The regime in Saigon was turning out to be more stable than anticipated, and in the spring of 1967 it announced that free elections would be held in the fall. The American-backed pacification program was beginning to take hold in the countryside. Hanoi feared that the U.S. was planning strikes into Cambodia, Laos, or even the North. The U.S. was engaging in a covert campaign to destabilize the government, and many in North Vietnam believed that there was an active internal resistance movement trying to bring down the Hanoi government.[10] Others feared that the VC might split off and find a separate accommodation with Saigon.[11] In some quarters in the North there began to be a hint of desperation.

There was no clear way out of the quandary. North Vietnamese General Tran Van Tra, field commander for operations in the South, stated that all the Communists could do was pursue a war of attrition, which ironically was the same conclusion Defense Secretary McNamara had reached. "We understood that the U.S. Army was superior to our own logistically, in weapons and in all things," Tran Van Tra wrote:

> So strategically we did not hope to defeat the U.S. Army completely. Our intentions were to fight a long time and cause heavy casualties to the United States, so the United States would see that the war was unwinnable and would leave. . . . Strategically it was a war of attrition. Tactically we tried to destroy U.S. units. We tried to cause heavy casualties

and damage the U.S. units so much that the U.S. side would realize that there would be no retreat and that the U.S. was waging war against a whole nation.[12]

Tran Van Tra believed the best the Communists could do was punish the United States until the Americans got tired and left. But Chinese Premier Zhou Enlai thought that the current conditions could not continue forever, and that something had to give. In April 1967 he offered his assessment to North Vietnamese Prime Minister Pham Van Dong:

> First, the war may continue and may even further expand.
> The rule of war is not determined by human will, neither
> that of the enemy's, nor that of ours. War has its own rule.
> Even when the enemy wants to stop, it is difficult for him to
> do so. . . . Another possibility is that the enemy may blockade
> the coastline. If he begins a overall blockade, that means it is
> preparing for expanding the war, a total war. . . . The third pos-
> sibility, as you two have mentioned, is that the dry season of
> the next year will be a crucial moment, and that it is possible
> to defeat the enemy, forcing him to recognize his defeat and
> to withdraw from Vietnam. Is it possible that the war would
> neither end nor expand, but would continue like it is now?
> This is impossible. The war will end sooner or later, this is
> only a matter of time. It is impossible that the war would be
> protracted like this, neither dead nor alive.[13]

The North Vietnamese Politburo held a series of key discussions in April 1967. After an extensive analysis of the battlefield situation, the Politburo members concluded that the war had to be won as quickly as possible. The Communist leadership assessed the situation in ways that McNamara would recognize and approve of. "Gradualism and attrition" was working. Hanoi was haunted by the "Crossover point." More of its men were being killed than could be sent south, and by some assessments more were dying than being born. The VC desertion rate had doubled every six months, and the burden of the war was being shifted to the PAVN. Supplies heading south were being interdicted, and the economy was suffering as more resources were being diverted toward the war. Criticism from Moscow and Beijing was mounting, the former pressing for negotiations, the latter demanding escalation. The war was showing no sign of progress, and Hanoi had to admit the failure of this stage of the struggle and move in a new direction.

The North Vietnamese discussed at least three strategic approaches: a regular force strategy; a guerrilla war strategy; and a negotiated settlement.[14] Politburo member and former Communist Party general secretary Truong Chinh counseled a long-term approach. He was an admirer of Mao, whose Communist Party code name was Vietnamese for "Long March." Because the Communists could not win by fighting major battles, they had to be patient. Truong Chinh argued that specific conditions forced their strategy to bend, and that this flexibility was true to their revolutionary doctrine. Others desired a more confrontational approach, and arguably Giap was in this camp, although this supposition is disputed. Giap reportedly desired a "continuous comprehensive offensive," a victory strategy, but only when the time was ripe. But there was no time to wait. Overall guidance came in Party Resolution Thirteen from the 13th Plenum of the Central Committee in April 1967, calling for a "spontaneous uprising in order to win a decisive victory in the shortest possible time." Hanoi was ordering a go-for-broke military strategy.

Most accounts credit the idea for Tet to General Nguyen Chi Thanh, head of the Central Office for South Vietnam (COSVN), the VC combatant commander.[15] Thanh and his planners came up with the concept at the 5th Conference of the Central Office of South Vietnam in May 1967 and briefed Hanoi in June. The basic plan was to draw the U.S. forces to the highlands with a series of attacks and while they were engaged there to strike at Saigon, Hue, and Da Nang. "Thanh's struggle philosophy was that 'America is wealthy but not resolute,' and 'squeeze tight to the American chest and attack,'" Bui Tin said.[16]

The developed plan for Tet was called *Tong Cong Kich, Tong Khoi Nghia* (TCK, TKN) or General Offensive/General Uprising.

Its premise was that a large-scale military strike would be the trip-wire for a general popular revolt against the Saigon government; the NLF would seize power; and the United States mission in Vietnam would be overcome by events. A U.S. withdrawal would then follow. The notion of a General Offensive/General Uprising had been around since at least 1960, and it had been in the planning cycle since 1964. Politburo debates in 1967 concluded that the time had come to implement the concept and that the uprising and offensive had to be simultaneous to succeed.

The key to the plan was the popular uprising. The North Vietnamese made four critical assumptions:

1. The South Vietnamese people felt no loyalty to the Thieu-Ky regime, and people would rally to the NLF given the opportunity;
2. The people in the South hated the American occupiers and would turn on them under the right circumstances;
3. The South Vietnamese armed forces were ineffective: they lacked motivation and loyalty and under pressure would flee, fold, or switch sides;
4. The General Offensive/General Uprising could be achieved quickly enough to present the Americans with a *fait accompli*, and they would then voluntarily leave the country.

These assumptions were rooted in both history and ideology. The Communists were inspired by the successful August 1945 Great Uprising against the Japanese and French. They also noted the success of Buddhist demonstrations in 1966, when much of South Vietnam was destabilized. They felt that the people of the South were ready to be led, needing only to be given the opportunity to rise up and throw off the Saigon regime's corrupt rule. With respect to the South Vietnamese armed forces, the Communists looked to the period before 1965 and the American intervention, when they were able to defeat ARVN units in large-scale engagements. They had no reason to believe anything had changed in this regard. And once the uprising was achieved and the situation looked hopeless, the Americans would logically choose to depart, just as the French had.

On the ideological level Hanoi believed that the South was in a prerevolutionary state and needed only a little help to spark the general uprising. The Communists had spent years preparing the groundwork at the political level and would now be able to harvest the results. From their doctrinaire point of view, the Thieu-Ky regime was an illegitimate puppet of imperialist occupiers, and the Communists believed that most people in the South shared this view. This sincerity of belief in their ideological framework gave them confidence that their premises were correct.[17]

Ironically, their views were buttressed by reports from the American press. The Hanoi regime followed American reportage on Vietnam closely, and what they read in American papers and heard from radio and TV convinced them that their assessment was correct. Lieutenant General Phillip B. Davidson, Westmoreland's chief of intelligence, wrote:

> Day after day, American reporters and television commentators belittled the United State effort in Vietnam and trumpeted its failures and shortcomings. They harped on the corrupt and dissolute nature of the Thieu regime and its lack of popular support. American reporters constantly derided ARVN and its combat effectiveness. So it was the American newsmen who contributed significantly to the misconceptions which led the Politburo to the monstrous defeat of Tet 1968.[18]

For example, Giap's monumental essay, "Big Victory/Great Task," cited the *New York Times* and the more conservative *U.S. News and World Report,* among others, to justify his assertion that his views of Communist successes were not simply "subjective."[19]

Tet was the centerpiece of an ambitious three-phased campaign plan. The first phase, to take place in the fall and winter of 1967, was a series of mainly PAVN attacks on the periphery of the country to draw American and South Vietnamese forces into the countryside. The second phase featured a countrywide assault on South Vietnamese cities, hitting key government and security targets. General engagement with American forces was to be avoided, although U.S. command and control targets in major cities were to be targeted if convenient. This assault would spark the general uprising. The Viet Cong would lead these attacks because they could more easily infiltrate; plus the VC would legitimize the uprising as a spontaneous Southern affair. The PAVN would eventually move in to consolidate. Phase II would also be attended by a massive propaganda campaign aimed at the South Vietnamese armed forces. Hanoi envisioned whole units disintegrating, joining the rebellion, and turning on the Americans. Also, there was the political *dau tranh*, which would overthrow the South Vietnamese government. Phase III was envisaged as a large set-piece battle, the decisive engagement that would end the war in the same way Dien Bien Phu did in 1954.[20]

It is noteworthy that the leadership had ordered that the war be won in the "shortest possible time." The December 1965 12th Plenum instructed that victory be sought in "a relatively short period of time," but by 1967 the Communists were in more of a hurry. One theory is that they were trying to influence the 1968 election. John Roche had predicted an election year attack in a 1967 memo to President Johnson based on the idea that the country would be at is weakest during a presidential campaign. Bui Tin agrees that the Communists wanted to "weaken American resolve during an election year."[21] Tran Van Tra states that the actual three phases of the campaign were intended to influence the election cycle: Phase I was Tet, Phase II was to commence May 5 and in practice was the eventual Little Tet, and Phase III was supposed to have taken place August 17-September 23 but was never executed because the first two phases had failed.

It was not the first time a guerrilla enemy had attempted to game the American political system. Philippine provisional President Emilio Aguinaldo pursued a conscious strategy to keep his insurgency in American headlines during the 1900 election. The Republicans were claiming victory in the war with Spain and had placed war hero Theodore Roosevelt in the second slot on the ticket with incumbent President William McKinley. But the Democrats argued—rightly, as it turned out—that the insurgency in the Philippines was just heating up, and Aguinaldo strove to buttress their case with facts on the ground.[21]

The timing of the attack during an election year raises the question of whether Tet was intended primarily as a means of targeting American public opinion. The Communists have been widely credited with pursuing a conscious strategy of attacking the American home front through generating negative headlines. It is true that in general terms the enemy was trying to influence the American public; democracy's enemies will always seek to target the seams and promote dissent. But there is no evidence that Tet was designed primarily or even secondarily to have any specific political effects inside the United States. This argument was more American invention than the enemy's intention.

General Tran Do denied that there was an attempt to wage a psychological war, calling any domestic American impact "an accidental byproduct." Captured Viet Cong Nam Dong, alias Can, said that Tet "was neither an ordinary campaign nor one staged with the intention of scoring a propaganda victory. It was a campaign designed to bring about a decisive victory and end the war." General Davidson said that during his tenure as MACV J-2 he never saw a captured document or prisoner statement indicating that influencing the will of the American people was an explicit objective of the attack.[23]

Another reason for the timing of the attack was the troop ceiling that President Johnson had set at the Guam Conference in March 1967. Westmoreland had requested 200,000 additional troops and was allowed less than half that number over the course of a year. Johnson's reticence to commit more forces signaled to the North Vietnamese that there were limits to how far the United States would go in an attrition war. "We realized that America had made its maximum military commitment to the war," Bui Tin said. "Vietnam was not sufficiently important for the United States to call up its reserves. We had stretched American power to a breaking point. When more frustration set in, all the Americans could do would be to withdraw; they had no more troops to send over."[24] The troop ceiling was an important though unintentional signal to Hanoi, and ironic, given the amount of attention the Administration gave to communication through diplomatic gestures. The White House seemed to have completely missed the impact of this decision on enemy decision-making.

A more immediate reason for seeking a rapid victory was the increasingly problematic state of Ho Chi Minh's health. He had turned 77 in May 1967, and his health had been in decline generally for two years. Ho was ill throughout 1967 and had traveled to China for treatments but was healthy enough to chair the Politburo meeting where the Tet proposal was discussed. He stayed in Hanoi the summer but returned to Beijing for more treatments from September to December. Ho had said that the war would last ten years, twenty years, or longer. But he wanted unification (or, from his point of view, reunification) of Vietnam in his lifetime, and Pham Van Dong said those around him "wanted him to live to see Vietnam unified."[25] Thus not all decisions in Hanoi were made according to an ideological master plan or because of facts on the ground. Sometimes the most basic human factors were judged to be more important.

OPPOSITION TO THE PLAN

Creating a "spontaneous" uprising required a great deal of planning. In June 1967 most of North Vietnam's ambassadors were called to Hanoi for meetings, a clear signal that something was going on. American intelligence analysts noted this development but assumed with more hope than evidence that the ambassadors were being told about a peace initiative. Viet Cong commanders met in Cambodia in late July to initiate planning Tet and began months of infiltration and stockpiling of weapons for the attack.

The Tet Offensive was being organized during a time of strife in the Communist world. China was wracked with turmoil in the summer of 1967, the height of the Cultural Revolution, which lasted from May 1966 to 1969, and the Communist government was facing a state of virtual civil war between the People's Liberation Army and the elite Red Guards.

At an April 11, 1967, meeting with Prime Minister Pham Van Dong and General Giap, Mao explained his view of the situation in the South: "We have a saying: 'If you preserve the mountain green, you will never have to worry about firewood.' The U.S. is afraid of your tactics. They wish that you would order your regular forces to fight, so they can destroy your main forces. But you were not deceived. Fighting a war of attrition is like having meals: [it is best] not to have too big a bite. In fighting the U.S. troops, you can have a bite the size of a platoon, a company, or a battalion. With regard to troops of the puppet regime, you can have a regiment-size bite. It means that fighting is similar to having meals, you should have one bite after another."[26]

"The Chinese believed in fighting only with guerrillas," Bui Tin said, "but we had a different approach. The Chinese were reluctant to help us. Soviet aid made the war possible. Le Duan [general secretary of the Vietnamese Communist Party] once told Mao Tse-tung that 'if you help us, we are sure to win; if you don't, we will still win, but we will have to sacrifice one or two million more soldiers to do so.'"[27] Later in the year Mao was in a bellicose mood and in late 1967 told Ho Chi Minh that he should "consider a strategy of annihilation," a suggestion Ho found "logical and reasonable."[28]

Meanwhile, Moscow was signaling that it would prefer the conflict to draw down. The Soviet Communists had supported Ho Chi Minh's efforts for decades, and maintained about 3,000 troops in North Vietnam as technical advisers.[29] But in 1967 Moscow believed that the best way forward was through negotiations, as was evident at the June 1967 Glassboro, New Jersey, summit conference between President Johnson and Soviet Premier Alexei Kosygin. The mood at the summit was generally upbeat, and the expression "the spirit of Glassboro" was a precursor to "détente" as a means of expressing a general mood of U.S./Soviet understanding and cooperation. The main topics at the summit were the recently concluded six-day war in the Middle East and ballistic missile defense, but they also discussed Vietnam. Kosygin noted archly that the United States had bombed Hanoi during his recent visit, and the President countered that it was nothing personal; he had no idea Kosygin was there, and, besides, it was a consequence of visiting war zones. Dean Rusk had been near a bombing in Saigon, for example. Kosygin wanted the United States to end bombing unconditionally as a condition for peace talks. Johnson was in favor of the idea if it could be implemented, as he always had been, but he was skeptical that Moscow could convince Hanoi to cooperate. He noted that during an earlier bombing halt the North had not responded with an agreement to negotiate. "You didn't have any influence in Hanoi," Johnson said. "The Chinese had taken over. You couldn't deliver them."[30]

Hanoi's conflicting guidance from Moscow and Beijing was set against the backdrop of the growing schism between the two Communist country giants. The days of monolithic communism were over. The Sino-Soviet rift began to appear in 1956 with the advent of the anti-Stalin campaign in the USSR and had reached critical proportions by the late 1960s.[31] Tensions peaked in the spring of 1969 with a series of border clashes that threatened all-out war.

The rivalry was played out in Hanoi as members of Chinese and Soviet factions in the Lao Dong Party campaigned against one another, with the Chinese faction prevailing. Members of the Chinese faction were able to use Moscow's reticence to help press the fight in the South to sow distrust of the Soviet Union among other members of the Hanoi leadership. An "anti-party plot" was "uncovered" in the summer and fall of 1967, and a major purge commenced just after the Glassboro Summit, during the period when the Tet plan was adopted. In September 1967, 200 senior North Vietnamese party officials were arrested for oppositionist activities, including the head of intelligence.[32] In November 1967 the national assembly published an edict about harshly punishing counter-revolutionary crimes. The Hanoi leadership was convinced that its government was riddled with potential traitors.

General Giap may have thought that he was one of the targets of the purge. At the height of the arrests he went to Hungary, ostensibly for medical treatment, although he may have been trying to avoid charges of being a counter-revolutionary for opposing the Tet plan.

Giap had long had a feud with General Thanh. They were the only two four-star general equivalents in the North Vietnamese Army, and both had strong political influence. As a Politburo member, Thanh was said to be aligned with the pro-Chinese faction, and Giap was known to be skeptical of the advice the leadership received from Beijing. Giap's approach to the war was more cautious than Thanh's, and the two had crossed swords before. In July 1966 Thanh publicly attacked Giap's views in the party newspaper, *Hoc Tap*. He did not criticize Giap by name but called the conservative ideas that he was promoting "old-fashioned" and "detached from reality." In January 1967 Truong Son, a Thanh spokesman, published a speech again emphasizing the importance of engaging the American forces, as opposed to the more defensive posture Giap recommended.[33]

Thanh's ideas had clearly gained significant support in Hanoi by the summer of 1967, and Giap might have found himself marginalized. But fate stepped in when Tranh died unexpectedly in July. First reports were that he had died from bomb fragments in his chest.[34] Thanh was conducting an inspection tour in Binh Duong Province in South Vietnam when the area was bombed by American aircraft. General Thanh was wounded by shrapnel and taken to North Vietnam via Cambodia for treatment, where he died. However, another story followed that Thanh died of a heart attack following a "long series of meetings" in Hanoi and two farewell parties on July 6, at which Thanh drank heavily.[35] An American analysis found that "for fear that other VC cadre would become demoralized, COSVN announced in July 1967 that the general died from a heart attack, rather than from wounds received during a bombing."[36] Bui Tin said that the deception operation was aimed at an external audience, that the heart attack story was floated to deny the Americans a key bit of good news. Ton That Can, a VC assistant propaganda officer captured in March 1968, said that Thanh's death in combat was well known among the VC. When Hanoi started to float the story about a heart attack following drinking at parties, senior officers in his unit "vehemently complained that the truth should be told, and that it was no disgrace for a military man to be killed in battle with his troops." The attempt to "conceal the fact that the [North Vietnamese Army] was indeed in the South was unworthy of the memory of Nguyen Chi Thanh."[37]

Tranh's death left Giap with the responsibility of executing the Tet plan. He had initially opposed it and may have counseled waiting or changing the plan. In his essay "Big Victory/ Great Task," first thought to be a rallying call for the Tet strategy, Giap clearly calls for an intensification of the military struggle, including a direct assault on enemy conventional forces, but not following the Tet template. "The military struggle of the South Vietnamese people has developed and is developing strongly, quickly, and steadfastly, in both forms—guerrilla warfare and large-scale combat," he wrote. Giap was opposed to the purely guerrilla approach and sought instead to combine guerrilla tactics with conventional battles. He listed the main objective of the military struggle as "to destroy the enemy military force," which was not an aspect of the Tet plan, at least not with respect to American forces, which were to be avoided. Giap mentions urban warfare, which was the centerpiece of the Tet plan, only in one short paragraph in the 52-page essay. And although he heaps praise on various other aspects of guerrilla war, he says the "tactic of attacking cities is being developed."[38] This was not a ringing endorsement for a plan that features city fighting as the central focus.

Giap also seems to argue that the timing was not right for such a massive attack. He asserts that the long-term strategy had been effective, and that the longer the United States stays in Vietnam the more difficult the fight becomes for them. He concludes that "the longer the fight, the more mature our forces become, and the weaker the enemy forces." Giap is arguing for continuing the protracted struggle, and perhaps seeking a decisive engagement later. But by the late summer of 1967 a defensive posture was considered not just overcautious but actively counter-revolutionary.

"Big Victory, Great Task" appeared in serial form at the same time as the anti-party group arrests and Giap's trip to Hungary, reportedly to seek medical attention for exhaustion after completing the essay. It may be significant that Giap went to a distant Soviet satellite state when the leadership frequently sought medical help in Beijing. It seems clear that Giap had never been a proponent of the Tet plan. Giap had always had his eyes on the ultimate and decisive conventional phase of the struggle. "Some engaged in wishful thinking without firmly grasping the rules of revolutionary uprisings and warfare," he wrote concerning Tet in 2005, "and there emerged a subjective view advocating a general uprising that would have exposed completely the revolutionary bases of the people right at a time when there were a million U.S. and Saigon troops and their allies on the battlefield." The city attacks "during the 1968 Tet Offensive ended up causing tremendous losses in terms of the revolution's position and strength."[39]

Tet's background, objectives, and assumptions are vital to understanding why the offensive took place and what the enemy expected. There has been a tendency since the Vietnam War to regard America's unconventional adversaries in almost superhuman terms. In this view, the terrorists and guerrillas are long-term thinkers who make plans spanning decades. They are methodical and precise. Their systems are complex and adaptive. They are motivated by institutional or ideological values rather than personality traits or emotions. Their attacks, whatever their effects, are calculated against an unfathomable plan, always cleverer than we can hope to understand and more dangerous than we realize.

But almost none of this is true, and attributing these qualities to the enemy is a serious shortcoming. It is exhibited by policymakers, national security and intelligence analysts, academics, the media, and the public. They assess the effectiveness of enemy actions not by measuring the results against what the attackers intended to do but by subjectively assessing how they affected policymakers, politicians, or the public. Assessments of impact are more commonly framed in the American domestic political context than in the more complex environment in which the conflict is being fought. If everything the enemy does is considered the successful execution of a comprehensive plan, and every outcome is believed to be that which the enemy intended, it is by definition impossible to achieve victory. This self-imposed asymmetry makes defeating an adversary much more difficult. Thus

a realistic appraisal of Tet must assess the offensive against what
the enemy planned to do and what it hoped to achieve, not in the
framework adopted by American policymakers, politicians, and
the media. The two most salient facts in this regard are that by
1967 the Communists knew they could not win the war without a
dramatic turn of events, and they believed Tet was their last-ditch
chance to prevail. It was not intended to be a symbolic attack, or
to send a message, or to give the Communists a better bargaining
posture. Tet was intended to win the war through sparking a mass
uprising, overthrowing the South Vietnamese government, and
making the position of the U.S. military untenable. That was
how the enemy defined victory, and none of it was achieved. "The
flawed application of the idea of revolutionary offense," General
Giap wrote, "was yet another costly lesson paid for in blood and
bone."[40]

V.

THE LIGHT AT THE END OF THE TUNNEL

One of the best-remembered expressions of the Vietnam War is "the light at the end of the tunnel," the fabled indication of progress that never seemed to arrive. It is often regarded as first being uttered in the months leading up to the Tet Offensive, and many cite an interview with National Security Adviser Walter W. Rostow in the December 1967 edition of *Look* magazine. Others cite William Westmoreland at his November 21, 1967, National Press Club speech. But the expression had been in play for years. Henry Cabot Lodge used it in January 1967; Hubert Humphrey said it in 1966; Rostow saw the light even in 1965; and in 1964 Vietnam skeptic

> We are winning the war.
>
> —GENERAL EARL G. WHEELER,
> CHAIRMAN OF THE
> JOINT CHIEFS OF STAFF

Walter Lippmann declared there was no light at the end of the Southeast Asian tunnel before the U.S. could properly be said to have entered it.[1] The expression had been used widely in the 1950s, with respect to the war in Korea in 1950 (again, before the true length of the tunnel was realized), Cyprus in 1954, the Congo crisis, various disputes over Formosa, and the Cold War in general. But it was most tellingly employed by French General Henri Navarre in May 1953, a year before lights out at Dien Bien Phu.

Lyndon Johnson's advisers may well have thought themselves in a tunnel, with the President's approval ratings for his conduct of the war at low ebb. Nevertheless, there was some reason for optimism. In March 1967 the Council of Ministers of the Republic of Vietnam approved a new constitution ten days ahead of schedule. A month later the South Vietnamese government announced it would hold free and open elections for president and vice president. The serving president was General Nguyen Van Thieu, who was generally considered a figurehead ruler. The real power in the country was General and Prime Minister Nguyen Cao Ky, a flamboyant former fighter pilot whose penchant for wearing black flight suits and a lavender scarf earned him the nickname "Captain Midnight." Ky was a capable ruler who had committed himself to rooting out corruption from Vietnamese politics, with mixed results. However, Washington favored Thieu, and after consultation with U.S. Ambassador Ellsworth Bunker, Ky unexpectedly chose not to run for president and accepted instead the second spot on the ticket behind Thieu. Ky later called this decision the biggest mistake of his life.

The election was held on September 3, 1967, under relatively peaceful conditions. Turnout was 83% of the registered voters, and most disruptions were caused not by the Viet Cong but by students and Buddhists. The Thieu/Ky ticket gained a plurality with 34.8% of the vote. Truong Dinh Dzu, a somewhat disreputable Buddhist lawyer nominated as the Popular Front peace candidate, came in second with 16% of the vote. His platform called for a coalition government with the Communists, and he used the dove as his symbol on the ballot.[2] A dispute arose over whether a plurality of the vote was adequate to elect Thieu, and the debate continued for some weeks until the Constituent Assembly voted 58–43 on October 2 to validate the election. Thieu was finally sworn in October 31.

Earlier in the year the budget for the U.S. pacification program had been increased, and on May 10, 1967, the Administration established the Civilian Operations and Revolutionary (later Rural) Development Support (CORDS) organization to oversee it. CORDS was run by Robert Komer, a former Army Intelligence officer, CIA operative, and NSC staffer who had a reputation as a skilled bureaucratic warrior who could get things done. He was awarded the sobriquet "Blowtorch Bob" by Henry Cabot Lodge, who said, "Arguing with Komer was like having a blowtorch aimed at the seat of your pants."[3] Like McNamara, he was a devotee of statistics and metrics. He developed a rating system known as the Hamlet Evaluation Survey (HES), based on monthly, 77-question surveys of each hamlet, filled out by senior district advisers.[4] The HES generated thousands of bits of economic, social, and security data, but the amount of information may have been overkill. As John Roche noted:

> [HES] was sociology's contribution to winning the war in Vietnam. The fact is that the military were pretty close to right when they said that the way to control the hearts and minds of the peasants is to guarantee them that they're not going to be shot at, because basically they're non-political. They want security. If you can guarantee them that, then they are happy.[5]

By the end of 1967, based on HES data, CORDS claimed that two thirds of South Vietnamese citizens lived under government control.[7]

Another major focus of the war effort at this time was building up the South Vietnamese military. This was a critical task, since the nation's armed forces would have to guarantee South Vietnamese freedom once the United States departed. By the end of 1967 the South Vietnamese armed forces had around 350,000 regular troops, 300,000 provincial and local militia, and 42,000 Civilian

Irregular Defense Groups (mainly Montagnard tribesmen). There were also 70,000 paramilitary National Police forces. However, Saigon faced the same type of challenges that continue to plague armed forces in the developing world: corruption, politicization, poor logistics and supply systems, inadequate training and doctrine, outdated equipment, substandard interoperability with U.S. forces, and, most critically, intelligence penetration by the enemy. General Palmer relates an experience when he visited the 25th ARVN Division headquarters at Duc Hoa:

> The division commander would discuss only trivial matters in his office; he took me outside well away from any building, with only the two of us present. Here he explained that he strongly suspected that his own Division G-2 (intelligence officer) was a Viet Cong agent; thus he dare not discuss operational matters in his own command post.[6]

Even given the difficulties its ally faced, the United States felt confident enough in South Vietnamese capabilities to turn over the defense of Saigon on December 15, 1967.

MCNAMARA'S DOWNFALL

Even as the situation in South Vietnam improved, one of the war's architects had already lost faith. In the fall of 1966, Robert McNamara returned from a four-day trip to South Vietnam and quietly recommended that Johnson freeze troop levels and seek a negotiated solution. In essence, he told the President that the war was unwinnable. The symbol of McNamara's disillusionment was his further recommendation that the United States construct a security barrier south of the DMZ along the border with the North, from the South China Sea to the Laotian border. The project soon became known as McNamara's Wall.

General Davidson called the barrier "one of the most preposterous concepts of this singular war."[7] It was conceived by

Robert Fisher of the Harvard Law School, and pitched to John McNaughton, the Assistant Secretary of Defense for International Security affairs, who then passed it on to the Secretary. McNamara saw the barrier as a useful alternative to bombing and a way to shift the policy debate. But the idea ran into strong opposition. The military argued that a static barrier was too costly to construct and maintain, and would ultimately be ineffective. John Roche observed at a meeting on the barrier that unless it stretched all the way to the Indian Ocean it could easily be circumvented, and in any case the Ho Chi Minh Trail already went around the planned terminus at Khe Sanh. "If you cut this thing off at the Laotian border, it's futile," he said. Roche later noted, "That was the last 'barrier' meeting I was invited to."[8]

The wall was also viewed as a symptom of McNamara's declining role in the Johnson administration. The Whiz Kid who entered office with energy, innovative concepts, and a mandate to change the way business was done in the Pentagon could come up with nothing better than a strategy the Romans used against the Picts, and which was already a very old idea in Vietnam. In the mid-1600s the Nguyen clan, a group of warlords with their seat at Hue, erected a double line of walls from the sea to the hills near the city of Dong Ha, not far from where McNamara wanted to build his barrier. The walls successfully defended the Nguyen from the northern Trinh clan for forty years, and helped guarantee a century-long peaceful division of Vietnam.

McNamara's Wall was debated through 1966, and by 1967 it had gained enough support to begin construction by linking the outposts that already existed along the DMZ. But by then Johnson was questioning whether McNamara could continue as Defense Secretary. As early as April 1967 Johnson began to look for another position to shift McNamara into, moving cautiously because he feared for the increasingly morose Secretary's mental health. As Roche observed, "McNamara had, for all intents and purposes, gone into a semi-comatose state by the summer of 1967." Johnson once told him, "I don't know about Bob. We can't have another Forrestal," referring to James Vincent Forrestal, the

first Secretary of Defense, who died May 22, 1949, under myste-
rious circumstances after having been fired by President Truman.
His death was ruled a suicide caused by depression. "Everything
that McNamara had believed in was going down in smoke," Roche
said.[9]

Sensing that his time at the Pentagon was short, McNamara
began to look to his legacy. In June 1967 he had his staff begin
a project to document the history of U.S. decision-making in
Vietnam. "It was prepared secretly by a team of about forty civilian
and military officials knowledgeable about Vietnam," General
Palmer noted. "Some of the authors were bitter, outspoken critics
of the war, and their bias is reflected in some parts of the report."[10]
The project ground on until January 1969, by which time McNamara was long gone, but its impact was felt in June 1971 when the
New York Times published excerpts leaked by Daniel Ellsworth in
what became known as the Pentagon Papers.[11]

From July 7 to 11, 1967, McNamara and General Wheeler traveled to Vietnam to assess the situation, and what they saw did not
give McNamara reason for hope. In late August McNamara testi-
fied before the Preparedness Subcommittee of the Senate Armed
Services Committee, and the members rebuked him for saying
among other things that the war could not be won by bombing
alone. Some senators believed the military situation was better
than what McNamara stated; others said that if his pessimistic
prognosis was correct the United States should withdraw. This
difference of opinion prompted press speculation that there were
deep divisions within the Administration regarding the bombing
campaign, which Johnson was obliged to deny at a September
1 Oval Office press briefing. A clearly agitated Johnson paced
back and forth behind his desk explaining to reporters that there
had been differences of opinion but no "deep division" and that
the situation had been "blown out of all proportion." He called
a report that McNamara would resign if the bombing campaign
was expanded "the most ridiculous report I have ever seen since
I became President."[12]

McNamara remained, but the bombing campaign intensified. Johnson knew the public wanted more concerted action

in Vietnam, and responded accordingly. He moved away from McNamara's gloomy prognosis and toward the more muscular position of the hawks. "When it came down to decision-making on Vietnam, from the summer of 1967 on," John Roche noted, "it was less and less McNamara, more and more Bus Wheeler, the Chairman of the Joint Chiefs of Staff, with Paul Nitze, who was Deputy Secretary of Defense, and Clark Clifford, who [were] two of the hardest hawks in town." When Roche questioned the utility of "this indeterminable blowing up of garages in North Vietnam by B-52s," he was called into a private meeting with the President and Clifford. Twenty years later he said, "I still have their footprints engraved on my ass."[13] When asked if he was a hawk or dove, Clifford responded, "I am not conscious of falling under any of those ornithological divisions."[14]

On August 3, 1967, Johnson announced that the troop ceiling would be raised to 525,000, and he also took the political risk of calling for a 10% surtax to support the war effort. In that same month, bombing raids were extended into downtown Hanoi, and Johnson began to overrule McNamara on other targeting decisions. Bombing was further escalated in late September and early October, which finally began to put pressure on North Vietnam's ability to support the VC and PAVN in the South. Bombing was no longer just an exercise in diplomatic signaling; it was increasingly a means of waging war.

Halting attempts at diplomacy continued, however. On September 29, 1967, in a speech before the National Legislative Conference in San Antonio, Johnson announced new conditions for negotiations, which became known as the "San Antonio Formula." In this proposal, which was crafted in the Office of the Secretary of Defense, the United States offered to halt bombing if the North Vietnamese would agree to prompt, productive talks and not "take advantage" of the bombing halt by continuing to send men and materiel to the South. The U.S. dropped its previous hard precondition that North Vietnam stop all infiltration, and instead merely reserved the right to respond if it continued. This proposal was swiftly rejected by Hanoi, as had been all previous proposals, regardless of the subtle softening in the American position.

For their part, the Joint Chiefs approved of Johnson's more aggressive approach and had an even bolder agenda. On October 17, 1967, the Chiefs submitted their answer to a question asked by the President on September 12: "What military actions consistent with present policy guidelines would serve to increase pressure on North Vietnam, thereby accelerating the rate of progress toward achievement of the U.S. objective in South Vietnam?" The Chiefs noted that while progress was being made, it "continued to be slow largely because U.S. military power has been constrained in a manner which had reduced significantly its impact and effectiveness." For it to speed up, "an appropriate increase in military pressure was required." The courses of action they recommended included removing bombing restrictions on militarily significant targets in the North; mining North Vietnamese deep-water ports and inland waterways; conducting offensive naval surface operations against North Vietnamese ships and suitable targets ashore; expanding operations in Laos and Cambodia; and expanding the covert operation code-named Footboy to destabilize the North Vietnamese government.[15] A Gallup poll from early October that gauged support for a similar plan but included the option to "go all out and use atomic weapons and bombs if the Army believes we should" attracted 42% support.[16] But there were limits to Johnson's taste for escalation. The old restrictions still applied. Recalling the 1965 meeting in which he dressed down his military commanders, Johnson responded that the Chiefs had "recommended actions which had previously been denied and would not now be approved." Meanwhile, on November 1, McNamara secretly recommended halting all bombing and limiting U.S. ground involvement. After careful consideration, Johnson rejected the proposal.

THE BORDER BATTLES

While U.S. Vietnam policy was shifting toward escalation, the Communists conducted a series of four nearly sequential major probing attacks from September to December 1967. They struck on the South Vietnamese frontier, and the engagements became known as "the border battles." According to General Tran Van

86

Tra, the battles were "feints to draw American troops away from Saigon and populated areas." They were also viewed as a means of testing command and control and other capabilities for the upcoming Tet Offensive.

The Communist fall offensive kicked off on September 11, 1967, with an attack on the Marine outpost at Con Thien, just south of the inaptly named demilitarized zone. Con Thien, set among a cluster of three prominent hills, was an important observation post and was locally known as the hill of angels, which took on a deeper meaning to its defenders, given the number of people killed in order to hold it. Con Thien had been the scene of a short but savage fight the previous May, when enemy troops breached the perimeter with flamethrowers before being driven back, and it had seen sporadic attacks since. In September the enemy bludgeoned the firebase with rockets and mortars placed illegally inside the DMZ. The shellfire was intense; at its peak on September 25 the enemy hit Con Thien with 1,190 rounds. Westmoreland responded with Operation Neutralize, a 49-day fire support campaign based on the SLAM concept (seek, locate, annihilate, monitor). The enemy around Con Thien was hit with every form of ordinance available—B-52s, naval fire, artillery, and tactical air—which pulverized its concentrated forces and disrupted any possible ground assault. The siege lasted until October 31, when the North Vietnamese gave up.

On October 27, the 88th PAVN regiment attacked the headquarters of the 9th ARVN Regiment at Song Be in III Corps near the Cambodian border; it was repulsed after a few days.[17] On October 29, the VC 273rd regiment attacked the Special Forces camp at Loc Ninh in III Corps near the Cambodian border and was beaten back after a battle lasting six days. The area was in heavy jungle, which made for some close-quarters fighting. At one point the enemy made a bayonet charge over the base airstrip directly into the guns of a U.S. artillery battery. The VC attackers were met with beehive munitions, similar to a 19th century canister round, and wiped out. Infantry units from the 1st Infantry Division were rushed to the battle, and the enemy was again defeated with heavy casualties.[18]

The most serious of the four attacks began on November 3 at Dak To in the Central Highlands, Kontum Province, in the northern part of II Corps. The PAVN had been quietly building up forces and defensive positions in the hills around Dak To, hoping to isolate and destroy a brigade-sized unit and pull reinforcements away from the cities and plains toward the border region. A document captured during the fighting revealed that the PAVN was trying to draw U.S. troops into the mountainous areas as well as test techniques of coordinated attack. But intelligence on enemy intentions, including information from a defector, a sergeant named Vu Hong, allowed the Americans to strike first. The battle developed into a series of assaults on enemy-defended hilltops, in which the PAVN was able to inflict heavier than normal casualties but typically suffered even more. The American 173rd Airborne Brigade and Fourth Infantry Division, plus several ARVN units, including the 3rd and 9th Airborne battalions, bore the brunt of the fighting. The dense foliage and hilly terrain were well suited to the enemy's concept of tactical defensive, and these conditions also made air and artillery support for the American attacks more difficult. The savage hill fights were some of the worst conventional encounters of the war. The enemy also launched periodic rocket and mortar attacks on the Dak To airstrip, the worst coming on November 12, destroying several aircraft and stockpiled ammunition and fuel. The fighting went on until December 1, when the last enemy units retreated west into Cambodia and Laos.[19]

General Davidson concluded that the main lesson the enemy learned from the border battles was "avoid any direct attacks on American positions." A Communist colonel who defected in 1968 called them "useless and bloody."[20] But the lesson the enemy drew was that Americans could in fact be drawn to the frontiers, one of its objectives in the months before Tet, and plans for the offensive continued to move ahead.

THE SUCCESS CAMPAIGN

In the fall of 1967 Johnson had reason to believe that the situation in Vietnam was improving. The enemy had been unable to win on the battlefield, and hopes were high that the new round of escalated bombing in the North would lead to the sought-after negotiations. However, Johnson was painfully aware of his lack of public support over the war effort. Try as he might to promote a positive view of the war, he was saddled with what had become known as the "credibility gap."

This expression is indelibly imprinted on the Johnson Administration, but it was introduced during the Kennedy era. In December 1962 Senator Kenneth B. Keating (R-NY) stated in a speech before the United States Inter-American Council that the United States had to "plug the credibility gap" regarding the Cuba issue and take a definitive stand so that the Soviet Union would know where the U.S. stood.[21] The expression was notably applied to Vietnam in 1965 in a *Washington Post* article by Murrey Marder, noting the "perceptively growing disquiet, misgiving or skepticism about the candor or validity of official declarations."[22] In late 1966, wag Jack Wilson defined "credibility gap" as "the shrinking distance between LBJ's foot and [Press Secretary] Bill Moyers' mouth."[23] The expression enjoyed frequent usage thereafter and by 1967 was firmly established as a cliché.

But the credibility gap reflected a genuine public concern; a March 1967 Gallup poll asked: "Do you think the Johnson administration is not telling the public all they should know about the Vietnam War?" Only 23% thought the Administration was telling the truth; 65% said it was not.[24] By October 1967 public confidence had fallen to 21%/71%[25] This skepticism prepared the ground for the events of the spring of 1968, which were seen as ultimate confirmation of the gap between Administration statements and the reality on the ground. Daniel Ellsberg later wrote, "The immense impact of Tet on the public consciousness and the attitude of Congress can be understood only against the background of the intense public lying over the preceding six months."[26]

Ellsberg was referring in part to a public relations blitz the Johnson Administration mounted in November 1967 dubbed the "success campaign." Ambassador Bunker, General Westmoreland, and others made a series of high-profile public appearances to highlight progress in Vietnam. The series' subject was called the "Success Campaign," allegedly after Army Chief of Staff General Harold K. Johnson said there was a "smell of success" in every aspect of the war effort during a two-week tour of military installations.

On November 13 Ambassador Bunker reported to the President that the U.S. was "making steady progress, not only militarily, but in other ways as well—in the evolution of the constitutional process and in pacification, which in my view is equally as important as military progress."[27] The next day he took this message to "The Today Show." On November 16 General Westmoreland reported to the House Armed Services Committee that progress had been made and that the United States might be able to begin to pull out of South Vietnam within two years if trends continued. Westmoreland delivered his most important speech to the National Press Club on November 21, in which he outlined U.S. war strategy and said the war had entered the final phase, "when the end begins to come into view." In one of the most quoted passages, he stated, "I am absolutely certain that whereas in 1965 the enemy was winning, today he is certainly losing." The next day the Washington Post headlined: "War's End in View."

The public began to respond to the idea that the situation in Vietnam was improving. Polls showed that in July 1967 only 34% of Americans believed the country was making progress in Vietnam, while 46% believed the U.S. was standing still and 11% believed we were losing. By the end of November 1967, 51% believed progress was being made, while 33% believed the war was stalemated and 8% thought we were losing.[28] A Harris poll from December showed that 62% opposed de-escalation as a way of showing peaceful intentions to get the enemy to negotiate, while 58% supported convincing the Communists they would lose the war if they continued fighting. Two thirds wanted to build up the South Vietnamese army to take over the fighting. General Westmoreland's performance in Vietnam was rated as "excellent" or "pretty good" by 68%, with only 16% rating his performance as "fair" or "poor."

By contrast, Robert McNamara's job performance was rated "fair" or "poor" by 45%. But by then it did not matter. Increasingly marginalized within the Administration, frustrated and upset with the new course of the war, and seeing his final proposal to wind down the war rejected, McNamara called it quits. On November 29, President Johnson announced that McNamara would step down as Secretary of Defense to become president of the World Bank. No successor was named, and McNamara agreed to stay on as Defense Secretary until he completed work on the FY 1969 Defense budget. His lame duck period would last three more agonizing months.

1967 ended with a burst of optimism about the war effort. In his end-of-year report Westmoreland reported that "the enemy [was] increasingly resorting to desperation tactics in attempting to achieve military/psychological victory; and he has experienced only failure in these attempts. Enemy bases, with sparse exception, are no longer safe havens and he has necessarily become increasingly reliant on Cambodian and Laotian sanctuaries. . . . The friendly picture gives rise to optimism for increased successes in 1968."[29] On December 23, during a visit to Vietnam, Johnson declared that "the enemy is not beaten, but he knows that he has met his master in the field." However, Administration optimism was tempered with the understanding that something was afoot. Early intelligence was indicating the enemy might have a dramatic move in mind. On December 18, 1967, General Wheeler spoke to the Detroit Economic Club and told the assembled that "we are winning the war." But he warned of possible future attacks. "There is still some heavy fighting ahead," Wheeler said; "it is entirely possible that there may be a Communist thrust similar to the desperate effort of the Germans in the Battle of the Bulge in Word War Two."[30]

On New Year's Eve 1967 a group of young attachés at the U.S. embassy in Saigon, calling themselves "The Flower People," held a "Light at the End of the Tunnel" costume party.[31] But as Ambassador Ellsworth Bunker said when he left Saigon in May 1973, "The tunnel was longer and the light was dimmer and farther away than any of us realized."

VI.

CODE NAME: BUTTERCUP

President Johnson's charm offensive in the fall of 1967, coupled with escalated bombing in North Vietnam, raised American confidence in his handling of the conflict. But during this same period America suffered a black eye with the South Vietnamese. The United States' embarrassment came at the hands of the chief of the South Vietnamese National Police, General Nguyen Ngoc Loan, the third most powerful political figure in South Vietnam, whom the Tet Offensive would make one of the most recognized and despised public figures in the world.

The controversy began in October 1967, when Loan's men picked up two

> I'll tell you what the signals from Hanoi are saying: "F**k you, Lyndon Johnson."
>
> —LYNDON JOHNSON

NLF emissaries headed for the U.S. embassy. One was a former Saigon school teacher named Nguyen Van Huan, alias Sau Ha.[1] Loan had information that Sau Ha and his accomplice were on their way to a meeting with American officials to discuss U.S./VC prisoner exchanges. Such direct, high-level contact between the U.S. and the insurgency without the participation of the South Vietnamese government was unprecedented and, in Loan's view, intolerable. His men apprehended the NLF envoys near the embassy and whisked them off to prison.

The arrest was kept out of the press until early December, but when the story broke it hit hard. The prospect of secret contacts between the U.S. and the NLF presumably without the consent of the South Vietnamese government greatly damaged America's reputation. Over the next few weeks rumors began to circulate about the circumstances surrounding the arrests. Some said Sau Ha was making initial contact with the Americans. Other reports said the U.S. and NLF already had held one secret meeting and that this was a follow-up. The United States consistently though not unequivocally denied that any such meetings had or were to have taken place, or that anything of the kind would occur without the prior knowledge of the RVN government. But there was more to the story than the American government was letting on. Reporters waiting in the outer offices of the Joint United States Public Affairs Office in Saigon heard officials behind closed doors raving about General Loan and repeatedly shouting, "That son of a bitch!"

GENERAL NGUYEN NGOC LOAN

Nguyen Ngoc Loan was born in 1930, the eldest of 11 children of a well-to-do family in Hue. His father was a successful mechanical engineer. Loan attended the prestigious Quoc Hoc High School, where he was a good student, and he excelled in music, becoming a skilled pianist with a taste for Chopin and Brahms. Loan fought for the Viet Minh in his teens but broke ties with the movement in 1949. He attended Hue University, where he was an honor student and received degrees in the natural sciences, pharmacy, and engineering. He also took a management course at MIT. After college Loan volunteered for officer training and graduated at the top of his class, which included future Prime Minister Nguyen Cao Ky. He was commissioned into the South Vietnamese Army as an infantryman but was soon singled out for his intelligence and initiative and sent to Morocco for flight training, then to the Ecole de l'Air, the French Air Force Academy in Salon de Provence.

Loan proved to be a daring and resourceful pilot who led the first South Vietnamese air mission against Hanoi. He had a fighter pilot's personality, not as flamboyant as Ky but highly competent, with a strong streak of independence and practical disobedience. John L. Hart, CIA Station Chief in Saigon from 1966 to 1968, wrote that "Loan was always a maverick who never conformed to anyone's stereotype of the compliant officer; trained by French and Americans, he greeted the preachments of both with the same restrained skepticism."[2] Loan became Ky's Chief of Staff when Ky commanded the South Vietnamese Air Force. Ky wrote that Loan "was fearless and carried out my orders with a great sense of responsibility. He always said what was on his mind and never cared about what anyone, including the U.S. media, wrote about him . . . [he was] a skilled, courageous, devoted and principled patriot."[3]

Loan's career trajectory tracked with Ky's, and his fortunes improved markedly when Ky was appointed prime minister in 1965. Loan had just returned from an air mission in May of that year when he was offered the job of chief of the Military Security Service (MSS), the military counter-intelligence bureau. The previous chief, named Chinh, had been arrested for allegedly plotting against the government. Loan was not particularly interested in the position, since flying was his passion, but he accepted it out of a sense of loyalty to his patron Ky.

Ky was determined to fight corruption in the South Vietnamese government and the society at large, and he saw Loan as a key instrument in this struggle. Ky noted that Loan was "the rarest of Vietnamese birds, an honest cop."[4] He said that "Loan was exactly the kind of man I needed to help me cleanse Vietnamese society. . . . [He was] one of the few completely honest and incorruptible men in Vietnam . . . the opportunities for graft and bribery were endless. Loan never took a cent."[5] Loan demonstrated his degree of professionalism by investigating Ky's sister Thi Ly, who was suspected of smuggling. He uncovered nothing but impressed many with his integrity and commitment to his job.

Loan was highly effective in his position as counter-intelligence chief and was rewarded with ever-increasing responsibilities. By 1966 he commanded the MSS, the National Police, Military Intelligence (G-2), and the Central Intelligence Organization (CIO). A CIA report on Loan's appointment to the latter post noted that "Ky chose Loan because Loan is trustworthy, has no political affiliations, and has kept clear of controversy." The CIA concluded that the greatest problem Loan faced was corruption and that he "may be able to correct the situation at CIO."[6] Another report noted: "Loan has a power apparatus that has substantial influence on virtually all the senior leaders and also on most province and district chiefs." He not only was responsible for the physical safety of the leadership but also was in a position to know about the channels of corruption and other extra-legal activities that politicians and military leaders were involved in, as well as their personal peccadilloes, private activities, and relationships. This gave Loan a substantial degree of influence, and generated marked enmity in some quarters.[7]

There were periodic calls for Loan's ouster, particularly from Ky's political opponents, who viewed Loan as one of the prime minister's critical pillars of political support. Loan was active in organizing political groups at the local level, and he set up situation rooms in each province to report on local activities. He established a dock workers union to compete with an established union he did not trust. And he controlled the nationalist newspaper *Cong Chung*, which served as an outlet for whatever information Loan wanted to publicize.

Loan played a critical role during a severe crisis in the north in the spring of 1966. Ky had dismissed General Nguyen Chanh Thi, commander of the South Vietnamese I Corps, a political rival and perennial coup plotter whom Ky accused of being a warlord.

Thi's removal sparked widespread rioting and civil disobedience, fanned by the Buddhist-led "Struggle Movement." Troops loyal to Thi in Da Nang, where his headquarters was located, also rebelled, establishing defensive perimeters around the Buddhist pagodas. Shots were exchanged between pro-Thi and pro-government troops. Major General Huynh Van Cao, the newly appointed commander of I Corps, hesitated to order a full-on attack against the dissidents. Outraged, President Ky sent in Loan, who relieved Cao of command and ordered the attack.[8] Scores were killed, yet Loan tried to keep casualties to a minimum. Rebels who had been holed up in the Da Nang radio station for months were convinced to surrender peacefully when Loan ordered a Patton tank to shoot a round into the roof.[9] In June 1966, while pacifying Hue, Loan took the city back slowly, block by block, with few shots being fired. During the final raid on the Buddhist headquarters at the Dieu De Pagoda, Loan passed out candies to children in the streets outside, then accompanied the Marine assault force that took the building and arrested the occupants with no casualties to either his men or the rebels.[10]

Given his degree of political involvement and the personal risks he had taken to stabilize the country, Loan was bitterly disappointed when Ky chose not to run for president in 1967 and instead took the second spot on a ticket with Thieu. That summer Loan said, "As long as Ky remains in power I will remain in power, and as long as I remain in power Ky will remain in power."[11] In October 1967, during the debate in the Constituent Assembly over the validity of the September election results, students demonstrating against Thieu and Ky were vigorously cleared by Loan's club-wielding police. As the Assembly voted on the election results, Loan's men roamed menacingly among the spectators while he was seen on the balcony, spinning the chambers of his revolver and sipping a beer.[12]

However, Loan was not predisposed to use violence unless he felt it was necessary. A few days after the vote in the Constituent Assembly, 500 Buddhists held a demonstration in the park across from Independence Palace, where their leader Thich Tri Quang was holding vigil under a tamarind tree. The Buddhists were protesting official recognition of the Buddhist Layman's League, an organization Loan had been instrumental in establishing behind the scenes, which was designed to enhance the authority of pro-government senior monk Thich Tam Chau. But Loan had a special relationship with Tri Quang; both were from Hue, they went to the same pagoda, and they had known each other for years.[13] Although the Buddhist gathering would have been illegal as a political demonstration, Loan chose to regard it as a prayer meeting. When asked why he was not breaking up the Buddhist gathering, as he had the student demonstration, Loan said, "It's a free country. Look yourself."[14]

Loan was an eccentric figure who accumulated nicknames like "The Cobra" or "The Hatchet." He was known on occasion to ride around Saigon in a jeep with a barber, forcing haircuts on long-haired youths he encountered in the streets. But he did not view himself as being a fearsome person. "My men always reproach me," Loan told Italian journalist Oriana Fallaci, famous for her interviews of famous people. "'You're too gentle for the job you do, you should be harder, more pitiless.' But I answer them, 'Politeness, my boys, politeness. Cruelty's no use in this job, one must be polite.'" But Loan had no use for the Viet Cong. "I know the Viet Cong; they're animals," he said. "Very human animals, but still animals."[15]

CIA Station Chief John Hart was impressed with Loan's leadership qualities. "He was an unassuming man even at the height of his authority," Hart said. Loan did not wear rank insignia, even on his dress uniform, and, as Hart noted, "he didn't need to because he was a born leader." Loan also saw to the welfare of his troops, which was atypical of high-ranking officers in that part of the world. "He was attentive to the little man," Hart said. "Unusual among Vietnamese officers, he fought harder for the well-being of his privates than for that of his colonels. Had South Vietnam had more leaders like him, it might still be independent."[16]

Oriana Fallaci met Loan in December 1967 and found him physically unprepossessing: "The ugliest little man I had ever seen, with a tiny twisted head screwed on to his meager shoulders," she wrote. "The only thing you noticed about the face was the mouth—so large and so out of proportion. From the mouth you looked directly down to the neck because the chin fell away so fast you wondered if it had existed. And the eyes, the eyes weren't really eyes; they were eyelids, that's all, scarcely visible through the slit. The nose, on the other hand, was a nose but so flat it was lost in the cheeks, which were also flat."[17] Sir Philip Goodhart, a British MP who visited South Vietnam in the summer of 1967, said that Loan "would scarcely win any prizes for popularity or good looks in Saigon—clumps of small, brown teeth appear to have been scattered quite haphazardly across his lower jaw. . . . But," Goodhart noted, "General Loan is not engaged in a beauty competition."[18] He had a hard job, and he did it well.

Goodhart observed that in the summer of 1967 Saigon had grown much safer on Loan's watch and that his 70,000-man force enjoyed "considerable success" in calming the city. Loan benefited from working with a team of British police advisers with experience in Africa. VC killings had dropped to as low as one per month. "The police special branch in Saigon has been notably effective in getting to grips with the local Communist infrastructure," Goodhart wrote, "and the flow of useful information has much improved."[19] To increase the information flow Loan had installed a suggestion box at the post office in Saigon that only he could open, and he encouraged citizens to help "foil dark schemes from subversive elements harmful to security."[20] Loan also set up an incentive program with rewards for tips that panned out.

But Loan's success did not earn him plaudits from the Americans. Some members of the press treated him with open hostility. R.W. Apple's October 1967 description was typical of those from people who disliked Loan; it called him "probably the most feared man in the country, and he has become, for the civilian political element at least, a symbol of illiberality and repression."[21] This was shortly after Loan's men had intentionally beaten three American reporters during the protests against the election of Thieu. Peter Arnett summed up Loan as "a feared man running a feared organization, with a flamboyant manner and a hair-trigger temper."[22] For his part, Loan did not go out of his way to court American reporters, and his stock response to their inquiries was "Silence

is golden." However, not all of Loan's press was bad. A January 19, 1968, *New York Times* article credited Loan with playing a "key role" in drastically cutting terror attacks in Saigon.[23] *Time* magazine called him "fearless, ruthless, but highly effective."[24] Horst Faas, the twice Pulitzer Prize-winning AP photo editor in Saigon and an old Vietnam hand, wrote: "U.S. commanders and newsmen who knew him respected him for his bravery and determination."[25] François Pelou, director of the Agence France-Presse office in Saigon, said "I find him a nice character . . . a very kind man."[26]

The U.S. government also had a mixed view of Loan. It was hard to argue with his success in stabilizing Saigon, but Loan was an ardent South Vietnamese nationalist who stood up to the U.S. when he felt it necessary. The CIA tracked his activities closely, and the Administration saw him as a troublemaker.[27] In December 1966 Loan had a run-in with the United States over the policing of Saigon. American MPs had detained and handcuffed the city's mayor, Van Van Cua, after he had fired a submachine gun into the air outside a floating restaurant called My Canh. The MPs who apprehended the mayor "detected an odor of alcohol" on him. But to Loan the issue was not public safety but jurisdiction. Loan issued a statement that thenceforward only the Vietnamese police could arrest Vietnamese civilians or members of the military. The South Vietnamese also held jurisdiction over American civilians. American MPs could arrest only American military personnel.[28] Loan was also skeptical of U.S. counterinsurgency methods. In late 1967 Loan was briefed on a U.S. plan to target the VC infrastructure called the Intelligence Coordination and Exploitation (ICEX) program, or Project Take-Off. Loan rejected South Vietnamese participation in the program but was overruled by Thieu in December 1967. This project was later renamed the Phoenix Program.

Johnson adviser Harry McPherson met Loan in May 1967 in Saigon at a dinner with Westmoreland's deputy General Creighton Abrams and some members of the Vietnamese government. "He showed up looking rather like a mischievous wild dog," McPherson said, "and he was treated as a kind of raffish scoundrel by the American I was with."[29] Station Chief John Hart, who was sympathetic to Loan, noted that "he was alive to the difficulties of imposing instant democracy upon an age-old hierarchical society embroiled in bitter civil war. But, shaking his head in doubt, he cooperated to the best of his understanding with the American politico-military game plan." [30]

CODE NAME: BUTTERCUP

The events surrounding the October 1967 arrest of the two NLF envoys heading for the U.S. embassy are a useful case study in the complex issues that can arise when assisting foreign states engaged in counterinsurgencies. Sometime in the fall of 1967 the NLF approached the United States to open a communications channel code-named Buttercup. The pretext for the opening was to discuss prisoner exchanges. This was a very sensitive issue to U.S. policymakers, and the opening was well timed. The South Vietnamese planned to execute three VC terrorists in Saigon in November 1967, and the Americans rushed to intervene, fearing that the Communists would commit reprisals against American POWs.[31]

This fear was justified. The Communists had begun reprisal killings two years earlier. On June 22, 1965, Viet Cong terrorist Tram Van Dong was executed publicly in Saigon, and two days later the NLF shot American POW Army Ranger Sergeant Harold G. Bennett. The NLF announced that the killing "serves to warn the U.S. aggressors and their henchmen who have committed acts of utmost barbarity in killing prisoners of war that the murderers must pay for their blood debts."[32] The U.S. denounced the murder as a war crime. In September, three VC agitators were executed in Da Nang, and the NLF responded by killing two captive members of the Special Forces, Sergeant First Class Kenneth M. Roraback and Captain Humbert Roque "Rocky" Versace.[33] Versace was well known among the POW community as an officer who went out of his way to show his contempt for his captors and engaged in various forms of resistance. Versace was posthumously awarded the Medal of Honor in 2002 for his conduct in captivity. After killing

Roraback and Versace, the North Vietnamese declared that thenceforward captured American flyers would be treated not as POWs but as war criminals and would be liable to be shot at any time. The North Vietnamese tactic of executing Americans rather than South Vietnamese was calculated to drive a wedge between Washington and Saigon. The Communists knew that the Americans would not respond to the tit-for-tat killings by executing their own prisoners but would seek to influence the South Vietnamese to ease up on their capital punishments. The Communists also balanced their threats and killings with high-profile incentives. On November 11, 1967, during the spat over the arrest of the two NLF emissaries to the U.S. embassy, the NLF handed over three U.S. POWs to antiwar activist Tom Hayden in Phnom Penh, Cambodia. The Communists said that this was part of their "humane and lenient" prisoner policy. Furthermore, two of the prisoners were African American, and the NLF declared that freeing the men was both in honor of the peace movement and of the "heroic struggle of the civil rights movement." This action prompted the State Department to pressure the South Vietnamese government to match the act as a goodwill gesture, which played into the hands of the Communists.[34]

The Buttercup opening seized the attention of Johnson's national security team. The years of strategic bombing and attrition warfare had made them impatient to find signs of diplomatic openings or initiatives from the North. Many believed that the Communist leadership would send some kind of subtle signal that negotiations were possible, and the hunt for signs of the great opening became an exercise in frustration. At a background briefing for reporters before the March 1967 Guam conference, Johnson was asked whether he had received signals from Hanoi. "Signals?" he said, "I'll tell you about signals. I got my antennae out in Washington. I got my antennae out in London. I got my antennae out in Paris. I got my antennae out in Tokyo. I even got my antennae out in *Rangoon*! You know what signals all my antennae are picking up from Hanoi? I'll tell you what the signals from Hanoi are saying: 'F**k you, Lyndon Johnson.'"[35]

Some were predisposed to see Buttercup as the first indication of the great diplomatic breakthrough they had been expecting. The Buttercup contact was read not simply as a channel to discuss prisoner exchanges but as a tentative feeler from the North that could lead to the advent of the sought-after armistice negotiations. Some more ambitious analysts further believed that the Buttercup channel indicated a split in the Communist leadership that could be exploited. Even the hawks bought into this psychology. Walt Rostow noted approvingly that the opening had occurred as the bombing campaign was stiffening, and argued that it indicated the effectiveness of escalation. LBJ adviser and Ambassador at Large Averill Harriman, a member of the Senior Group, gave an enthusiastic assessment of the Buttercup channel in a personal memo to Johnson separate from the official advisory group report. He noted that while some in the group believed that suggesting the possibility of a negotiated peace only encouraged Hanoi to hold out for a better deal, "there is no evidence whatever supporting this contention."[36]

The drive to divine positive signs in statements emanating from the Communists reached absurd proportions. When the U.S. received a message from the NLF that it was willing to discuss prisoner exchanges and broader issues but that "now is not the right time to talk peace," the message was interpreted by the State Department to be simply "an attempt to show [the] NLF in [a] position of strength" because the Communists in fact did want to discuss peace.[37] State's main concern was that the prisoner exchanges not look like prisoner exchanges or it would reveal that secret contacts between the two sides were underway. "One method might be to have NLF notify us that POWs in poor health will be at designated area at designated time for evacuation by U.S. helicopter," State recommended. "The release could be portrayed as humanitarian gesture."[38]

Meanwhile, on November 2, 1967, the North Vietnamese communicated through a cutout—Pakistan's ambassador in Beijing—that they had no desire to install a Communist government in the South but simply wanted to negotiate a coalition government and seek unity only when it was acceptable to the South Vietnamese people. As well, they said, an unconditional bombing halt by the U.S. could lead to negotiations on the Geneva model.[39] So when Loan arrested the NLF envoys and disrupted the Buttercup channel it was seen by those Americans who chose to believe it as derailing a potential major breakthrough in communications that could lead to the end of the war.

Loan's actions were understandable under the circumstances. The Saigon government was always watchful for signs that the United States was going to sell its ally out. Many South Vietnamese had cultivated a healthy mistrust of the Americans, whom they believed would betray them eventually, either by design or incompetence. General Loan in particular had little regard for American policymakers, whom he considered a necessary evil. The feeling was mutual. Thus when Loan's intelligence service picked up information on the secret contacts between the U.S. and the NLF, he watched for an opportunity, and when it presented itself in the form of Sau Ha and his accomplice, he had them arrested. Minister of Information Nguyen Ngoc Linh said the arrests "will teach [the Americans] to be a little more polite with us Vietnamese." He added, "It's not good manners to ask a guest to come to dinner without first consulting your wife. Especially if the guest is an enemy."[40]

The South Vietnamese had changed the state of play regarding the contact with the NLF, but they had not gone so far as to embarrass the United States by making the events public. Nodding to political reality, the U.S. drew the South Vietnamese government and General Loan into the secret discussions over what should be done with the potential opening to the North. Behind the scenes, Loan said he "did not give a damn" about Sau Ha's release but felt that to do so on the NLF's terms was a mistake. He said that Sau Ha had been very cooperative in captivity and had given up a great deal of information that was injurious to the VC. He believed that Sau Ha would be afraid to return to the NLF, given the extent of his cooperation, and Loan was instead considering sending him around the country in an anti-VC public relations drive. Loan felt that if the NLF made a show of good faith—for example, releasing an American flyer and soldier—then something useful might be achieved, but he was skeptical of the possibility of Buttercup developing into a channel for major ceasefire initiatives from the Communist leadership.[41]

On November 3, 1967, in honor of the RVN's National Day, the South freed 6,270 prisoners, including 4,320 Viet Cong suspects (mainly peasants) in a traditional goodwill gesture. (Note that the vast numbers of those freed underscored the disproportionate efforts the United States was making on behalf of a few NLF cadres, who were actually guilty.) In the list of promotions issued the same day, Loan was raised from temporary to permanent brigadier general. He had recently augmented his public profile by leading an air strike on Viet Cong forces at Bo Duc near the Cambodian border. The promotion displeased American officials, who considered Loan "a definite liability."[42] In late November, however, Loan unexpectedly submitted his resignation, claiming health reasons. Several Cabinet ministers and other officials associated with Ky threatened to resign unless Loan was retained.[43] Shortly thereafter the Buttercup story was leaked to the press, and Loan was publicly identified as the one who leaked it. Many of the stories came from the Saigon daily *Song*, the Loan-controlled *Cong Chung*, and from statements in the National Assembly.[44] The matter became a major public controversy in South Vietnam. It was widely believed that Loan was being forced out by the Americans for exposing their dealings with the VC, or that he was taking a stand on principle because the U.S. was trying to compel the government to release Sau Ha.

The Cabinet rejected Loan's resignation on November 30. The issue simmered for several more weeks as reports continued in the Saigon press about the planned U.S./NLF negotiations and another meeting that allegedly had already taken place. The fact that the U.S. government would not, and in fact could not, comment on the controversy generated further rumors and fueled suspicion that the U.S. was trying to sell the South out. *Cong Chung* took a particularly strident anti-American line, with one article declaring that "patriotic Vietnamese must struggle directly against the Americans to preserve their national sovereignty and dignity."[45] Behind the scenes Vice President Ky advised Loan to tone down the rhetoric. But Loan was being hailed by some segments of Vietnamese society as a nationalist hero who was brave enough to stand up to the Americans, and rumors of U.S. pressure to have him replaced made it impossible for President Thieu to take any action against Loan or even to accept his resignation because it would have made Thieu look like a U.S. puppet.[46]

Buttercup quickly wilted. The United States was helpless against Loan's political jujitsu. A secret cable from the Saigon U.S. embassy to the Secretary of State dated December 27, 1967, called Loan's actions "unfortunate."[47] But the U.S. hopes for a major diplomatic breakthrough at this time were the product of wish fulfillment. The Communists were in the final preparatory stages for Tet, and it is more likely that Buttercup was an attempt at political warfare, an information operation intended to distract the United States on the eve of a major offensive, rather than a serious outreach effort. In that respect it was very effective, in that it seemed to have made the intended impression on American policymakers. It played to the biases of those who had been waiting for years for a major diplomatic opening to develop. They wanted to see a sign, and the North obligingly gave it to them.

But the damage was done to America's reputation in the South. In early January 1968, South Vietnamese Representative Nguyen The Linh denounced the United States as "the second enemy of the South Vietnamese people after the Communists."[48] The National Assembly adopted a resolution against a "false peace" or any coalition with the NLF. Whatever might have come from Buttercup was dead. But the affair was a major political victory for General Loan and a lesson to the United States on how not to deal with its junior partner.

VII.

INTELLIGENCE FAILURE

The Tet Offensive is often cited as an example of intelligence failure in war, ranking with the Pearl Harbor attack, the Ardennes Offensive, the outbreak of the Korean War, and the 9/11 attacks. Dramatic events often draw the tag "intelligence failure," since the shock of the event implies some sort of breakdown in the early warning system. Hindsight then supplies the explanation of what should have happened, which is often obvious only after the fact.

Tet, however, was not a surprise on the level of the attacks noted above, which were wholly unanticipated at one or more levels of war. MACV and the White House knew a great deal about the

> We've been predicting the possibility of attacks such as this.
>
> —ROBERT MCNAMARA

Tet Offensive long before the attack was launched. At the strategic level it was clear by the winter of 1967–68 that the enemy was preparing for a major push. At the operational level, U.S. forces knew the broad outlines of the attack plan and were deployed to counter large-scale enemy moves, particularly in the north but also around Saigon and in other cities. At the tactical level, allied units in a number of targeted cities were fully prepared for the attacks when they came, in some cases having seen detailed Communist attack plans in advance. And the Communists sacrificed the element of surprise by an apparent last-minute timing change that led to some units opening the battle early, others stepping off on time, and still others attacking late.

The primary shock came on the home front. Although military planners and civilian decision-makers were aware that an attack was developing, they chose not to share this information with the American people. Thus, while allied fighting forces were for the most part prepared for the attack, people in the United States were caught by surprise.

WHAT WE KNEW

Ward Just wrote in the *Washington Post* February 2, 1968, that there was "general agreement that real intelligence on the raids had been nonexistent."[2] But there was no such general agreement. Secretary McNamara and General Wheeler appeared that day before an executive session of the Senate Armed Services Committee to declare the Tet Offensive a Communist failure, and afterward McNamara told reporters, "We've been predicting the possibility of attacks such as this." General Wheeler said that there had been no "intelligence failure," and added, "I feel that our information was accurate. It was timely."[3] Later that day at his first press conference on Tet, President Johnson said that "we have known for several months now that the Communists planned a massive winter-spring offensive. We have detailed information on Ho Chi Minh's order governing that offensive."

"Everyone in the White House knew it was coming," Rostow later observed. "We knew, through our intelligence network, that the North Vietnamese were preparing what they called 'a maximum effort.' We also alerted our military forces."[4]

There was talk of a major Communist attack as soon as the orders for Tet began to go out through Communist channels in the summer of 1967. On August 15, 1967, Robert Pisor reported in the *Detroit News* that there were rumors in Saigon of a "massive, countrywide military strike" coming. October 25, 1967, the Central Committee passed Resolution 14 calling for the General Offensive/General Uprising. A copy of the General Offensive/General Uprising order was captured in Quang Tri Province on November 13, 1967, by elements of the 101st Airborne. In late November 1967 the CIA station in Saigon produced a report called "The Big Gamble," which asserted that a change of Communist strategy was afoot, pointing toward a major attack. But the CIA's fall 1967 national intelligence estimate for Vietnam did not contain any specific indications of an attack brewing, and MACV was initially skeptical of the "Big Gamble" theory. However, Westmoreland later came to conclude that a nationwide effort was possible, but that the objective would be to seize areas along the frontier and in the I Corps area in the northern part of the country.

Other more specific indications followed. In December 1967 the North Vietnamese Politburo passed a resolution moving the revolution in the South into "the phase of winning decisive victory," and traffic on the Ho Chi Minh Trail surged 200%. Around the same time the notion that a desperation attack was coming made its way into Administration talking points. As noted earlier, in his otherwise optimistic speech to the Detroit Economic Club on December 18, 1967, General Wheeler noted the possibility of a Battle of the Bulge style desperation strike. On December 20 Westmoreland sent a communiqué to the Pentagon and White House predicting "an intensified countrywide effort, perhaps a maximum effort, over a relatively short period." And on December 22 President Johnson told a closed meeting with the Australian

Cabinet that he "foresaw the North Vietnamese using 'kamikaze' tactics in the weeks ahead."[5]

In early January 1968 the U.S. embassy issued a press release on the Communist order to attack Saigon and launch the General Offensive/General Uprising, based on the document captured November 13. The press release noted that the VC central headquarters "have ordered the entire army and people of South Vietnam to implement a general offensive and general uprising in order to achieve a decisive victory for the revolution." AP reported that the embassy "distributed a translation of what it described as a captured enemy notebook saying the opportunity for a general uprising was within reach in South Vietnam. The mission implied, however, this was not as significant as it sounded."[6] But some commentators understood the implications of the plan. The Camden, South Carolina *Chronicle* ran a prescient editorial based on the document:

> The Vietcong confidently expects to win, not through defeating America's armed forces but through a general uprising in Vietnam, plus considerable inside help from soulmates in the United States. They're counting on stirring up things in Vietnam so that there will be an uprising and then "U.S. forces must be withdrawn" and a "coalition government" formed.[7]

By then detailed attack plans were being uncovered. On January 5, 4th Infantry Division troops operating in Pleiku captured a copy of "Urgent Order Number One," which outlined the planned attack on the city during Tet by the H-15 Viet Cong Battalion and the North Vietnamese 95B Regiment. Over the course of January the U.S. also captured the attack plans for other targets, including Con Thien, Ban Me Thuot, and Phu Cuong. In response to these developments, the chief of the South Vietnamese Joint General Staff, General Cao Van Vien, informed Westmoreland on January 8 that he would try to limit the Tet ceasefire to 24 hours instead of the planned 48 hours. He was overruled by President Thieu, who nevertheless cut the ceasefire back to 36 hours.

Signs of an impending Communist attack caught the attention of Army Lieutenant General Frederick C. Weyand, who took over from General Palmer as commander of II Field Force in July 1967 and was responsible for the 11 provinces around Saigon that made up the III Corps Tactical Zone. Weyand had a strong intelligence background, dating back to his days as assistant chief of staff for intelligence in the China-Burma-India Theater during World War II. He had seen signs that the Viet Cong were moving out of their sanctuaries in Cambodia toward Saigon and assembling in and around the city. Weyand met with Westmoreland on January 10 and convinced him to postpone a proposed action in Phuoc Long Province, near the Cambodian border, in favor of deploying to positions around Saigon. Westmoreland concurred, and by the time of the Tet attacks Weyand had moved about half of his combat forces to positions outside the capital. On January 15, Westmoreland formally warned the U.S. Mission Council in Saigon that Communist attacks might occur either immediately before or after the Tet truce.

On January 18, 1968, North Vietnamese Communist Party General Secretary Le Duan sent a letter to the Communists in the South explaining that the Americans had reached the point of strategic stalemate and that it was up to them to seize the initiative. He foresaw three possible outcomes for the coming battle: total victory in Saigon; victory in other cities and rural areas but not Saigon; a number of lesser victories but not enough to expel the Americans. He also noted that Ho Chi Minh had wanted to move south to encourage the fighters personally, but the Politburo convinced him his health was not up to the trip. Le Duan encouraged the VC to win "the greatest victory to welcome Uncle Ho in the South."[8]

Even the press knew some kind of attack was coming. "For months any journalist with decent sources was expecting something big at Tet," wrote Don North of ABC News. "The ABC bureau and most other news agencies were on full alert, R&Rs were canceled and I had celebrated Christmas with my family in nearby Kuala Lumpur, Malaysia, on December 1 so I could be in

Vietnam, ready for the big enemy push when it came sometime before, during or after Tet." North noted that General Weyand spoke at length with journalists about the coming offensive and even told them off the record that he was maneuvering his forces to counter an expected attack on Saigon.[9]

HOW INTELLIGENCE FAILED

By late January the United States and South Vietnamese had amassed much information on the enemy's movements, plans, and intentions. They knew a great deal about the planned attack and had taken important steps to counter it. But intelligence failure often has less to do with what information the U.S. has or does not have, and more with failure of the analytical process or the unwillingness of policymakers to accept the findings.[10] The same information viewed through different analytical lenses can yield differing interpretations and conclusions. Four premises in particular contributed to the failure of the allied forces to understand the scope of the Tet Offensive.

The most important premise that led to discounting Tet was the assumption that the offensive as planned had no chance of succeeding, and that the enemy knew it. The basic outlines of the attack and the General Offensive/General Uprising were fairly well understood by mid-January 1968. The problem was that the plan was too flawed to be taken seriously. The guerrillas would be able to be pinned down, and would be too weak to defend themselves. The number of planned attacks seemed too large; they would divide the enemy's forces and make victory impossible in any single city. The urban focus was also discounted, since it would sacrifice mobility, the guerrillas' main strength. And the overall scale of the attack did not seem reasonable, since it would diminish VC strength nationwide and leave the organization without reserves.[11]

All these factors—urban focus, nationwide scope, general scale of attacks—violated too many of the classic principles of war for analysts to believe the plan was real. The captured documents generated a sense of disbelief; the idea was so foolhardy that it was difficult to accept that what had been uncovered was the actual attack plan. Many, including Westmoreland, concluded that the city attacks had to be simply a diversionary move because they could not possibly succeed. Westmoreland said that he did not believe the enemy would attempt "suicidal attacks in the face of our power."[12] General Davidson later wrote, "Even had I known exactly what was to take place, it was so preposterous that I probably would have been unable to sell it." The only way the offensive could work was if the general uprising took place as expected and the entire country rose up in support of the Communists. U.S. analysts rightly discounted this scenario as an unrealistic assumption but concluded that the plan was probably just propaganda. Nevertheless, the Communists did not think their plan was preposterous or suicidal. The United States reached an erroneous conclusion by not accepting the idea that the enemy had made a fatally flawed assessment, namely that it had a chance of winning.

Since the plan clearly lacked merit from a military point of view, many concluded that the attack would be only an attempt to gain positional advantage for future negotiations. In other words, since the Communists must have known they could not win, whatever they were doing had to be in pursuit of something else. In this case, intelligence failed because of a faulty premise that led to the United States to attribute much less ambitious objectives to the enemy, objectives it could actually reach.

The North Vietnamese encouraged the idea that they were seeking a diplomatic opening. During the Buttercup imbroglio the North had suggested through Pakistan's ambassador to China that a bombing halt could lead to talks, a position consistent with the North's long-time posture that ceasing the attacks was a necessary but not necessarily sufficient precondition to talks. On December 30, 1967, North Vietnamese Foreign Minister Nguyen Duy Trinh said in a speech that if Washington halted its strategic bombing campaign, Hanoi "would"—not "could"—be prepared to enter into negotiations. This subtle shift created a new round of anticipation in the diplomatic community, which had been disappointed after the Buttercup channel was disrupted. Hanoi seemed to be signaling that it accepted the terms reached at the June 1967 U.S.-Soviet Glassboro Summit. Johnson reiterated the San Antonio Formula in his State of the Union address on January 17, saying that "the bombing would stop immediately if talks would take place promptly and with reasonable hopes that they would be productive; and the other side must not take advantage of our restraint, as they have in the past."

Preparations for the Tet Offensive were moving forward, so it is reasonable to conclude that Hanoi's apparent diplomatic opening was just a diversionary effort. However, even the well-known fact that the enemy had an attack in the works did not dissuade those who believed that the Communists' ultimate object was negotiation. A lengthy analysis by Chalmers M. Roberts in the *Washington Post* on January 28, 1968, noted Hanoi's preparations for a continuation of the "Winter-Spring 1967–8 Offensive" and even quoted the plan for the General Offensive/General Uprising captured in November 1967. But Roberts reported that the Administration believed the enemy was not actually seeking to win through sparking an uprising but would use the offensive to advance a diplomatic posture:

> This, then, is where the situation is today as the Communists appear to be preparing for a major push in their winter-spring offensive. Washington senses a degree of urgency in the current Communist push, designed perhaps to improve the military situation which in turn could enhance the Communist negotiating position.[13]

So just days before the Tet Offensive began the Administration had already downgraded perceptions of the enemy's objectives and expectations.

On January 29 the U.S. offered to halt bombing and open peace negotiations if the North Vietnamese would not raise infiltration and supply shipments beyond "normal levels." Commentators charged that this offer was a retreat from the conditions of the San Antonio Formula, which the Administration denied.[14] A debate arose over what constituted "normal levels" and whether they took advantage of U.S. restraint. The implication was that the North Vietnamese could continue with business as usual after the U.S. stopped bombing, which seemed to be a unilateral concession. On January 30 the *New York Times* ran a column-one front-page story on this homegrown controversy, next to a story headlined "Vietcong Attack 7 Cities: Allies Call Off Tet Truce." The Tet Offensive was on, and the debate over diplomatic signaling was moot.

A second inaccurate premise concerned the location of the attack. Despite abundant information suggesting that the Communists were preparing a nationwide effort, this was seen as a mere diversion. The consensus grew that the main thrust of the attack would be in the I Corps area, at or around the Marine outpost at Khe Sanh.

Signs of a buildup in I Corps were evident weeks before the battle commenced. On January 2, 1968, six high-ranking North Vietnamese officers were ambushed near Khe Sanh, which suggested the presence of large units. Signals intelligence developed by the NSA and other technical means showed that large numbers of North Vietnamese regulars were moving into the area. Signals intercepts indicated that the 2nd NVA division, which was already inside South Vietnam, was moving its operations toward Da Nang. A PAVN regiment was detected moving toward Hue. By mid-January there were an estimated four divisions with 40,000 men committed to the area. The intelligence in this case was good, but subtly deceptive. Conventional forces generated more signals than guerrillas, so while these intercepts supported the thesis that I Corps would be the main effort, it was only because of the lesser concentration of such signals elsewhere, not because of the absence of troops.[15]

In response to the enemy movements, the Marines implemented Operation Checkers, moving forces north to repel the anticipated PAVN attack. On January 12 the AP reported that "senior Marine officers said there are indications that the Communist troops will concentrate on the provinces of Quang Tri, which fronts the DMZ, and Thua Thien, just south of it, in their *expected spring offensive in the north*" [emphasis added]. Sources said that "the Communists are getting ready for a wave of attacks on allied outposts, especially in the northernmost provinces, in the next few weeks."[16] Meanwhile General Westmoreland moved the 1st Cavalry Division north to Phu Bai, and by the end of the month more than half the U.S. combat maneuver battalions had moved into I Corps.

The conclusion that Khe Sanh would be the main Communist effort was also a product of mirror-imaging. A MACV war game in December-January concluded that a massed, coordinated attack in the north was the enemy's best move. When it began to appear that this was what the Communists were planning, it seemed to confirm what U.S. military analysts already believed. And Khe Sanh was the type of contest the Americans wanted to fight, a conventional battle against regular troops in a fixed location. When the North Vietnamese opened the attack on Khe Sanh on January 21, the action seemed to validate both the assumptions of the timing of the attack (shortly before Tet) and its location (in the north). On January 22 Westmoreland reported, "I believe the enemy will attempt a country-wide show of strength just prior to Tet, with Khe Sanh being the main event." Several attacks were seen in store for various smaller cities, and he believed that "terrorism will probably increase in and around Saigon." In another message he noted that the enemy buildup was "unusual in its urgency and intensity. The bulk of our evidence suggests that the enemy is conducting a short-term surge effort, possibly designed to improve his chance of gaining his ends through political means, perhaps through negotiations leading to some form of coalition government." The belief that the enemy was seeking victory in the upcoming Tet Offensive was considered so unlikely it did not even make the list. Yet at that time there was no talk of intelligence failure but a general sense that the analysis had been correct.

A complicating factor then arose. North Korean commandoes attacked the South Korean presidential mansion on January 21, the same day the assault on Khe Sanh began. Two days later North Korean Marines seized the surveillance ship U.S.S Pueblo in international waters off the North Korean coast. Some speculated that the North Korean attacks may have been intended to support the North Vietnamese move against Khe Sanh by distracting policymakers. Decades later former KGB operative Oleg Kalugin revealed that the *Pueblo* was seized on orders from Moscow in order to verify intelligence given to them by John Anthony Walker, Jr., a Navy NCO who became one of the most notorious spies of the Cold War. The crisis overshadowed the approach of Tet and the possibility of a Communist attack. On January 25 Johnson mobilized nearly 15,000 reservists for active duty to be sent to Korea and dispatched the nuclear aircraft carrier *U.S.S Enterprise* to the area as a show of force. (Ironically, the Korean crisis was the main agenda item for the President's "Tuesday lunch" with his top advisers on January 30, along with a discussion of some potential peace feelers to Hanoi through Romania. The "lunch" convened at 5:50 p.m.; by then January 31 was dawning in Saigon, and the Tet attacks had already begun.)

Evidence continued to mount in late January that a major attack was coming, but policymakers remained focused on the northern part of South Vietnam. On January 24 Ambassador Bunker and General Westmoreland informed Washington that the Communists might break the Tet truce and recommended that the South Vietnamese government cancel leaves in I Corps, the part of the country they thought was most at risk. The next day Westmoreland reported that the situation at Khe Sanh was critical and could be the turning point of the war. And Westmoreland's first report to the Pentagon after the outbreak of the Tet Offensive and the attack on Saigon showed that he still clung to the idea that the countrywide attacks were diversionary. "[The enemy's] aim," he wrote, "appears to be to cause movement of friendly units and to divert attention from what I believe will be his main effort, the Khe Sanh/DMZ area."[17]

Another failure, though a lesser one, was the belief that the attack would take place either just before or just after the Tet holiday, but not during it. Tet is an important holiday in Vietnamese culture, not just the start of the new year but a holiday with religious overtones and the beginning of three weeks of celebrations. Analysts apparently had concluded that the holiday was so popular and had such religious significance that the Communists did not want to risk causing an affront by marring it with violence. But battles had been opened on Tet before. In 1418 there was an attack during Tet by General (later Emperor) Le Loi against the Chinese Ming occupiers. In 1789 Emperor Quang Trung surprised and defeated a Chinese force at Thang Long under the slogan "swift fight, swift win." He let his troops celebrate Tet a day in advance.[18] So the planned Communist offensive fit in this tradition, and the Communists used the symbolism of Quang Trung's attack in their propaganda.

The Communists generally did not honor truces. In 1967 there were 202 violations of the Tet truce, in which nine U.S. and five allied troops were killed. Those violations were unsystematic and the result of the fluid nature of the battlefront, according to a State Department report.[19] Truces were more often used for less violent purposes. On November 17, 1967, the NLF proclaimed three-day ceasefires for Christmas and the Western New Year, which they used to conduct reconnaissance missions on locations targeted for attacks during Tet. The VC moved between the countryside and cities pretending to be civilians traveling home for the holidays. They also exploited the ceasefires to smuggle arms disguised as merchandise. One VC arms smuggler named Ngo Van Giang determined that the primary trade on Route 1 into Saigon was in fruits and vegetables, so he filled baskets with arms and ammunition and concealed the contraband with layers of tomatoes. Along Route 13 the principal trade was in rubber and firewood, so the VC stacked firewood in vehicles to create cavities in which arms were secreted. Arms and ammunition were also transported inside hollowed-out logs. Ngo Van Giang's smuggling operation had at least 24 hours' warning of sweeps against them because they could intercept and decode secret ARVN communications.[20]

However, whatever tactical surprise the North Vietnamese might have enjoyed they forfeited by bungling their timing at the opening of the battle. The Communists began their holiday ceasefire on January 27, which gave their units time to get into their attack positions. Also that day the North Vietnamese announced they would free three captured U.S. pilots in observance of Tet. But the AP reported that the Communists conducted a number of attacks leading up to the truce period, and that "the prospect was for little, if any, lessening of the fighting that has marked the last week."[21] On January 28, Westmoreland wired the White House that "there are indications that the enemy may not cease military operations during Tet. In fact, he is now well into his announced Tet stand-down period with no discernible decrease in significant activity in the northern two corps areas." That same day a raid on an enemy cell in Qui Nhon in Binh Dinh Province netted 11 Viet Cong with prepared audio tapes calling for a people's uprising, which they were to play after capturing the local radio station.

The allied ceasefire began at 6 p.m. on January 29, except in the I Corps Tactical Zone, where it had been canceled. Many South Vietnamese soldiers were spending the holiday with family members, and most ARVN units were at half strength. President Thieu and his family were at his wife's parents' house at My Tho in the Mekong Delta region. As the allied ceasefire began, North Vietnamese radio broadcast a poem by Ho Chi Minh entitled "Tet Mau Than," or "Year of the Monkey":

> This spring far outshines previous springs
> Of triumphs throughout the land come happy tidings
> Let North and South emulate each other in fighting the U.S.
>> aggressors
> Forward!
> Total victory will be ours.

The poem was the order of the day for the Tet Offensive. The attack was supposed to start after the first day of the lunar new year, which in South Vietnam was January 30. But shortly before Tet began, North Vietnamese radio made an unusual announcement. Hanoi stated that because of a fortuitous alignment of the sun, moon, and earth, the Tet holiday would begin on January 29, not January 30. This was a strange signal. One theory was that it was intended to give the citizens of the North a day of holiday before the offensive began. Another theory was that this was a last-minute attempt to gain surprise since the planned attack date had been compromised, and Hanoi was trying to communicate to troops already dispersed in their ready positions that the attack was being moved up a day. But the real explanation hinged on a minor revision in the calendar that had an unforeseen but critical impact.

On August 8, 1967, Hanoi approved a lunar calendar based on Indochina Time (UTC +7) instead of the traditional China Standard Time (UTC +8). South Vietnam remained on China Standard Time. This small shift fatefully placed the new moon at 2329 hours on January 29 in the North and 0015 hours January 30 in the South. North Vietnamese military planners probably did not notice this discrepancy until shortly before the attack kicked off when it became clear that the launch date they had set for "after the first day of the lunar new year" meant different dates to different units.[22]

The result of this confusing last-minute signal was a rolling series of initial attacks that spoiled the Communists' chance at achieving tactical surprise. One particularly premature attack took place January 29, when Communist forces mortared Da Nang. Later that day General Weyand sent word to II Field Force that "there are a number of positive intelligence indicators that the enemy will deliberately violate the truce by attacking friendly installations during the night of January 29 or during the early morning hours of 30 January. Addressees will take action to insure maximum alert postures throughout the Tet period. Be particularly alert for enemy deception involving the use of friendly vehicles or uniforms."[23]

As Weyand predicted, more attacks followed after midnight on January 30. Eight hundred troops of the 18B North Vietnamese Regiment hit Nha Trang and were defeated by ARVN forces in under a day. PAVN political officer Huynh Tung later said that they were defeated because promised reinforcements did not arrive. Two thousand troops of the 33rd PAVN Regiment attacked Ban Me Thuot in the Central Highlands and met with some initial success before being countered by elements of the ARVN 8th Cavalry and 45th Infantry Regiments.[24] The PAVN also attacked Pleiku and Kontum, and, over all, Communist forces assaulted six cities and towns in the early morning of January 30. By daylight the attackers had mostly been contained or driven off.[25]

At 0700 that day General Davidson, the MACV J-2, briefed Westmoreland on the assaults and told him to expect more that night. Westmoreland concurred, and placed all U.S. forces on high alert. He briefed President Thieu, who likewise issued an alert and recalled the South Vietnamese troops on leave. By 1100 hours on January 30 the Tet truce was canceled everywhere in South Vietnam, and allied forces were preparing for the assault expected the next day. Thus, before the main weight of the Tet attacks had been felt, allied forces were already awaiting them. If there had ever been a chance for a surprise attack, the Communists had lost it through miscalculating the calendar.

The peace movement later used the staggered attack schedule to blame the United States and South Vietnam for the outbreak of fighting during the putative ceasefire. It argued that the NLF had implemented a seven-day truce while the U.S. would honor only 36 hours, and then only in the Central Highlands and the south of the country. Communist attacks in the north on the first day were simply a justifiable response to the fact that the U.S. had canceled the truce in I Corps, even though most of the January 30 attacks took place in the Central Highlands in II Corps. When the South Vietnamese government called off the truce altogether in response to the January 30 attacks, the VC was in its rights to simply continue "spontaneously" attacking nationwide. In short, peace proponents argued that the Tet Offensive was America's fault.[26]

SURPRISE ON THE HOME FRONT

The greatest impact the Tet Offensive had was on the home front. The Johnson Administration had known a great deal about the Communist attack plan but decided not to share it with the American people. Instead, the government stressed good news from Vietnam, building on the fall 1967 "Success Campaign." Secretary of State Dean Rusk told the *Washington Post* that "the war was being won by the allies" and that it "would be won if America had the will to win it." President Johnson outlined several reasons for optimism in his January 17, 1968, State of the Union message, including the three elections that had been held, enemy defeats on the battlefield, and the success in expanding the number of people living in areas under government control. However, he noted that "the enemy continues to pour men and material across frontiers and into battle, despite his continuous heavy losses," and "continues to hope that America's will to persevere can be broken. Well, he is wrong. America will persevere. Our patience and our perseverance will match our power. Aggression will never prevail." President Thieu's January 25 state of the union message in Saigon was very upbeat and resonated with the same issue that face contemporary states undergoing democratization in difficult circumstances. However, he noted that 1968 was an American election year and that the Communists could be counted on to try to use that fact to their advantage.

There can be good reasons for not letting the public know what the enemy is planning—for example, if a planned counter-stroke depends on the adversary being unaware of one's knowledge of the attack plan. Walt Rostow later observed that the reason for staying quiet about the attack was that the U.S. "didn't want to let the other side know what we knew. I know that doesn't sound too sensible, and it certainly proved to be a big mistake, but that's the way it was."[27] If the enemy is planning a massed attack that can easily be countered, it makes sense to let the enemy execute it and suffer the consequences. This was precisely what happened in the north and around Saigon. Lieutenant Colonel Edward C. Peter, who at the time served in the headquarters of II Field Force, noted somewhat archly in 1969 that "it is true that we did not announce with a fanfare that we were concentrating forces near the National Priority area. Apparently the military experts of the newspapers did not realize what was transpiring in this regard."[28]

However, concealing knowledge of the scale of the imminent attacks and maintaining a positive outlook raised expectations at home that the end of the war was at hand. Failure to share information about the coming offensive with the American people magnified its domestic impact when it arrived. The American people were unprepared psychologically for the attacks, regardless of the fact that the enemy failed to achieve its objectives. This outcome demonstrated that the appearance of intelligence failure can be as bad as or worse than the real thing.

The lesson from Tet is that policymakers have to balance operational secrecy against the critical variable of public perception. The government and the military were not by and large surprised by the Tet attacks, but the public and members of the press were shocked. This meant that later allied claims of victory were met with a general sense of skepticism. In this sense, Tet was less a case of intelligence failure than a public relations fiasco. The Johnson Administration did a poor job of alerting the public that something was about to happen in Vietnam, and the sudden attack, as ineffective as it was, seemed to belie the previous justifiable claims of progress in the war. Furthermore, symbolism quickly overcame substance. The first stateside report about the Tet Offensive that most people heard was that the Viet Cong had seized the U.S. embassy in Saigon.

VIII.

THE EMBASSY ATTACK

The Viet Cong assault on the U.S. embassy in Saigon is almost unique in military history. It was a failed raid by an ad hoc team hitting a secondary target of no particular military significance that became one of the most widely noted, best remembered, least understood attacks in the Vietnam War. It was emblematic of the entire Tet Offensive, a microcosm of the Viet Cong operation. The attack was a skirmish involving 19 enemy troops that lasted a few hours and had no military impact. But the symbolic value was beyond measure, and the attack is one of the most noted incidents of the entire war.

Saigon is secure now.

—AMBASSADOR
ELLSWORTH BUNKER

CONCEPT AND PREPARATION

The embassy assault was part of the general attack plan for Saigon. South Vietnam's capital city was home to 2,000,000 people at the time, half of them displaced persons. In mid-1967 the U.S. felt confident enough in South Vietnamese forces to turn over defense of the city to them. There were ten ARVN battalions in and around Saigon, and 17,000 paramilitary National Police under the command of General Loan. The ARVN 5th Ranger Group was also based in the city near the sprawling Tan Son Nhut air base complex. The United States had 23 battalions near Saigon, and the 716th Military Police battalion was based inside the city under the command of Lieutenant Colonel Gordon D. Rowe.

The total enemy force in the area was around 35 battalions, including the 5th and 7th Viet Cong divisions. There were also 3,000 local force guerrillas inside the city. The local commander was General Tran Do. The plan was to make diversionary attacks north of the city to lure U.S. forces away from Saigon, then attack targets inside the capital and raise the popular uprising. Naturally, Saigon was the most important target of the entire offensive, since success there would mean the downfall of the government and the fulfillment of the plan to place the United States in an untenable political position, guests in a country where the host no longer wanted them.

The assault force was led by the Viet Cong T700 Unit (previously known as the C-10 Sapper Battalion), mostly recruited from locals. Among the objectives were seizing the American embassy, the presidential palace, and the Saigon radio station. Viet Cong forces began to move into their attack positions around midnight on January 30, dressed as civilians, using the celebrating crowds on the streets to mask their movements.

The team that attacked the U.S. embassy was something less than the elite force one might expect to have been given such a critical task. It was a pick-up group with no specific training related to the target and no knowledge of its mission until the last minute. Its journey to the embassy grounds was something of a comedy of errors.

Among the attack group was Ngo Van Giang, a.k.a. Ba Van, age 43, commander of the J9 Special Action Unit, subordinate to the T700 Unit, a Northerner who had been with the Viet Cong since 1960.[1] Another was Nguyen Van Sau, alias Chuc, who was forcibly recruited by the Viet Cong in 1964 when the force surrounded his village and seized 20 young men. Life was very difficult in the force, particularly because of a lack of adequate rations, but Chuc stayed with the VC out of a sense of obligation to his friends and also a developing sense of purpose that they were doing the right thing. He had been in the C-10 Battalion since September 1965 and was trained in low crawling, scaling walls, using explosives, and other skills of the sappers' art. But mainly he delivered messages.

On January 28 at 2100 hours Ba Van was in Trang Dau hamlet in Hau Nghia Province, just west of Saigon. The Chief of Staff of the T700 unit, Ba Tam, told him that he would participate in an unspecified attack "within the next few days." Senior Captain Bay Tuyen would command the mission, with Ba Van and Captain Ut Nho assisting him. The same day Chuc was also told he would participate in an unspecified attack.[2] Later that night they were brought weapons and ammunition concealed in rolled-up bamboo mats and baskets under a layer of tomatoes. Ut Nho was in charge of smuggling the weapons. He gave Ba Van the address of a safe house in Saigon and told him to say he was "a friend of Mr. Ba." At 1300 hours on January 29 a truck arrived, driven by Nguyen Van Ba, a chauffeur for the U.S. embassy. Ba Van and four others got into the truck and made the three-hour journey to Saigon.[3]

When they arrived in the city, Ba Van discovered he had lost the address of the safe house, but he remembered it was on Nguyen Dinh Chieu St. near the Tan Dinh market, so the group drove around the area looking for a likely house. They spotted one they thought was the safe house, and the five VC went to the door while the driver remained with the truck. A child answered, and Ba Van said he was "a friend of Mr. Ba." A man and woman then appeared at the door and asked the five men to come in. The woman drew the blinds and closed the doors while the man left the room.

Ba Van suddenly had a bad feeling, believing the man was going to flee the house and report the visitors to the National Police. He told the other members of the team they had to get out, and the five men ran from the house. Four of them darted down the street toward the Tan Dinh Market while Ba Van went to the truck and told the driver what was happening. He hopped in the truck, and the two drove around trying to find the rest of the unit, who were concealed nearby. One of the four, named Sau, said he knew a place where they could hole up. They flagged down taxis and departed in pairs. Ba Van and the driver then headed back to Trang Dau, arriving at 1900 hours.[4]

The next morning, at 10 a.m., Ba Van received word from Ut Nho that a contact was coming for him. It turned out to be the same driver, Nguyen Van Ba, who turned up at noon on a Honda motorcycle. They drove to Saigon, arriving at 1500 hours. Nguyen Van Ba dropped Ba Van off at the Cu Market and told him to wait. He returned 15 minutes later driving a yellow-and-light blue station wagon. They drove down Thong Nhat Blvd. by the U.S. embassy, circled the block, and stopped at the corner of Mac Dinh Chi St., across the street from the embassy compound. Nguyen Van Ba dropped off Ba Van, told him that he should come back to that corner at 2300 hours, and drove away.

Ba Van walked down the block past the embassy front gate, then took a taxi to the Saigon Market, arriving around 1600. He bought some firecrackers and walked to the Bach Dang River to light them off, celebrating the new year. He drank some beers at a sidewalk café, then hired a taxi to take him by the house where he and his family had lived six years earlier. He then returned to the Saigon Market and drank beers until it was time to return to the rendezvous point.

Ut Nho picked up Ba Van at 2300 hours in a truck and drove him to an auto repair shop garage at 59 Phan Thanh Gian St., near an ARVN compound in Da Kao, Tan Dinh area, five blocks from the U.S. embassy. There were 17 men present, plus the woman who owned the garage. For most of them this was the first time they had met, and few knew what their impending mission was.

They were not a picked force, not particularly skilled at infiltration or urban combat. Ba Van, Chuc, and team members Giang, Teo, and Van all had at least three months of sapper training. Others had less reason for being there. Two team members, Duc and Vinh, were office workers. Sergeant Dang Van Son, age 44, was a cook with the C-40 security company.[5] His American interrogator rated him as "below average intelligence." He was a Northerner, who previously had been a farmer. He fought with the Viet Minh from 1947 to 1951. In 1964 he was drafted into the PAVN and sent south the next year. On January 26, 1968, five days before the Tet Offensive, he volunteered for "a mission to liberate Saigon." He and another member of the unit, Ngo Thanh Sang, offered to go because they were "tired of the hardships of living in the jungle." By January 30 they were secreted in a three-story safe house in Saigon, with no word about their mission or the other members of their team. They arrived at the garage at 0100 hours on January 31, were handed weapons, and told to wait.[6]

Between midnight and 0245 hours, Bay Tuyen and Ut Nho briefed the team on its mission. The team members learned that their target was the U.S. embassy. The information had been kept from them out of elevated concern for operational security. In general, the Viet Cong did not think the Tet missions required much in the way of preparation for the foot soldiers, since the teams had only to seize and hold their objectives, then await reinforcements and the popular uprising. But this degree of secrecy added to the confusion when the plans were executed, and the lack of training and team cohesion also greatly hampered operations. However, the American embassy may not have even been on the original VC target list, since the assault force was assembled only at the last minute. Had the embassy been considered a critical target, the enemy would presumably have dedicated some of its best people to the mission and devised a more thorough plan, particularly involving intelligence exploitation of whatever sensitive documents they might capture. But there were no such experts involved in the assault.

The team was issued weapons: seven new AK-47s, six assorted pistols, two well-used B-40 rocket launchers with five rounds each, 30kg of C-4 explosives, and 120 rifle rounds per man. The attack was set for 0300 hours. Bay Tuyen would lead. Ut Nho and six or seven others were to seize control of the main gate and hold it. Ba Van would lead his four men, Sau, Vinh, Mang, and Teo, to take the side gate. The other five or six men would take over the embassy proper. They were told to overrun the embassy compound, enter and seize the building, and hold it for 36 hours. They were then to withdraw. They were given no instructions what to do once they got inside the embassy, if or when reinforcements would arrive, or how to escape the embassy area. Presumably Bay Tuyen knew at least some of these details, but he did not brief his team. The attackers were not given information on the size or composition of the expected defending force. They were simply told to kill anyone who resisted but to take prisoners if any of the defenders surrendered and were unarmed. Chuc later said he was not sure why they were attacking the embassy and thought it was an unimportant target. He doubted they could seize the building and did not expect to survive the attack.

THE EMBASSY ATTACK ✕

At 0250 hours on January 31, the attackers left for the embassy in two vehicles, a blue taxi in the lead, followed by a Peugeot truck. They wore white or blue shirts, black or blue slacks, red armbands on the left arm and blue, white, and yellow neckerchiefs. The lead vehicle carried Bay Tuyen, Ut Nho, and his team. In the truck were Ba Van and the rest. The taxi pulled up in front of the embassy and stopped, while the truck stopped farther down the wall. The two teams immediately deployed and began their attacks.

The U.S. embassy in Saigon was a six-story structure, one of several buildings in a four-acre compound surrounded by a high reinforced-concrete wall. This chancery building was opened in September 1967, on the same day President Johnson announced the San Antonio Formula. It replaced the old chancery building, which had been car-bombed by the Viet Cong on March 29, 1965.[7] (The 1965 bombing, now barely remembered, killed two Americans, one Filipino, and 19 Vietnamese and wounded 183 others.) The new embassy had $2.6 million in improvements and was a much harder target. Two MPs were on duty, Specialist 4th Class Charles L. Daniel and PFC William M. Sebast. They were expecting trouble. When they saw the attack force pull up they slammed the embassy gates and sent code "Signal 300"—embassy under attack.

One of Ut Nho's men detonated a 15-pound C-4 charge at the base of the embassy wall 120 meters to the right of the front gate. The blast created a small but serviceable hole low to the ground. The VC fired a few B-40 rounds randomly into the upper floors of the embassy building while Ut Nho's team crawled through the hole and began fighting. Daniel shouted into his radio, "They're coming in—help me!" and the two MPs opened fire. He and Sebast gunned down two men, probably Bay Tuyen and Ut Nho, before they were killed. Sergeant Jonnie B. Thomas and Specialist 4th Class Owen E. Mebust sped up outside in a jeep, responding to the call, and were mowed down. Other Americans opened up from positions in the upper floors of the embassy. Ngo Thanh Sang, one of the first in the compound, was quickly killed. Dang Van Son also went down almost immediately, shot in the head and leg. Bay Tuyen and Ut Nho soon were down, and Chuc was wounded in the first ten minutes. The remaining VC took cover behind large round shrubbery pots on the embassy grounds. MPs took positions on rooftops of nearby houses and poured fire onto the exposed VC positions.

Meanwhile Ba Van led his men to the side gate, but found the sentry post deserted and the gate secured. Ba Van shortly received word to go back to the front of the embassy and enter the compound through the hole in the wall blown by Ut Nho's group. He crawled through the hole and immediately saw the bodies of two VC and an American MP. Shortly thereafter Ba Van was severely wounded and taken to the far side of the building, where he remained semi-conscious until he was captured at 0730. Nguyen

Van Ba, the embassy chauffeur who had cooperated with the VC and probably killed Daniel and Sebast, lay next to him, also gravely wounded. The chauffeur later died.

Inside the chancery Marine Sgt. Ronald W. Harper and Cpl. George B. Zahuranic closed the marble and iron doors as the first gunfire erupted. The VC fired a B-40 rocket, which shattered the marble and wounded Zahuranic but failed to force an opening.[8] On the roof Marine Sgt. Rudy A. Soto radioed a distress call to Captain Robert J. O'Brien, commander of the Marine embassy detachment, five blocks away at the Marine quarters. O'Brien rousted his men, and they rushed to the scene. Marines, Army MPs, South Vietnamese National Police, and ARVN troops quickly surrounded the embassy. Inside were six Americans and two South Vietnamese watchmen.

Trapped, leaderless, under fire, and with nowhere to go, the Viet Cong began dying one by one. Spotters on surrounding rooftops directed fire against attackers seeking cover in the courtyard. The main firefight lasted two to three hours as the enemy attackers were slowly picked off. After several aborted attempts, a helicopter landed on the chancery roof with Army troops from the 502nd Infantry at Bien Hoa. By then the Viet Cong attacking force was down to its last man. He had made his way into the embassy living quarters and was heading up the stairs to the second floor. Retired Army Lieutenant Colonel George Jacobsen, the embassy mission coordinator, was upstairs on the second floor but unarmed. He went to his window and shouted to the MPs outside for help. In a dramatic sequence that was filmed and aired on American television, an MP threw Jacobsen a pistol. A few minutes later tear gas was pumped into the villa to drive the VC attacker out, but he fled up the stairs. "With all the luck that I've had all of my life, I got him before he got me," Jacobsen told reporters that morning.

The embassy attack was over. At 0915 the compound was declared secure. General Westmoreland arrived, and footage showed him walking among the enemy bodies scattered about the courtyard. Blood was pooled on the lawn. The corpse-strewn garden in the compound looked "like a butcher shop in Eden," according to UPI's Kate Webb. U.S. casualties were five killed and five wounded. The dead were MPs Daniel, Sebast, Thomas, and Mebus, and Marine Corporal James C. Marshall. Four South Vietnamese civilian workers were also killed. Of the enemy force, three were wounded and captured, the rest killed.

PRESS COVERAGE OF THE EMBASSY ATTACK

Images of the embassy attack dominated the news for the first few days of the Tet Offensive. Seeing Americans defending the embassy grounds from VC attackers suggested that the Communists were more powerful than the Administration had been claiming. If the front lines were in Saigon, it seemed that no place was safe; the entire country was under threat and there was nowhere the enemy could not hit if it wanted to.

The embassy assault story dominated the early Tet reportage. AP filed the first story at 3:15 a.m. local time, shortly after the VC blew the hole in the embassy wall. Many other reports and updates soon followed. U.S. Army LTC Edward C. Peter said that "there seemed to be more information on the accomplishments of the [nineteen] Viet Cong who attacked the American Embassy than on the other four thousand enemy who hit the city."[9] The first wire reports on the embassy assault appeared in January 30 evening editions in some west coast U.S. papers, usually appended to copy originally filed about the previous day's attacks. This was an artifact of the time difference and International Date Line. Much of the early reporting got the details wrong. For example, AP's Edwin Q. White's first sentence read: "A Viet Cong suicide squad seized and held parts of the U.S. embassy in the heart of Saigon for six hours today before being wiped out by American forces." The caption of the accompanying photo said that the VC "had stormed the U.S. embassy compound and holed up inside the embassy building," which Peter Arnett said he had overheard in another reporter's interview with an unnamed MP.[10]

Reports like this shaped perceptions of the extent to which the VC had accomplished its objectives. Press reports consistently referred to the team that attacked the embassy as a "suicide squad," which they were not. Use of that term conjured visions of the

Japanese kamikazes, a term President Johnson had used himself in Australia the previous December. In doing so, the press redefined the VC objective—seizing and holding the embassy—down to what the team actually achieved—dying on the spot. Wiping out attackers bent on suicide is less of a victory than defeating an enemy seeking to occupy the embassy compound and await reinforcements from the popular uprising. This small bit of poetic license on the part of the press greatly misrepresented the Viet Cong intentions.

A more important question became whether or not the VC had penetrated the embassy chancery building. Edwin Q. White reported that "Gen. Westmoreland said the Viet Cong did not get inside the gleaming, white, new building itself. *However, dozens of persons on the scene said some of the Viet Cong were in the lower floors of the main building. Vietnamese police sources also said some of them had made their way into the building.*" (emphasis in original) This was typical of the accounts that ran in morning papers in the U.S.

John Roche was in the White House when the first press reports came in. "The AP runs a story on the ticker that the Vietnamese are inside the American embassy," he recalled. "I happened to be on the phone at that point with [Embassy Political Counselor] John Archibald Calhoun, who was sitting in his office on the ground floor. The stories that came out said that the rugs were stained with blood from the battle that was going on in the foyer. There were no rugs. It was all linoleum. But who cares about little points like that? They never got inside the building." Roche called downstairs to the press room to AP general manager Wes Gallagher, who was the head of the AP bureau. Roche said, "Look, this is cockeyed. Come on up to my office and I'll put you on the phone with the political officer, Arch Calhoun, in his office in the embassy that you people say has been captured by the North Vietnamese." Gallagher replied, "No, how do I know he isn't in Camranh Bay or someplace else?"[11]

If the VC had penetrated the chancery it would have made no great difference to the outcome of the battle. But the fact that the press was saying one thing and the Administration another

134

reopened the credibility gap. In the war of symbols, this was a crucial disconnect, however irrelevant to any military concerns. This debate kept the matter alive and distracted attention from the critical fact that the VC attack had failed.

There were other perception problems. At 9:30 General Westmoreland spoke to the press outside the chancery entrance. His air of confidence contrasted with the evidence of a vicious struggle surrounding him. The seal of the United States had been blasted from over the entrance and lay bent and blackened before the door. A reporter asked, "General, how would you assess yesterday's activities and today's, what is the enemy doing, are these major attacks or . . ." At that point the sound of an explosion interrupted. Westmoreland looked toward it quickly, then turned back to the cameras. "That's, uh, EOD setting off a cache of M-79, uh, duds I believe," Westmoreland said, smiling. The reporter continued his question to the sound of further explosions. Westmoreland said that the enemy "very deceitfully" attacked during the Tet truce in an effort "to create maximum consternation," but had failed. He said that the attack was "diversionary" from the main effort in Quang Tri Province. But there was a conspicuous sense of contrast between Westmoreland's answer and the atmosphere at the embassy. The timing of the first detonation could not have been more dramatic.

Meanwhile Ambassador Ellsworth Bunker spoke to reporters at the back steps of the embassy and announced, "Saigon is secure now." The fact that he chose to hold his press briefing in the rear of the chancery was noted by most reports and seen as significant. His bold statement about Saigon being secure amid clear sounds of combat elsewhere in the city was unfortunate and helped reinforce the idea that the Administration either had no idea what was going on or was lying to the American people.

Thus through a combination of inaccurate reporting, erroneous official statements, poor visuals, and bad luck, the embassy attack was elevated from a botched raid to a strategic victory for the Communists. In a Harris poll conducted the weekend of February 3-4, 61% agreed that the "successful Vietcong penetration of the United States Embassy compound . . . showed that we were not prepared" for the attack. The facts surrounding the event were by that point irrelevant.

BATTLEGROUND SAIGON

Ambassador Bunker had impulsively declared Saigon secure, but the city was in turmoil. Attacks were taking place throughout the city and in the surrounding countryside. General Weyand said that his electric situation map looked like "a pinball machine, one light after another going on as it was hit."[12] In the chaos of battle unconfirmed reports of enemy activity were pouring in from across the city. In one humorous episode an aerial spotter saw VC dragging mortar tubes across a field using hand carts; closer examination revealed them to be golfers at a Saigon golf course, which earlier had been the scene of some sharp conflict.[13] At 1730 on January 31 President Thieu declared martial law and imposed a 24-hour curfew and press censorship. The edict was confirmed by the Council of Ministers the next day.

Most of the Saigon attacks mirrored the poor planning and execution of the embassy assault. Shortly before the embassy attack, 34 VC in three vehicles pulled up outside the presidential palace on Tu Do St. and demanded entry. The palace guard opened fire, backed by two tanks, and the raiders were stopped. Two American military police came on the scene and were killed by the VC. The enemy took its weapons and retreated to a high-rise building across the street. This entrenchment commenced a two-day siege as the VC men were rooted out in room-to-room fighting. Only three of the attackers survived.

The radio station attack was more successful. Twenty VC approached the building at three in the morning dressed as police, led by Dang Xuan Tao. They killed the few security staffers and took control of their objective. The surrounding buildings were to be secured by an infantry and engineer platoon, but these units were intercepted en route to the radio station and had to abort the mission.[14] Dang Xuan Tao and his team set about playing their prepared tapes calling for the mass uprising in support of the general offensive, but the message was never broadcast. Technicians at the transmitter, which was located 14 miles away and was apparently not on the Communist target list, cut the radio station off. This action had been prearranged by station director general Lieutenant Colonel Vu Duc Vinh, who had anticipated the VC attack. The crew at the alternate studio site went on the air with whatever they had on hand—selections from the Beatles, the Rolling Stones, Viennese waltzes, and Vietnamese marches.[15] The radio station was quickly put under siege, and the VC held out for around eight hours. Most were killed.

The largest and militarily most significant battle took place at Tan Son Nhut air base. Tan Son Nhut was a sprawling complex, the primary airfield for Saigon and the locus of the American presence in South Vietnam. The MACV headquarters, known as "Pentagon East," was located there, along with the 7th Air Force headquarters, the South Vietnamese Joint General Staff complex, and the South Vietnamese Armor force headquarters. Many high-ranking U.S. and South Vietnamese officers had homes there or nearby, and the complex was a critical target for the VC.

In contrast with some of the other, smaller-scale attacks, such as at the U.S. embassy or the presidential palace, planning and preparation for the Tan Son Nhut attack had been detailed and thorough.[16] Colonel Nam Thuyen, commander of the 9th VC Division, had visited Tan Son Nhut during the Christmas truce, pretending to be a student. One of his sub-commanders regularly visited a family grave near the airport to pay his respects to the dead and also to reconnoiter the best access points through the perimeter. This graveyard later became an ammo dump when weapons were smuggled in coffins and buried there prior to the attack.[17] Detailed information was collected on targets inside the base, such as residences of high-ranking American and South Vietnamese officers. As Tet neared, three battalions of VC took their positions inside the Vinatexco textile mill across the street from the air base. But not all the units participating in the attack were well prepared. The 269th VC Battalion arrived in the area at 0300 on January 30 and only then learned that their mission was to participate in the attack on Tan Son Nhut. Their orders were simply to penetrate the perimeter at a predetermined point, advance to the flight line, and dig in. They were to hold the area for 48 hours, and then they'd be given further instructions.[18]

The vicious battle that broke out there the morning of January 31 contrasted with the rag-tag embassy assault that was dominating press coverage. The enemy burst through Gate 51 and into the complex. Tan Son Nhut was defended by the U.S. Air Force 377th Security Police Squadron, the MACV headquarters guards, and some South Vietnamese forces, including Vice President Ky's guard detachment. The Americans had rehearsed a contingency plan to defend the complex against just such an attack five days earlier, but the scale of the assault was larger than expected. The enemy swarmed onto the airfield. But by chance, the 8th ARVN Airborne Battalion was present that morning, awaiting a flight to Da Nang. The South Vietnamese paratroopers charged across the tarmac at the invading enemy and commenced a bloody hand-to-hand fight. After a few minutes of savage struggle, the VC assault was blunted.

Elsewhere all available American support personnel were rousted from sleep and thrown into the defense. Army communications specialist Nick Graziano was given a rifle and dropped off with other rear-echelon troops along the wired perimeter; they were ordered to repel any attackers who came in their direction. "None of us had been trained for combat," he said. But soon they were in the thick of it as a wave of Viet Cong swept toward them. "I saw them plain," he recalled. "They were screaming guys in black pajamas, and they came right at us. The only thing separating them from us was the fence." Helicopter gunships came to their assistance, and the VC attackers were driven back. Graziano recalled,

> We would open up with everything we had, and loads of them would drop. But it wasn't anything like what you see in movies or on television. Nobody goes 'ohhh' and falls gracefully to the ground. Bullets do a lot of damage to the human body. I saw arms and other body parts flying off, and a lot of those guys were ground into what looked like hamburger meat. [19]

On the north side of the air base, the 101st VC Regiment was charged with seizing the ARVN depot complex at Go Vap. The complex contained a number of heavy weapons, tanks at the Phu Dong armor headquarters and howitzers at the Cao Lo artillery compound. Trained armor crews and artillery troops accompanied the assault troops, and were on hand to use the weapons to support the assault on Tan Son Nhut. The VC managed to overrun both positions, but the attackers' plans were foiled when they found that the tanks were not there—they had been moved two months previously—and gunners at Co Lao had removed the breech blocks from the 12 105mm guns they captured. The 4th South Vietnamese Marines retook the complex later that afternoon after heavy fighting.

A Viet Cong assault force attacked the South Vietnamese Joint General Staff complex, and a tough fight ensued with heavy casualties on both sides. The Communists penetrated the compound and seized a building marked "General HQ Company," believing it to be the main Joint General Staff headquarters, where they dug in. But it was actually only the headquarters of the headquarters company, the unit that provided staff support. Meanwhile, around noon President Thieu arrived at the air base and met with his top commanders in the actual headquarters and began coordinating the South Vietnamese response to the Tet Offensive to the sounds of fighting outside.

American reinforcement troops were on the scene within hours. The 3rd squadron of the 3rd U.S. Cavalry attacked the enemy at 6 a.m. Elements of the 25th U.S. Infantry Division based 15 miles away at Cu Chi sped toward Tan Son Nhut, being guided through the darkness by their commander, who flew in a helicopter above and in front of the column dropping signal flares. By noon the Viet Cong troops had retreated back to the textile mill, where they were besieged, pounded by fire from artillery, fighter aircraft, and helicopter gunships.[20]

The heart of the Viet Cong position in Saigon was in the Cholon neighborhood in the southwestern part of the city, on the west bank of the Saigon River. Cholon was a large, densely populated, mostly poor part of the city with a large ethnically Chinese population. The name means "big market," and the neighborhood was known for its thriving black market activity. It was also the most sympathetic part of the city to the Viet Cong, and Communist planners looked to it to spark the general uprising.

The VC had established a command post and field hospital at the Phu Tho racetrack, known for its drugged horses and rigged races. U.S. infantry and ARVN Rangers seized the track on the first day of the assault, but the enemy considered it a critical position and kept feeding reinforcements into a futile contest for control. The openness of the racetrack area worked to the advantage of the allied forces, which could bring in more firepower than in the more densely built up urban areas. The fighting there continued for several days as the VC attempted to hold the position, a fruitless and pointless effort on its part that resulted in a large number of casualties.

Within a few days the VC retreated into the slums of Cholon. Civilians were asked to evacuate so sections of the neighborhood could be leveled to drive out or kill the Communists, as had been done in the Gia Dinh neighborhood to the northeast.[21] But pro-VC sentiment was strong in the central part of the neighborhood, which was a traditional ethnic Chinese enclave, and the people refused to leave. Fighting went house to house briefly but proved to be too costly. On February 4 Cholon was declared a free-fire zone, and citizens were ordered to evacuate, although not all of them did, and many were killed. Large swaths of Cholon were devastated. John Roche recalled that American helicopter gunships were "shooting away like mad. I wrote Johnson a memo saying for God's sake, before you use any of this stuff, any of these Cobras and the rest of them, they have to get clearance from the commander. Don't just let these guys go out because at this point they'll shoot at anything that moves. It's unfortunately often the case. So we did a lot of harm to ourselves through the rather indiscriminate use of firepower."[22] Oriana Fallaci observed after a visit to the neighborhood, "at least half of Cholon is razed to the ground, you can't even recognize the streets. Where the streets used to be all you can see is stretches of charred earth and mud."[23] The last organized VC fighters were rooted out of the area by February 10, but by then the fighting in Cholon had contributed the most enduring image of the war.

Perception

oven by 2/10 — 6p the
7 vards

IX.

"THE SHOT SEEN ROUND THE WORLD"

There is both power and peril in images. One sees what the photographer wants the viewer to see and trusts that the image is a true reflection of the events, not staged or altered after the fact. But the viewer also brings to the image that which he would like to believe, which has nothing to do with the photographer or sometimes even the event, and therein lies the most compelling force of photography.

Pulitzer Prize-winning combat photographer Eddie Adams once said, "Photos lie." He was referring to his own work, the picture for which he was most known, the image he once said he came to Vietnam to get. It shows a man with

Buddha will understand.

—GENERAL NGUYEN
NGOC LOAN

his right arm extended, holding a pistol, in the act of shooting a bound prisoner in civilian clothes. The perspective of the viewer is behind the armed man in a rumpled, dirty uniform, showing part of his blank profile; the viewer can see the face of the man being shot, his full expression, his pain, his shock, his humanity. At the left of the photo, sometimes cropped out, a helmeted man looks on, smiling, or grimacing, or surprised; in any case, he is showing his teeth. At the right another man walks by, taking no notice. He is always cropped out.

The photograph, entitled "Saigon Execution," is wildly famous. Discussing Vietnam, one can say "the photo of the guy shooting that guy," or "the shooting photo," or just refer to a photo and raise one's arm and listeners will understand. Rarely does an image become so iconic or have such impact, transcending the event it portrays, redefining it, even obscuring it. Joe Rosenthal's picture of the Marines raising the flag on Mount Suribachi, at Iwo Jima, on February 23, 1945, was such a photo. It had an effect that is difficult to explain rationally, coalescing a national sense of pride, purpose, and strength. David Rubinger's 1967 photo of three Israeli paratroopers overcome with emotion at the liberation of the Wailing Wall in East Jerusalem moments after having engaged in vicious hand-to-hand fighting with Jordanian troops, encapsulated Israel's national myth, martial prowess, and belief in God and destiny. Another instant icon was Thomas E. Franklin's picture of three Brooklyn-based firefighters raising an American flag among the rubble of the World Trade Center site on the afternoon of September 11, 2001. The angle of the flagpole evoked Rosenthal's Iwo Jima photo, and prints of the two were sometimes displayed together. Such images transcend what the photographer may have intended, if in fact he intended anything. They are taken over by photo editors, caption writers, copy desks, reporters and broadcasters, by people who see them and write their own mental narratives. That is ultimately where the meaning of the photos resides, and it is the source of their power, the ability to spark the desire in the viewer to conjure a compelling story.

There are no Americans in the two most famous photos of the war, "Saigon Execution" and Nick Ut's 1972 "Vietnam Napalm," showing young, naked, nine-year-old Kim Phuc fleeing a village under attack. Again, if one mentions "the naked girl" in the context of the Vietnam War, people understand instantly. There are some soldiers in the latter photo, but they are ARVN troops, not Americans. Most versions crop out the second cameraman standing to the left and behind Kim, calmly reloading his camera; his presence, and preoccupation, tends to dampen the drama of the scene, much as the disinterested passerby does in "Saigon Execution."

The most famous Vietnam photo featuring an American is Hugh Van Es's picture of the evacuation by helicopter of Vietnamese officials and their families from the roof of the Pittman Apartments, 22 Gia Long St. in Saigon, a building that had been used by the CIA and USAID. The picture is usually misidentified as Americans being choppered from the roof of the U.S. embassy. But the only American clearly in the shot is CIA employee O. B. Harnage, who was helping the refugees aboard.[1] These most-recognized photos of Vietnam all convey strongly negative messages taken at face value. But there is usually much more to the story than a photograph can convey. "Saigon Execution" was such a picture. The image communicates brutality, finality, hopelessness—the viewer can sense the heat and sweat and stink of the scene. But one comes away with only a vague notion of what happened.

THE ASSASSIN

The shooter in "Saigon Execution" is General Nguyen Ngoc Loan, the head of the South Vietnamese National Police, who had caused the United States such difficulties during the Buttercup affair. The man Loan is in the act of shooting is Viet Cong Captain Nguyen Van Lem, whose code name was Bay Lop—Bay for being a seventh son, Lop after his new wife, Nguyen Thi Lop.[2] Bay Lop was born in 1933, and had a record as an insurgent stretching back to the days of the Viet Minh. In January 1967 he was a company executive officer in the Viet Cong K-20 unit.[3] During Tet his mission was to eliminate those the Communists had identified as enemies of the people. Bay Lop was an assassin.

145

Assassination was a key component of the Communist plan to foment the popular uprising against the South Vietnamese government. The VC had marked most senior leaders for death, including Ambassador Bunker, General Westmoreland, President Thieu, Vice President Ky, Interior Minister General Linh Quang Vien, and of course General Loan. Loan's intelligence network had already informed him that the enemy was out to murder him. "Who isn't afraid of being killed in Saigon?" he said a few weeks before Tet. "Each day I'm walking a tightrope. Each day I'm gambling with my life. Of course they want to kill me and maybe they'll manage to."[4]

The VC had conducted assassinations for years. They were an important aspect of the terrorism campaign it carried out as part of its larger guerrilla struggle.[5] Between 1958 and the first ten months of 1966 the Viet Cong assassinated 11,200 civilians and kidnapped a further 39,750.[6] VC assassins were particularly active in the months leading up to the 1967 elections.[7] One dynamic assassin was a 24-year-old woman named Phung Ngoc Anh, known as the "Dragon Lady," who gunned down her victims with a .45 caliber pistol while perched on the back of a motorcycle driven by an accomplice. She was apprehended in September 1967.[8] In all of 1967 there were 3,706 VC assassinations and 5,369 abductions. The next year VC assassinations topped 9,000.

The principal targets of the assassins were village government officials, tribal and other nongovernment leaders, unfriendly reporters and editors, and, when available, Americans. The assassination program operated in cities, villages, and hamlets, wherever the VC was present. The VC tended to target both the best and worst South Vietnamese officials; it killed the effective and popular administrators to deny their talents to the regime, and killed the ineffective and corrupt administrators to appeal to popular sympathies.

An enemy document entitled "The Task of Breaking the Enemy Control and Eliminating the Tyrants in the City," captured January 8, 1968, gives insight into the tactics, techniques, and procedures of the assassination program.[9] The assassins did not

146

plan random acts of violence but carefully targeted terrorism. Recommended weapons included "explosive charges, grenade, pistol, and other locally made weapons such as hammer, stick, scissors, swords, poisonous arrows, pincers, [and] clubs." The document suggested various scenarios for the killings:

> We can kill a person at his own house or at his office. For this
> purpose we must disguise ourselves and secretly penetrate
> through the fences into the house. We can kill him when he
> is going to work, or on his way home from his office, when he
> is riding a bicycle or driving a car. We can lure him into a love
> trap or kill him during a party.[10]

The assassins were instructed to employ teams of no more than thee people. Detailed guidance was given on how to conduct surveillance of the target (e.g., "Where is his house? What is his job? Where does he usually take his meals and sleep? With whom does he usually spend his time?"), his house, his movements, his hobbies ("prostitutes, music, dancing, movies, sports, bicycle racing, wine or opium?"), whether or not he is usually armed or knows martial arts, and other pertinent information.

Assassinations had three phases—approach, combat, and retreat. On the approach, "to lie in wait is much better than to walk towards him to attack his front, his flank, or his back." In combat—the attack—the assassins were instructed, "If we meet the enemy, try to execute him at once; we will pass up an opportunity if we don't kill him. If Comrade #1 meets the enemy, he must kill him immediately. If he encounters any difficulties, Comrade #2 must kill the enemy. Both of them must kill the enemy as soon as possible, in order to have enough time to cope with the situation outside." During the retreat, "escape in crowded streets and mingle with the people." Assassins should move down crowded streets, not deserted ones, and use smoke grenades if needed. They were told not to initiate combat with a pursuing enemy, and absolutely avoid capture. They were to go to a new safe house, not the one the team left from. And upon return, "the party chapter must provide immediate ideological guidance" presumably just in case the assassin had an emotional reaction to the act he just committed.

The document reiterates: "Kill the enemy at once." The assassin "must be determined and act bravely without hesitation or mercy." Depending on the situation, the assassin might leave a note explaining the reason for the "execution."

THE TET ASSASSINATIONS

Assassination was a key component of the VC plan to paralyze the government and disrupt its response during Tet. It was also intended to make reconstituting the government difficult if the VC fighters were driven out. The assassination plan for Saigon was approved in December 1967. It was a full-phased program that included killing high-level leaders, liquidating middle- and lower-level officials when possible, and suppressing antirevolutionary elements among the people. [11] Assassination teams went to homes of marked officials, officers, and others and killed them and, when possible, their families. When VC troops briefly secured some neighborhoods, mock trials were held for "traitors" who were quickly "executed." Captured soldiers, home for the holidays and out of uniform, were shot on the spot. But the assassination teams suffered the same difficulties that other VC units did. Planning was not uniformly rigorous, and even when it was, the plans were not always carried out.

Captain Le Van Nguyen, a Hanoi native and former Viet Minh, served in a security unit in the North. He had infiltrated to the South in the summer of 1965 in Quang Tri Province, and afterward served in various security detachments. On December 31, 1967, he was assigned to a seven-man squad whose mission was to assassinate or capture government figures in Saigon. The team leader was named Tu Thanh. They infiltrated Saigon sometime during January and stayed in a safe house. On January 29 at 1800 hours Le Van Nguyen was issued a K-54 pistol and 40 rounds of ammunition, and told of the attack plan. His mission was to go to the Gia Dinh police station and kill or capture the police chief, Nguyen Duc Kham, and his assistants. Tu Thanh assured him that the citizens of Saigon would rise up soon after the attack commenced. Le Van Nguyen was skeptical, and shortly before the mission was to be executed both he and Tu Thanh, who had also had a change of heart, deserted. He was captured two days later.[12]

Extensive observation had been carried out at Tan Son Nhut airfield, where many high-ranking U.S. and Vietnamese officers and officials lived. The Communists had plans to attack the MACV command structure. VC sappers knew where all the high-ranking American officers in Saigon lived and how they were guarded. A lengthy planning document for the assault in the area notes to "Organize to destroy the enemy helicopters on the roof of General Ky's and General Westmoreland's residences, because they can flee by means of helicopter."[13] Westmoreland had a security detail, but most generals and colonels were assigned only South Vietnamese "watchmen" who kept an eye on things at night, or "lethargically hung around the billets." These men disappeared the evening of January 30, a fact that was noticed with some suspicion. Many American officers kept their sidearms close by that night just in case, but the assassins never arrived.[14]

A remarkably candid VC after-action report of the assassination program in Saigon admitted a comprehensive and systemic failure in the effort to take out the key leaders targeted. "The number of anti-revolutionary personnel exterminated by us was still small," the report said. "The reason for this failure stems from a collection of inaccurate information on the addresses of the [targets], the vigilance and careful security measures taken in the protection of these persons, the hasty assignment of missions to our cadres and units in charge, the non-availability of forces to operate in some areas, the inexperience of personnel who implemented the plan, the shortage of weapons, the delay in the receipt of the orders . . . and lack of determination to fight."[15] The efforts at other levels were similarly ineffective, although the VC nevertheless claimed to have killed thousands of policemen and security personnel. However, even given the failure of the assassination program, there would be an unintended victory through the photo and film of Bay Lop's death. Unintended consequences of the assassination program gave us the most vivid image of the Tet Offensive and probably of the war.

THE AN QUANG PAGODA

The Tet Offensive came as no surprise to General Loan. He had been holding contingency planning sessions for three days prior to the attack on Saigon, and spent his nights on combat alert prowling the city in a jeep until 2 a.m. He was about to retire for the night on January 31 when the attacks started. President Thieu was at his villa, and Vice President Ky was at Tan Son Nhut. Loan advised Ky to stay there and dispatched two armored companies to protect him. Then Loan put together a platoon of men from the Police Field Force and sped to the radio station with two armored cars. The government needed to take back the station quickly to communicate to the people and squelch rumors of a coup or worse. Loan personally led the assault on the building at 6 a.m. They retook the main floor quickly, and the VC retreated from the studio to the upper floors, where they maintained a spirited defense. "We take it back," Loan recalled, "and the man right next to me is shot dead and falls on top of me."[16] In 45 minutes Loan called Ky and told him the station was secure. The government sent a tape to be played, announcing a curfew and asking people to stay indoors while the attackers were dealt with.

Loan got little rest the next few days as he coordinated the defense of the capital. He was constantly on the move, visiting every trouble spot and keeping his men organized and motivated. He was paying particular attention to the fierce fighting in Cholon, especially in the vicinity of the An Quang pagoda, which the VC were using as a headquarters. An Quang was a complex of buildings off Ly Thai To St. about a mile east of the Phu Tho racetrack, and was the home of Thich Tri Quang. VC flags fluttered from the buildings of the complex and snipers were on the rooftops. Rumor had it that a Viet Cong two-star general was holed up inside.

Two South Vietnamese Marine companies and six tanks were ordered to take the pagoda. The Marines were reticent to use the amount of force necessary to expel the occupiers. Loan told the

Marines that if they were unwilling to take back the pagoda his men would do it themselves. The National Police mounted the assault and were met by heavy weapons fire. A short time later, 30 monks and nuns began to protest at another pagoda in support of the Viet Cong. Loan told the protestors that if they did not clear the area he would clear it with tear gas. The monks and nuns refused, and Loan's men dispersed them.[17] The pagoda fell on February 1 around 5 p.m. after heavy fighting. Many Viet Cong escaped out the rear.

Don Webster of CBS news, who was on the scene, doubted that An Quang had actually been a VC headquarters because "there's little record of the Buddhists and the Vietcong working very closely together," apparently heedless of the VC flags flying from the structure, with or without the permission of the Buddhists. "If the purpose of this war is to win the hearts and minds of the people," he continued, "the capture of the An Quang pagoda can be considered a defeat."[18] Had the South Vietnamese failed to take the objective, of course, that would also have been reported a defeat.

ENTER EDDIE ADAMS

On the scene that day was 35-year-old AP photographer Eddie Adams. He was an award-winning journalist and former Marine who had learned his trade as a combat photographer during the Korean conflict. Adams had first come to Vietnam in 1965, and during Tet he was on his third "tour" for the AP. Adams was intensely competitive and fearless, and he was often close to the action. He had a knack for showing up at the right place at the right time, and his contacts in the Marine Corps proved to be invaluable for gaining him access. AP correspondent George Esper recalled, "What struck me was Eddie's ability to get to the big stories before anyone, even the military. I recall several amphibious landings the Marines made; I accompanied the Marines on some of those operations. As we landed, there was Eddie already on the beachhead awaiting us with a big smile. He drove the military crazy trying to figure out how he got there before them on these secret operations. To this day I don't know myself. Eddie had so many sources in Vietnam, from generals to the grunts in the field. He always shared his information with me, both from them and from what he saw on the battlefield, and got me access to key operations and field commanders."[19] In fact, Adams was friendly with General Lewis W. Walt, who had been commander of III MAF in Vietnam and at the time of Tet was the Assistant Commandant of the Marine Corps.

Hal Buell, who was AP photo chief in New York at the time and Adams's boss, said that "Eddie was especially suited to AP. He had no political or social agenda. He was dedicated to telling the story truthfully and straightforwardly. No picture was barred, but there was no spin either, no special selection that got in the way of what was real. His mind was open to any idea for a multi-picture story or a single oddity that would make for a good image. It was always the image that counted."[20] Photojournalist and fellow former Marine Wally McNamee said there was "a sort of cult of personality about Adams. Eddie had great success with his war coverage and seemed to attract other hacks. Maybe it was because of the brooding intensity I think he had developed. Eddie was no longer the fresh-faced 19-year-old from New Kensington. He was a world-class, super-competitive photographer covering the biggest and most dangerous story in the world, achieving great success and notoriety."[21]

Peter Arnett, who worked frequently with Adams, observed that he "was a social animal who reveled in organizing offbeat entertainment for his buddies."[22] In 1966 the two were covering the Buddhist uprisings in the South. Once during a riot a nervous young American MP drew his pistol and held it on Arnett, who with Bob Schieffer was asserting his rights to cover the story. Adams, who was photographing the scene, said, "Come on, shoot the fucker. It'll make a better picture." "Eddie's comment broke the ice," Arnett recalled. "The MP relaxed, and we hung around until the demonstration was over." When Arnett later questioned the wisdom of Adams's comment, he joked, "I was just practicing for a real execution."[23]

On January 31 Adams covered the embassy attack, which took place a few blocks from the AP offices on the fourth floor of the Eden building. It was dangerous for American photographers to travel the streets of Saigon, and most photos were taken by Vietnamese freelancers, but Adams was unfazed by the action. On the morning of February 1, tips arrived that there was heavy fighting about four miles west around the An Quang pagoda. Adams teamed up with NBC correspondent Howard Tuckner, cameramen Vo Suu and his brother Vo Huynh, and soundman Le Phuc Dinh. The NBC offices were adjacent to AP's, and the organizations sometimes teamed up for stories. They were driven to the Cholon section and walked toward the sound of the fighting. Correspondents from ABC and CBS were also on the scene. The crews stayed near An Quang for some time taking pictures, but it did not seem as though they would get anything interesting, so around noon they decided to leave. Adams and the others were about to depart when they noticed a man being led up the street and thought maybe there would be something worth shooting.

Bay Lop was being brought in by some South Vietnamese Marines. He was dressed in a checked shirt and dark pants, his arms bound. One Marine carried a pistol they had taken from him. Adams moved toward them and took some pictures. The Vo brothers were filming the scene from each side of the street. "When they were close—maybe five feet away—the soldiers stopped and backed away," Adams said. "I saw a man walk into my camera viewfinder from the left." It was General Loan, who had been directing action near the pagoda. Adams did not know who he was at first. Loan appraised the situation briefly, then told one of his regimental commanders to shoot Bay Lop. The man hesitated, so Loan drew his weapon.

NBC's Howard Tuckner saw the pistol in Loan's hand and told cameraman Vo Suu, "Keep rolling. Keep rolling."[24] An ABC cameraman filmed the walk-up but stopped when Loan took his pistol out because he was afraid of him. The CBS crew was elsewhere. "There was not one word," Tuckner recalled. "Loan did not try to talk to him nor to scare him. He did not wave his gun at his face or his head. He did not put the gun to his temple. He just blew his brains out."[25]

"I had no idea he would shoot," Adams said. "It was common to hold a pistol to the head of prisoners during questioning. So I prepared to make that picture—the threat, the interrogation. But it didn't happen. The man just pulled a pistol out of his holster, raised it to the VC's head and shot him in the temple. I made a picture at the same time."[26]

Bay Lop fell and the camera followed him. A stream of blood pulsed from the head wound, diminishing with each beat of his fading heart and plummeting blood pressure. Loan turned to the assembled journalists. "Many Americans have been killed these last few days, and many of my best Vietnamese friends," he said. "Now do you understand? Buddha will understand."[27] A Marine placed a VC propaganda leaflet on Bay Lop's face, and the body was left in the street. The corpse was soon thrown on the back of a flatbed truck and taken to one of the mass graves outside Saigon where the dead VC were being dumped.

Why did General Loan shoot Bay Lop? In part it was because the man he had told to shoot him had vacillated. "I think, 'Then I must do it,'" Loan recalled. "If you hesitate, if you didn't do your duty, the men won't follow you."[28] But why did Bay Lop merit death? In 1972 Loan told Tom Buckley, "When you see a man in civilian clothes with a revolver killing your people . . . when many of your people have already been killed, then what are you supposed to do? . . . He killed a policeman. He spit in the face of the men who captured him. What do you want us to do? Put him in jail for two or three years and then let him go back to the enemy?" Loan noted that those Communists who fought in uniform were given the treatment they were guaranteed by international agreements, "but when they are not in uniform they are criminals and the rule of war is death."[29]

Loan knew about Bay Lop before the fateful moment, who he was and what he had been doing. Colonel Tran Minh Cong, police chief of the 2nd district (which included the U.S. embassy and presidential palace) said that Bay Lop had been captured shortly before in the act of killing the families of police officers. He had shot "about 34 people and dumped them in a ditch."[30] Ky said Bay Lop was witnessed among piles of bodies as he killed a police sergeant, his wife, and three children. "The Geneva Conventions do not extend the protections of prisoner of war status to spies, mercenaries and guerrillas who fail to distinguish themselves from civilians," Ky said.[31] By some accounts some of the victims were family members of General Loan's deputy and close friend.

Eyewitness Corrado Pizzinelli, an Italian, said, "When they look at the picture of General Nguyen Ngoc Loan executing Captain Lop, they think it was disgraceful. But it was right. I never understood the masochism that became part of your national spirit. I was near Loan that day. I know why he fired. One second before, he happened to see his best friend falling down, killed by a Viet Cong sniper. I will never condemn General Loan. I ask whether he could have acted differently. That's war."[32]

Nguyen Truong Toai, a 25-year-old student who joined the ARVN in June 1968 out of a sense of national spirit in response to the Communist attacks during Tet, said that Americans writing about the shooting "didn't understand the reality of the war, the truth of what was going on in Vietnam." Nguyen Truong Toai was present at the shooting, and knew Bay Lop. "I knew that Communist and I knew what he did," he said. "In 1968 in Saigon he pushed the children out during the fighting—innocent children— as a wave of people so that his own people could escape from the fighting. During the heaviest fighting he used children as shields, and the soldiers could no longer shoot when he did that. And General Loan could not take that . . . [W]hen [General Loan] saw the corpses of the children he asked, 'Why? What happened?' and when he found out why those children died and who was responsible for this act, this tragedy, he shot the man . . . I would have done the same thing; I would have shot this monstrous guy if I had caught him that way . . . I don't think the American people ever truly knew what was going on in Vietnam."[33] NBC cameraman Vo Suu said he never forgot General Loan's words after he shot Bay Lop, and that he had seen many worse things during the war. "That war is terrible," he said. "I think just part of it was exposed to the world. Many parts of it, it's behind a jungle.

Nobody knows. I'm talking about atrocity," he said. Memories of slain villagers and dead babies haunted him thirty years later. "So many, so many, so many," he said. "Even now I remember."[34]

There were other accounts of the crimes of Bay Lop. Tran Minh Cong says that earlier in the Tet Offensive Bay Lop had led a team taking hostages at the armored corps training school compound. He ordered the commander, ARVN Lieutenant Colonel Nguyen Tuan, to show the VC how to start up the tanks. When Tuan refused Bay Lop killed him and his family, "including his 80 year old grandmother."[35] A version of the story published in 1972 by the AP noted that Tuan was Loan's friend. Tuan was beheaded and his wife and five of their six children were "killed by grenades thrown into their house."[36]

Susan Sontag claimed without evidence or clear rationale that the picture was a photo op arranged for the media. "It was staged by General Loan," she claimed, "who had led the prisoner, hands tied behind his back, out to the street where journalists had gathered; he would not have carried out the summary execution there had they not been available to witness it."[37]

"The General was a very sentimental guy," Colonel Cong said. "I didn't believe he could shoot that guy. Frankly he wasn't the type." But Loan was "angry and emotional in that moment. In a very quick moment he had no time to think. To tell you the truth I don't know why he did it. But I would have done the same thing."[38]

But the reason or reasons General Loan pulled the trigger would soon be rendered moot.

GETTING THE STORY OUT

Eddie Adams rushed into the AP offices. "Goddamn it, General Loan shot a man right in front of my eyes," he said, holding up a roll of film. "I think I may have got it right here. Hey, I hope so."[39] Adams handed the film to a darkroom attendant, and Peter Arnett interviewed him about what he had witnessed. Soon the man emerged from the darkroom and handed the film strip to AP photo editor Horst Faas. Faas looked at the film with a magnifying glass and muttered, "Damn." He handed the film to Adams, who examined it and "let out a whoop."[40]

"Running my Nikon eyeball quickly over a roll of black-and-white film from Eddie Adams," Haas recalled, "I saw what I had never seen before on the lightbox of my Saigon editing desk: The perfect newspicture—the perfectly framed and exposed 'frozen moment' of an event which I felt instantly would become representative of the brutality of the Vietnam War."[41] The timing of the picture was incredible; it captured the instant when the bullet was passing through Bay Lo's head.

Faas chose four of 20 pictures to send out by radiophone. Adams objected, wanting them all to be sent, but they were up against technical limitations. In those days transmitting a picture took 20 minutes. "The single radiotelephone circuit to Paris, shared with UPI, was closing down after three hours. AP's radiophoto operator, Tran Van Hung, already had gone to sleep beneath his transmitter because of the curfew and continued fighting."[42] So it took another day for the full 20-picture sequence to be transmitted. But the first photos, including the execution shot, were available in the U.S. 11 hours after the event, in time for same-day evening news broadcasts and next-morning editions of newspapers.

NBC ran a series of stills, including the Adams photo, on its February 1 evening broadcast, narrated by John Chancellor: "There was awful savagery. Here the Viet Cong killed a South Vietnamese Colonel and murdered his wife and six children. And this South Vietnamese officer came home during a lull in the fighting to find the bodies of his murdered children. There was awful retribution. Here the infamous chief of the South Vietnamese National Police, General Loan, executed a captured Viet Cong officer. Rough justice on a Saigon street as the charmed life of the city of Saigon comes to a bloody end."[43] NBC showed the Loan photo again toward the end of the broadcast. Johnson adviser Harry McPherson recalled, "I remember being impressed in some way by the fact that [the Adams photograph] was shown twice in the same newscast that they showed it. Described what we were seeing, then went back and showed it again. Most unusual for any television. And this seemed to be saying, watch this. This is important."[44]

The *New York Times* ran the Adams photo on the front page on February 2 with the caption "Guerrilla Dies." A longer sequence of the Adams photos ran on page 12. Below the front-page execution photo was a picture of a stunned South Vietnamese soldier carrying the body of his daughter, captioned "His Family Slain by Vietcong." The man's quarters had been overrun and his wife and children killed. William F. Buckley, Jr. described the scene as "a desolate soldier, his face lined with grief, carrying the corpse of a little girl with a face like a Madonna's."[45]

The next day in a village outside Saigon some people gathered to read the *Saigon News*, which featured the Adams picture. "Look at Loan killing a VC," one man said, handing the paper to his neighbor, Nguyen Thi Lop. She immediately recognized the man being shot as her husband. "I knew instantly it was Lem," she said. "But I couldn't say anything, I had to hide my grief and shoulder it like a hawker's burden as I wandered about the city trying to quietly find out what happened. I was too terrified to approach his unit for fear of being identified." She later renamed her daughter Loan to help cleanse the General's soul. "If [Lem] had been killed in a running battle or by a foreign GI I would not have minded so much," she said. "It was war after all. But the way he was shot after being wounded and captured by another Vietnamese was too much to bear."[46]

There were other such images from Tet. Horst Faas recalled that "the days after Adams' execution photo, Vietnamese photographers competed with a whole horror scenario of similar events. AP's Le Ngoc Cung came up with a heartbreaking sequence showing a South Vietnamese soldier sharing a sandwich and water from a canteen with a Vietcong prisoner. The last pictures show how he shot him. Dang Van Phuoc, also roaming the city for AP, had photos of diehard Vietcong dragged from the ruins and then summarily shot. No pardons were given, and the photos showed that for days."[47] But the Adams photo did not simply document an event. It stood alone as a work of art. "Eddie was after more than just good day-to-day newsphoto coverage of the war," Faas said. "He was after the perfect, meaningful photograph expressing the frustrations, the bravery, the suffering of the war—all expressed in one image. He had tried for three years, on countless military operations, and would become very moody and depressed when it did not work out perfectly. New York headquarters was happy with his work—but Eddie wasn't. Until February 1, 1968." Said Adams, "I got what I came to Vietnam for."[48]

NBC had film of the execution but did not know it at first. The NBC crew stayed to film the afternoon fight at the pagoda, then Howard Tuckner shot the "stand-upper" to introduce the execution piece. Vo Suu had changed the film cartridge quickly after the shooting, fearing the film might be confiscated, but Loan's men made no such attempt. Back at NBC's Saigon bureau, chief Ron Steinman rescripted the event, playing the final fight at the pagoda first and the execution scene second, to heighten the drama and make the story line more linear. He also lost the "stand-upper." But he had not seen the developed film, and Tuckner doubted that they had the death shot. Vo Suu, however, was positive he got it. Steinman wired New York a description of the scene as related by the eyewitnesses. "If he has it all, it's startling stuff," Steinman wrote. "If he has part of it, it's still more than anyone else has."[49]

Getting the film back to New York was difficult. Regular commercial air transport was impossible under the circumstances. The undeveloped film was sent out Friday, February 2, in a special military escort vehicle, and flown to Tokyo on a medevac flight. There was only one color film-processing lab in Tokyo, and it operated on a first-come, first-served basis. In order to beat the competition, NBC hired a Grand Prix motorcycle racer to courier its films from the airport. Vo Suu had shot 115 minutes of footage, which was reduced to 7 minutes 40 seconds that aired. Tuckner's report on the pagoda fighting and the Loan execution was edited from an original raw 30 minutes to 3 minutes 55 seconds.

Robert Northshield, executive producer of the Huntley-Brinkley Report, watched the film as it came in from Tokyo via satellite, along with John Chancellor. "I thought that was awful rough," Northshield said. Chancellor could hardly speak. The original execution sequence was 23 seconds long, but when the footage aired it was edited to six seconds, and later four seconds. The screen went to black for three seconds, then to a title slide, and then a commercial. The NBC report identified Bay Lop as "the commander of the Viet Cong commando unit." It was 46 hours from the event to the airing of the film.

Northshield made the call to cut away after the body fell. The close-up of Bay Lop lying on the pavement as blood gushed from his head was considered too graphic for airing. However, one NBC staffer later said that the full scene should have been shown, that the view the American people were getting of the war was "too sanitized" and that they "'should have had their noses rubbed in' the violence and gore."[50]

REACTION TO THE SHOOTING

Tom Buckley, writing in *Harper's* in 1972, cited the dissemination of Adams's grisly photograph as "the turning point, the moment when the American public turned against the war." "The Tet Offensive destroyed confidence in the men who were directing [the war effort]; the murder committed by Loan sealed its moral bankruptcy."[51] David D. Perlmutter, writing in 2003, noted that there was "no evidence of any public fury in reaction to the image" or evidence that it turned public opinion against the war, but there was evidence that "political and military leaders in 1968 assumed that the picture had a public-opinion effect and acted on that assumption."[52]

Robert Kennedy quickly exploited the situation. Six days after the photo appeared he gave a major speech on Vietnam in which he spoke at length about the event and what he thought it implied about the United States and the Vietnam War:

> Last week, a Viet Cong suspect was turned over to the chief
> of the Vietnamese Security Services, one of our leading allies,
> who executed him on the spot, a flat violation of the Geneva
> Convention on the Rules of War. And what has been done
> about it? Of course, the enemy is brutal and cruel, and has
> done the same thing many times. But we are not fighting the
> Communists in order to become more like them—we fight
> to preserve our differences. The photograph of the execution

was on front pages all around the world—leading our best and oldest friends to ask, more in sorrow than in anger, what has happened to America? I believe we asked the same question of ourselves that morning and the fact is that we do not have a satisfactory answer.

The International Red Cross issued a protest against the summary execution of prisoners. The International Commission of Jurists in Geneva published a report condemning brutality in the Vietnamese conflict and singled out General Loan specifically.[53] Journalist Tom Buckley observed that the execution could be seen as merciful, sparing Bay Lop "the gruesome torture that would have almost certainly been a prelude to his death in captivity."[54] The North Vietnamese immediately recognized the propaganda value of the picture and made it part of a traveling exposition. The Viet Cong threatened to take retaliatory action against prisoners, which had already been its policy, but in response the U.S. discussed the treatment of detainees with the South Vietnamese and also made a point of letting the press know about the discussions.[55]

The Saigon government was embarrassed but tried to keep the event in perspective. At a February 5 new conference, Vice President Ky said he had given orders forbidding these types of "brutal acts." But he also noted the atrocities the VC had perpetrated targeting the security forces. "I know the foreign press makes a lot of noise about this death," he said, "but when you see your friends die it is hard to control your reactions." He also noted the double standard in the fact that photos of VC atrocities had not gained as wide a circulation as the Adams photo had.[56] South Vietnamese Ambassador to the United States, Bui Diem, said that the images of Bay Lop's killing "crystallized the war's brutality without providing a context within which to understand the events they depicted."[57] Colonel Cong said "people felt frustrated and angry that the U.S. media made such a big deal about that picture. Most Vietnamese thought the killing of the Viet Cong was justified. He deserved to die—that's how they felt."[58]

The earliest reports of the event in fact provided a great deal of context, but that context faded over time. The details of the story were lost, but the image remained. The February 1 Huntley-Brinkley Report, showing stills of violence by the Viet Cong as well as the Adams photo, had given broad context to the situation. When NBC ran the film on February 2, the report also placed it in the context of the fight at the pagoda, though losing the story of the VC execution squads. On March 10, NBC ran a special on the war hosted by Frank McGee. This report discarded the known context of the event and replaced it with a negative and dishonest setup: "South Vietnam's national police chief had killed a man who had been captured carrying a pistol," McGee said. "This was taken as sufficient evidence that he was a Viet Cong officer, so the police chief put a bullet in his brain. He's still the chief of police."[59] Democratic Senators Paul Douglas (IL) and Gale McGee (WY) were invited to be on the program, and William Bundy wrote talking points for them that among other things explained the context of the shooting. Bundy argued that "nobody will excuse this act, but it must be looked at in the light of a situation where Loan undoubtedly knew, as everybody did, that the VC had just been murdering civilians, including the wives and families of officials all over Saigon. He acted in hot blood, and this is not the first time that there have been such summary executions in wars in Asia or elsewhere."[60] Over time, however, this line of argument faded, and the event was remembered as a stark and senseless act of brutality.

The execution was not a defining moment; rather, the photo defined the moment. For his part Adams was unaffected by the event. "My own feeling was at the time, somebody got shot in the head, so what?" he said. "You become very callous over there . . . Even when I'd seen it when it was transmitted I didn't think much of it."[61] When the photo became famous Adams said he didn't understand why. Reporters asked him why he didn't intervene to stop the shooting, which he called "an idiotic question." Harry McPherson said, "When I saw [Loan] do this it did not altogether surprise me. I'd heard he was a brutal fellow." [62] But for him, as for many others, the killing helped delegitimize the war and discredit the Saigon government. It was the other shoe that dropped. The fact of the Tet Offensive made it appear as though the government was lying about the course of the war; the Adams photo made it seem as though the war was not worth fighting. "Americans saw not only the inhumanity of an ally but also confirmation of an impression that had been building for years," McPherson said. "We were sunk in a war between alien peoples, with whom we shared few human values. . . . I felt that this [was] proof that we were backing a regime without scruples. It proved too that we were involved up to our necks in a war between alien cultures, alien to us in which we had very little in common. . . . One felt simply that we shouldn't be there."[63]

Walt Rostow recalled, years later, "If you captured a man in that tense, urban civil war context and shot him, in that highly irregular and tense circumstance, [it] did not strike me as an act of wickedness. It's an act, a very sad act, but it's an act of war, in that context. Now without knowing who the one was or what the police were up against at that particular time in the battle of Saigon I can understand that it could be misinterpreted by others, but that was my judgment." Vice President Ky noted in his memoir, "In the click of a shutter, our struggle for independence and self-determination was transformed into an image of a seemingly senseless and brutal execution."[64]

X.

ASSESSING THE BROADER OFFENSIVE

By the end of the first week most Communist assault troops were either on the defensive, surrounded, driven off, or destroyed. They had failed to reach their military objectives in almost all of their attacks, many of them failing in the first few hours. In broad terms, the Tet Offensive was a military catastrophe.

Between 64,000 and 84,000 Viet Cong and PAVN troops took part in the offensive. They attacked 36 provincial capitals, 5 of 6 autonomous cities, 64 of 242 district capitals, and 50 hamlets. This tally shows the extent to which Giap divided his forces and underscores the fact that North Vietnamese planners

We had to destroy Ben Tre in order to save it.

—MAJOR BOORIS, 3/39TH INFANTRY BATTALION, 9TH INFANTRY DIVISION saw them as a tipping force, a vanguard that would be joined by masses of South Vietnamese seeking "liberation" from U.S. "occupiers" and their "lackeys" in Saigon. But when the hoped-for general uprising failed to materialize, the general offensive was crushed.

The bulk of the attacks were aimed at South Vietnamese forces, not Americans. The Communists generally sought to avoid head-to-head confrontations with U.S. troops, which experience since 1965 had taught them was not a sound policy. To the extent possible they sought to lure the U.S. into the countryside or bypass American troops while pursuing attacks against the ARVN and trying to foment the popular uprising. But the North Vietnamese had severely underestimated the fighting spirit of the ARVN, and they fatally overestimated the desire of the South Vietnamese people to rally to their cause. In the end, the ARVN did not desert to the Communists, and the popular uprising never took place. The former development harmed the plan; the latter was fatal.

Other Tet engagements followed the confused pattern of the embassy attack. Twelve Viet Cong sappers attacked the South Vietnamese Navy headquarters at Bach Dang Quay at 2:55 a.m. on January 31. They blew a hole in the wall and tried to force an entry. Within five minutes ten were killed, and the remaining two were captured. Two VC companies attacked the ARVN III Corps headquarters at Bin Hoa airfield. They had been ordered to liberate a prisoner of war compound in the area. Their rally point was a nearby rubber plantation, but U.S. troops had cut down the rubber trees to provide fields of fire for the expected attack. Not finding the grove, the VC got disoriented and attacked the headquarters by way of improvisation. They were wiped out. At Pleiku American troops had the benefit of having captured a copy of "Urgent Order Number One" on January 5, which detailed the attack plan on the city by the H-15 VC Battalion and the NVA 95B Regiment. They prepared a defense, and the attack came exactly as stated. Nevertheless, the battle at Pleiku was a hard fight, and half the town was destroyed.

South Vietnamese troops generally fought well, especially when defending. General Abrams reviewed the performance of the ARVN units and found that only eight of 149 battalions were unsatisfactory, 30 battalions distinguished themselves, and the rest performed satisfactorily. Abrams noted that this ranking exceeded the low expectations of most Americans.[1] American and ARVN units cooperated in the defense of Quang Tri near Hue. The Province Adviser, Robert Brewer, had a double agent who gave him the blueprint for the Tet attacks in the area. Brewer had preplanned the defense with the commander of the 1st Brigade 1st Air Cavalry Division, which had been positioned as a reserve force for Khe Sanh. The local ARVN commander kept his men from going home for leave on Tet, and when the Communist force attacked, the 1st ARVN Regiment and 9th ARVN Airborne mounted a strong counterattack. Meanwhile, American air cavalry exploited the morning fog to conceal a movement to the enemy rear, where they attacked and routed the Communists.

America's coalition partners in Vietnam also played a role in Tet. When the VC seized the town of Ba Ria, the 3rd Battalion of the Royal Australian Regiment led an ARVN unit in retaking the city. At Da Nang, U.S. Marines and ARVN troops fought side by side with South Korean Marines.

Not all of the engagements were settled in a matter of a few hours or days. A ten-day battle raged at Da Lat, a historic resort city in Lam Dong Province that was also the site of the South Vietnamese National Military Academy. There was also a nuclear reactor at Da Lat that had been operating since 1960, which caused American policymakers some concern that nuclear materials would fall into enemy hands. The city had not previously seen much action, but the VC devoted two battalions, the 145 and 186, to the Tet assault. They moved quickly to the center of the town and seized the marketplace. They were attacked by two regional militia companies with two armored cars, assisted by a cadet company from the military academy and a helicopter gunship. The VC troops were stunned by the ferocity of the attack from an inferior force and retreated to the Pasteur Institute, where they dug in. There was a standoff in the town until reinforcements arrived from the ARVN 23rd Ranger Battalion. More ARVN Rangers were sent to Da Lat over the following days, and the city was finally secured on February 11. The nuclear facility was later shut down and the fuel removed before the North Vietnamese takeover in 1975.

The hard fight at the provincial capital of Ben Tre in the Mekong Delta gave the war one of its most memorable quotations. A small VC force attacked the city on January 31 and was driven out by ARVN forces. A few days later a Viet Cong reinforced regiment of 2,500 men, including the 516 and 518 Battalions, attacked and quickly overran most of the city. The government buildings and the U.S. military compound were surrounded, and the enemy pressed the attack. Local American units from the 3/39th Infantry battalion of the 9th Infantry Division had been diverted to the battle in Saigon and were not immediately available to relieve the besieged defenders, and two companies of the 2/39th were sent into the city to stave off disaster. They were immediately engaged in fierce house-to-house fighting and could not dislodge the enemy. The commander on the scene called for air and artillery support to engage the VC, even with the certainty that broad swaths of the city would be damaged and the lives of noncombatants threatened.

At first higher command balked at the possible damage that might be inflicted. "We had to argue with our corps headquarters at Can Tho. They didn't like the idea," a captain said. "But they were convinced when we explained that it was rockets and bombing, or the end for us."[2] Fighter bombers and attack helicopters swarmed on the city, seeking targets and hitting enemy positions with bombs and rockets. Napalm scorched the wooden buildings and thatch-roofed houses. Artillery from the 9th Infantry base at Dong Tam pounded the center of the city. Persistent fire stalled the enemy attack but at great cost. Air Force Major Chester L. Brown, a forward air controller over the city, said "It is always a pity about the civilians. In the mass confusion of this kind of thing, the people don't know where the lines are, they don't know where to hide. And some of the weapons we use are area weapons, spraying a general area instead of a specific target."[3]

On the second day of the battle elements of the 3/39th Infantry conducted an air assault on the center of the town and began to clear the enemy forces. By then many had been killed or had begun to retreat outside the city, where they were hunted by helicopter gunships. Ben Tre was declared secure after a 50-hour battle, but an estimated 45% of the city lay in ruins. After the city was secured, the 3/39th held an after-action press briefing in the living room of a house they were using as one of their headquarters. Major Booris, S-3 of the 3/39th, gave the briefing. Journalists badgered Major Booris on the question of the indiscriminate use of heavy firepower; they apparently had determined that this was a more newsworthy narrative than the heroic stand of outnumbered American troops. Captain Michael D. Miller of the 46th Engineer Battalion 159th Engineer Group was present at the briefing and described the scene:

> At one point the journalists were pressing Major Booris to explain why it had been necessary to wipe out the town. They were definitely pressing the point that perhaps too much force had been applied by the U.S. forces. Major Booris was trying his best to put a good face on the situation. But at one point he got flustered, and blurted out, "We had to destroy Ben Tre in order to save it."[4]

Perhaps sensing that Major Booris was losing control of the briefing, his commanding officer, Lieutenant Colonel Anthony P. Deluca, quickly but smoothly intervened and took over the rest of the proceedings. But the damage had been done. Major Booris contributed the most memorable quote to Peter Arnett's AP report on the battle and its cost to the people of Ben Tre:

> At what point do you turn your heavy guns and jet fighter-bombers on the streets of your own city? When does the infliction of civilian casualties become irrelevant as long as the enemy is destroyed? The answers to both these questions came in the first few hours of the battle for Ben Tre, a once

placid Mekong Delta city of 35,000. "It became necessary to destroy the town to save it," a U.S. major says.

The expression "destroy the town in order to save it" supplied the headline for Arnett's story, which ran on front pages across the country. It immediately entered the Vietnam War lexicon and was a particular favorite of war critics, who wielded it with abandon as an example of the absurdity and waste of war. It was often misquoted as "destroy the village in order to save it," conjuring images of a needless scorched-earth attack on a small hamlet rather than a last-resort measure to save embattled and outnumbered American and South Vietnamese troops about to be overrun in a major urban fight. But the details and context became irrelevant in the face of the instant notoriety of the quote. "I have to admit that I almost laughed when [Booris] said that," Captain Miller said, "It was a really unfortunate comment. But Major Booris, in his defense, was trying his best to defend his battalion's honor."[5]

THE COMMUNIST VIEW

The day after the Ben Tre briefing the Communists declared the Tet Offensive a major victory. On February 8, 1968, Radio Hanoi claimed that "hundreds of thousands of people have risen up and destroyed enemy positions, wiped out whole fragments of the puppet administration, punished cruel agents of the enemy, and took control of many important sectors, constantly narrowing the enemy's control of the city. . . . The revolutionary forces and the Saigon population of various strata are resolutely maintaining the revolutionary administration, shattering the enemy's counterattacks, and winning even greater victories."[6] This image was pure fantasy. By then most of Saigon was secure and the revolutionary administration nonexistent, but this was an accurate reflection of the North Vietnamese vision of how the Tet Offensive was supposed to have unfolded. Failure on the battlefield had not blunted the Communist propaganda machine. Radio Hanoi broadcast accounts of significant Viet Cong victories that bore no relation to reality, based on scripts probably written well in advance. But their public face admitted no problems. A COSVN statement from February 10 declared that after ten days of attacks it was achieving "tremendous and all-sided victories." A communiqué from a February 12 meeting of the Central Committee of the NLF held to assess the situation claimed that devastating blows had been delivered on the enemy armed forces and that millions of people in the South had risen up "animated by a seething revolutionary spirit." The regime forces were in a "critical, confused and seriously obstructed situation," and the NLF pledged to "progress forward to achieve complete victory."

Initial American press coverage gave high marks to the Viet Cong for the conduct of the Tet attacks. Orr Kelly wrote in the *Washington Star* that "U.S. military commanders were surprised by the intensity and precise coordination of the Viet Cong's offensive."[7] Peter Arnett wrote for AP that "the Communists proved to be masters of the little details necessary for success."[8] But this was not the case. The attacks were generally not well planned, the teams sent to undertake them were briefed at the last minute and were unfamiliar with their targets, and there was precious little success that the Viet Cong could point to.

A Viet Cong first-day assessment of the battle from the evening of January 31 contrasted with Radio Hanoi's optimistic tone.[9] After some boilerplate statements about the "glorious success" and the defeat of the "imperialists' neocolonialist war of aggression," the assessment grew more sober on the specifics. "We failed to seize a number of primary objectives and to completely destroy mobile and defensive units of the enemy," the author notes. "We also failed to hold the occupied areas. In the political field we failed to motivate the people to stage uprisings and break the enemy's oppressive control." In other words, the general uprising had not occurred. In a brilliant example of understatement the report states that Communist forces "did not succeed in completely destroying many [enemy] mobile and defensive units at the very start" and "if in coming days we fail to quickly motivate a large and powerful force of the masses to stand up against the enemy in time" as well as concentrate new attacks, the enemy will recover his strength and "counterattack us more strongly." This will "limit the impact of our victories" the report said, as well as "create new difficulties for us."[10]

The author of the assessment was saying in as plain language as the totalitarian system would allow that the initial attacks had failed to achieve the major objectives of the offensive, and if the uprising did not happen soon, the entire offensive was lost. The report says the VC forces were "fully able to successfully achieve our plan," but because of the initial setbacks "we cannot yet, therefore, achieve total victory in a short period." The assessment recommended increased efforts to strengthen morale; continuous, concentrated attacks on enemy forces and infrastructure; motivating the people to rise up in the countryside and cities; mobilizing new armed cadres and civilian laborers to support the effort; consolidating liberated areas; and improving command and control. But this was a wish list. Instructions such as "when [enemy forces] counterattack us, we must be determined to annihilate them" were not so much specific tactical plans as orders to stand and die in place. Significantly, the "stand and fight" order was limited to the Viet Cong; the report stated that "in order to avoid casualties, we must not use main-force units to attack [the enemy]."[11]

The Communist field commanders were under no illusions about the looming disaster they were facing. They had not abandoned their plan, but by the end of the second full day they knew that critical elements, most significantly the general uprising, were not taking place. But they continued to follow the plan because they were not allowed to change it. By February 6 the first pulse of the offensive was over, and that day Viet Cong units moving openly toward the city of Tay Ninh were ambushed by ARVN troops. The VC units were routed, and U.S. helicopter gunships hunted down the survivors. At the battle site ARVN troops found discarded banners the Viet Cong had planned to carry in a victory parade after taking the city.

The COSVN ordered the provincial groups to assess the situation in their areas in the first full week of the battle. A February 10 assessment captured in Bien Hoa Province put a brave face on the "victories" being achieved during the offensive. But the author soberly noted the absence of large-scale cooperation from the South Vietnamese people. "The people's spirit for uprising is still very weak compared with the requirements and with the new capabilities and advantages," the report reads. The uprising was "not well coordinated with the military offensive." A February 3 political assessment from Hau Nghia Province noted the failure of propaganda efforts to raise the people to support the VC or to convince South Vietnamese troops to defect. "From the outbreak of fire at an 'X' hour until now, our political and troop proselytizing effort, on the whole, has not been brought into full force and we have not been very successful." The document urged greater propaganda efforts to correct the situation. An assessment from the Mekong Delta advised VC fighters that the fight had just begun, and they should not expect to achieve victory quickly; "fierce, seesaw attacks" could be expected, and the battle might continue for three or four months.[12]

Hanoi's erroneous belief that the South was on the verge of a popular uprising and that a simple demonstration of strength would rally the people to its cause was fatal to the plan. Not only did the uprising not take place but the Communist failure also generated a sense in the South that the VC was much weaker than its years of propaganda and terrorism had led people to believe. Political scientist Samuel Popkin, author of a study of rural Vietnam entitled *The Rational Peasant*, concluded that Tet "totally destroyed the idea of the inevitability of an N.L.F. victory in the villages . . . When the villagers saw the stacks of Vietcong bodies in Saigon on their local TV sets, they rushed to get their sons into local defense forces so that they would not be drafted by the Vietcong."[13] A U.S. adviser to the ARVN 5th Division stated that "psychologically Tet had a most therapeutic impact on his unit."[14] The Viet Cong also attempted to convince the South Vietnamese people that the Tet attacks were part of a plan coordinated with the United States to oust the Saigon government. This was a major propaganda effort that apparently sought to exploit anti-American feeling that had been brewing since the previous fall and the Buttercup affair. Some people accepted this notion, based on the reasoning that such a large-scale attack could not have happened without U.S. complicity. The VC made broadcasts to the effect that the U.S. and NLF were seeking to build a coalition government, which forced Ambassador Bunker to issue a statement on February 2 denying this. But a study conducted after Tet showed that many people in Saigon had heard this rumor, and a number believed it.

The problems the Communists faced in executing their attack plan were caused by some of the same flaws that made U.S. intelligence skeptical that the plans they had analyzed were real. North Vietnamese planners had made assumptions that led them to violate basic principles of war. The most important of these was the belief that they could spark a general uprising, which was critical for them to achieve their objective of overthrowing the government and defeating the Americans without having to fight them. They assumed that they could generate the uprising nationwide through tripwire attacks in all the major cities. But in order to do this they severely divided their forces. In almost every attack there were too few troops available for ensuring success. Each attack was compartmentalized, and none of them were able mutually to support others. The dispersed nature of the attacks also created difficulties in command, control, and coordination.

The Americans, on the other hand, possessed a great deal of mobility and were able quickly to shift forces and resources where needed. The Communist plan to draw the United States into the countryside was ineffective, partly because U.S. commanders understood that an assault was coming and deployed their forces accordingly, but also because once the battle was joined even those American forces out of position were able to move quickly toward enemy concentrations in and around the cities, something for which the enemy had no effective response.

Many Viet Cong forces were not well trained or prepared for the attacks. Cadres who went into the cities for the most part had no experience with urban warfare or conventional combat generally. They were seldom given training specific to their missions and were inadequately briefed on their plans of attack. "They were all peasants," noted François Mazour of Agence France-Presse, who was in Saigon during Tet. "Many of these were in the city for the first time. They knew nothing of life in Saigon—the traffic, for instance. They'd never seen such tall buildings, so many cars, such wide streets. They knew only the country, little roads and rice fields, and they knew only one thing: that they'd come to liberate Saigon. . . . They failed almost everywhere. They failed because they were peasants; they didn't know the snares of the big city."[15]

The General Offensive could not succeed without the General Uprising, and it was planned with the expectation that the uprising would take place. Consequently, the attacking forces were used as catalysts, not as main battle forces to seize and hold ground beyond a few days. There were few reinforcement or replacement plans. The Communists were counting on the general uprising, hoping that the South Vietnamese masses would either join their troops in holding key objectives in the cities and spontaneously overthrow the government apparatus or create such chaos that the matter would become academic. The VC assault teams that were told to take their objectives and await reinforcements thus were pinned down waiting for troops that not only never arrived but also were never even allocated. The planners simply assumed they would be mobilized from the rising masses at some point.

The plan forfeited the primary advantage of the guerrilla warrior, which is his mobility. Instead of hit and run, the Tet tactical plan was to hit and hold. In this way the enemy solved for the Americans one of the most difficult problems for a military force fighting a counterinsurgency, namely locating and fixing the insurgents. Once an insurgent force has massed and revealed itself the advantage falls to the side with superior firepower, which in the case was the United States. Finally, the Communist plan was an all-or-nothing proposition. Every aspect of the plan had to work perfectly for it to succeed, and there was no contingency plan for failure. The magnitude of the Communists' defeat in Tet was thus a direct reflection of their conceptual failings, erroneous premises, poor assessment, inadequate planning, and lackluster execution.

The United States quickly declared Tet a Communist defeat, for reasons that mirrored the conclusions the enemy had reached in its internal reviews. Westmoreland reported back to Washington that the offensive was spent after two days. Secretary McNamara and General Wheeler downplayed Tet at the February 2 hearing before the executive session of the Senate Armed Services Committee, and President Johnson declared the offensive "a complete failure" in his news conference the same day. "[T]he stated purposes of the general uprising have failed," Johnson declared. "Communist leaders counted on popular support in the cities for their effort. They found little or none." Johnson tried to minimize the impact of the Communist attacks by comparing their effects to the traffic jams caused by domestic protestors. "I think we know that the march on the Pentagon can tie up things and disrupt things here," he said. "I think we can see what happened in Detroit. I think we can see what happened in Saigon." But he cautioned that there might be more action at Khe Sanh or near the DMZ.

The scope of the Communists' failure is best measured against what they had hoped to achieve. In the second week after Tet began Douglas Pike noted the importance of the enemy's objectives as a determinant of the scale of their defeat:

> Assessment of the degree of failure must be built on an assessment of the enemy's intentions. If intentions in the offensive were limited, then the failure was also a limited one; if more ambitious, then the failure was a major one. And if the enemy intention was a knock-out punch then, quite obviously, the failure was monumental.[16]

What Pike did not consider was that American analysts would invent a new category of intentions that the enemy had not considered, a category in which they did not fail—the psychological domain.

Tet was declared a Communist "psychological victory" early in the battle. To some it seemed obvious. Don North of ABC filmed a closer while covering the attack on the U.S. embassy in which he said, "Since the lunar new year, the Viet Cong and North Vietnamese have proved they are capable of bold and impressive military moves that Americans here never dreamed could be achieved. Whether they can sustain this onslaught for long remains to be seen. But whatever turn the war now takes, the capture of the U.S. embassy here for almost seven hours is a psychological victory that will rally and inspire the Viet Cong." He explained later that "ABC expected the story as well as some perspective even in those early hours of the offensive—a first rough draft of history." But his editorial take on the attack never aired. "Worried about editorializing by a correspondent on a sensitive story," he wrote, "someone at ABC headquarters in New York killed the on-camera closer."[17] Days later, however, the "psychological triumph" theme was well established. Murrey Marder's observation from the February 3 *Washington Post* was typical of this type of press commentary: "Claims of 'military success' in Washington and Saigon put the best possible face on a jarring political and psychological setback."[18]

The notion of Tet as a psychological victory is one of the reasons the battle has inspired America's enemies ever since. Rather than holding the enemy up to its planned objectives, as Pike recommended, the United States lowered the bar, and defined the level of victory down to the point where the enemy actually met it. This propensity to give America's enemies credit simply for trying is not limited to Tet, and it is a fatal practice in wars of perception. It gives the enemy power and recognition unearned and undeserved.

The idea that Tet was intended as a symbolic attack did not originate with the media but with American policymakers. The notion was fed to the press in Johnson Administration talking points from the first day of battle, and it had been percolating even before Tet began. General Westmoreland had invoked the idea of a coming Communist attack geared toward psychological or political advantage in his 1967 end-of-year report. Analysts had concluded that it was self-evidently absurd that the Communists were hoping to win, since this was impossible, so they concluded that the enemy had to be aiming for something else. The Johnson Administration succumbed to mirror-imaging; since the United States used force not to achieve victory but to "send a message," it assumed the enemy was doing the same thing.

The conclusion that Tet was intended primarily if not exclusively as a symbolic attack originated with the CIA. The evening of

January 29, as reports of the January 30 attacks in Vietnam were coming in to the White House, Walt Rostow met with Director of the CIA Richard Helms and requested a report on the attacks. The next morning Rostow received a five-page situation memo stating that the "flurry of enemy activity was intended primarily for the psychological impact it would have on the South Vietnamese on Vietnam's most important holiday."[19] The memo cited no evidence to back the assertion and ignored substantial evidence to the contrary. A Top Secret CIA Intelligence Memorandum dated January 31 further developed the psychological impact thesis, stating that the offensive "appears primarily designed for maximum psychological impact" and to "seriously disrupt the country, if only temporarily." The memo noted the extensive preparations for an offensive and the possibility that the Communists were seeking some battlefield victories. But the CIA also asserted that the Communists hoped to "improve their political and military image" in the event of negotiations and that the "campaign itself was linked, directly or by implication, to the possibility of a political settlement." The report concluded that the offensive intended to "convey the impression" that despite their many problems "the Communists are still powerful and capable of waging war."[20] Of course from Hanoi's perspective they were actually waging war, not simply conveying the impression of it. The mania for interpreting the use of force as a signal for something else reached its epitome in this memo.

The "psychological impact" notion appealed to policymakers who had been trying to achieve their own psychological effects through strategic bombing. Lyndon Johnson adopted the CIA assessment of Communist intentions and made the argument at his February 2 press conference:

> Their second objective, obviously from the—what you can see from not only Vietnam but from other Communist capitals—even from some unknowing people here at home— is a psychological victory. We have to realize that in moments of tenseness and trial—as we will have today and as we had

in the past days—that there will be a great effort to exploit
that and let that substitute for military victory they have not
achieved. I do not believe when the American people know the
facts, when the world knows the facts and when the results
are laid out for them to examine, I do not believe that they will
achieve a psychological victory.

That same day Secretary McNamara said that a psychological
victory was the enemy's "fall-back objective." He added, "We can
deny this too."[21] General Weyand said the enemy's objectives
were "more 'political and psychological' than military, and to
some extent, at least, the enemy achieved his goals." He observed
that while the attacks failed militarily, "the psychological and
political impact of the onslaught would be considerable, obviously." A senior civilian official at the U.S. embassy was quoted
as saying, "Sure, the people are impressed" with the VC assault.[22]
An unnamed federal official told the *Washington Post* it was "a fan-
tastic achievement for the Viet Cong."[23] The intelligence community also leaked its conclusion directly to the press. Such official
and semi-official statements fueled the "psychological victory"
story line, and the press simply echoed what the government had
concluded the enemy was trying to do.

This conclusion was pure supposition, unsupported by captured documents or information gained from interrogations of
captured VC. The North Vietnamese never stated that their goals
were psychological and never intended their attacks to be merely
symbolic. But the quick failure of almost all the Communists' initial assaults drove U.S. analysts and policymakers to believe that
the enemy in fact had never intended to succeed. The Americans
unilaterally redefined enemy victory to a level the enemy could
actually achieve, thereby helping the enemy achieve it. High-
profile but hopeless attacks, such as that on the U.S. embassy in
Saigon, set the wheels in motion, and the Administration began
talking about this alleged psychological objective; press coverage
did the rest. Why a wholly misguided military venture that failed
to reach any of its intended objectives can be thought of as any

kind of victory is a mystery. But the "psychological impact" theme became a self-inflicted wound, and was a much more damaging case of intelligence failure than any connected with Tet.

McNamara believed this analysis for some time. In a February 6, 1968, conversation with President Johnson, he reiterated the view that the Tet attack was not a last-gasp measure but was intended to improve the Communist bargaining position prior to the peace initiative that our decision-makers had by then concluded was imminent. And while the Communists had been defeated on the battlefield, McNamara believed that as a propaganda and public opinion effort the attack was somewhat successful and the enemy would gain strength. In particular, he thought the attacks demonstrated that the enemy was stronger than the U.S. had imagined.[24]

Thus, although the enemy continued to claim phantom victories and hope for a mass uprising that never came, the United States handed it a symbolic victory by failing to recognize the magnitude of its defeat. And by mid-February the Tet Offensive was not yet concluded. The enemy continued to hold out in the only city where it had even a semblance of success, the former imperial capital of Hue.

XI.

THE BATTLE OF HUE

Chinese military theorist Sun Tzu wrote that "the lowest form of war is to attack cities." His dictum was proved in the battle of Hue. Hue stands apart in the Vietnam War, a scene of 26 days of brutal, close-quarters urban combat. It was the largest city fight the United States had engaged in since the recapture of Seoul, South Korea, in late September 1950, and it remains an important case study of military operations on urban terrain. At Marine Corps Mess Night ceremonies, it is one of only two Vietnam battles in the traditional toast honoring the Corps' most important engagements—the other being Khe Sanh.[2]

Hue! Refuge of romantic loves.

—TRAN VAN TUNG

Hue was set among the northern hill country along the banks of the Perfume River, 50 miles up Highway 1 from Da Nang, and about the same distance south of the DMZ. It was the seat of the Nguyen dynasty in the 19th century, and the citadel—the "old city"—was built by the unifier of modern Vietnam, Emperor Gia Long. The old city was three square miles in area, walled and moated in a modified Chinese style similar to the neoclassical "star fort" design. The old imperial palace was near the southern wall. The "new city," south of the Perfume River, was half the size of the old city and for the most part constructed by the French. In 1968 Hue was home to 135,000 residents.

Hue was the center of South Vietnamese intellectual life and had been the educational and cultural heart of the country since the 19th century. The city was steeped in tradition, and its citizens were conscious of their role as leaders of Vietnamese culture. Writer Tran Van Tung waxed on the romance of pre-war Hue:

> See Hue! With its craftsmen, singers, scholars and maidens. Who can forget the memory of those dainty figures—those living flowers? How enchanting the moonlight, to walk leisurely along the River of Perfumes, the soul open to poetry, the heart bursting forth with tenderness. Hue! Refuge of romantic loves.[3]

Hue's Quoc Hoc High School, the first secondary school in Vietnam, nurtured the Vietnamese elite from the time of its founding as a school for princes and dynastic bureaucrats. Its graduates included Ngo Dinh Diem, Ho Chi Minh, Vo Nguyen Giap, North Vietnamese Prime Minister Pham Van Dog, Communist Party Secretary Le Duan, and General Nguyen Ngoc Loan, among others. The city's intellectual climate gave birth to many reform movements, one of the most notable being Buddhist leader Thich Tri Quang's drive to overthrow President Diem. The 1966 "Struggle Movement," noted earlier, was also a product of Hue. From the Communist perspective, given Hue's recent history of rebellion, it seemed to have the best chance of any major city of experiencing the popular uprising necessary for the Tet Offensive to succeed.

Hue was also an important military target since it was a choke point and transportation hub along Highway 1, with a rail line and a port with access downriver to the sea. Capturing Hue would sever the direct ground link between Da Nang and Quang Tri Province and make supplying the northern part of I Corps much more difficult.

The Communist attack plan for Hue was finalized in January. The mixed North Vietnamese and Viet Cong assault force totaled 7,500 troops, and included two infantry regiments, two shock commandos, and two reserve regiments, divided into Groups 5 and 6, attacking the southern and northern parts of the city respectively. At the height of the fighting the enemy would have close to 15,000 troops engaged. The principal objective was to seize and hold the walled citadel, which necessitated first taking the entrance gates on the north and west sides. I Corps intelligence reports at the time focused on enemy movements around Khe Sanh; Hue was judged to be a secondary or tertiary target. Thus the enemy was able to move larger than expected forces into position mostly undetected and was able to gain some element of surprise.

The first warning of impending attack came when elements of a Marine reconnaissance company encountered a large enemy force three miles southwest of Hue at 10 p.m. on January 30 and reported the movement to the ARVN 1st Division headquarters. Brigadier General Ngo Quang Truong, the division commander, had earlier suspected that an attack was brewing and had raised the alert status as well as sent out word recalling his troops on leave. However, General Truong expected the attack to come from south of the city and deployed many of his troops there. North Vietnamese communications indicating imminent attack were picked up by an Army radio intercept field station at Phu Bai, just south of Hue, but protocol dictated the messages be sent to Da Nang for analysis, and by the time they were processed the attack had begun.

Four hours later, in the early hours of January 31, the PAVN force was in position. Sapper units had infiltrated the city two days earlier. A red flare at 0340 signaled the attack. Group 6 moved on the old city from the west and northwest, seized the An

Hoa (north) gate, and blew up the Chanh Tay (west) gate. Group 5 moved on the south side of the city from the south and southeast, meeting light resistance. These initial attacks by regulars were well coordinated and effective, unlike the VC movements in Saigon and elsewhere.

After securing the north and west gates the troops in Group 6 moved on to their main objectives, which included the I Tactical Zone headquarters, the Tay Loc airfield, the Dong Da training center, the VII Tank Corps headquarters, and the 1st ARVN Division headquarters in the northeast corner of the citadel. Most of the 1st Division headquarters personnel were on holiday leave, but those who remained barricaded themselves in the building as soon as they realized they were under attack. The headquarters staff was soon joined by the Hac Bao, or Black Panther Company, which had been guarding the airfield. The NVA balked at the fierce resistance the defenders put up and placed the headquarters under siege. Meanwhile, other Group 6 units crossed the citadel, seized the Bach Ho (southwest) gate, and blew up the rail bridge over the Perfume River. Sporadic fighting broke out across the citadel as NVA forces encountered ARVN units trying to organize some form of coordinated defense, but the surprised South Vietnamese troops could not hold. By 0700 the Communist flag flew on a tall flagpole over the former imperial capital, and the enemy had gained control of the entire northern half of Hue except for the beleaguered but stubborn holdouts in the ARVN 1st Division headquarters.

The initial South Vietnamese response was spirited but ineffective. Units in positions outside Hue had to fight their way toward the city even before engaging the main enemy force. Reinforcements were slow in coming, and the first counterattacks were fruitless. The 7th ARVN Airborne Battalion made three assaults on enemy positions in the first day and were repulsed. In one case, three ARVN M113 armored personnel carriers rolled boldly toward the city and were rocketed into oblivion. The 2nd Battalion 3rd ARVN Regiment moved east along the north bank of the river toward the railway bridge near the citadel and was caught in heavy fighting. One company was isolated from the bat-

The Tet Offensive was a major allied victory during the Vietnam War that is remembered as a strategic defeat. Here U.S. Marines move up a street in Hue, February 5, 1968. *Credit: Photo by Kyoichi Sawada, © Bettmann/CORBIS.*

Lyndon Johnson meets with (l. to r.) General Earl G. "Bus" Wheeler, Chairman of the Joint Chiefs of Staff, MACV commander General William Westmoreland, and Secretary of Defense Robert S. McNamara. *Credit: Photograph VA021173, Larry Berman Collection (Personal Papers), The Vietnam Archive, Texas Tech University.*

Special assistant John P. Roche told the president that to maintain public support for the war the American people needed to know that it was right to be in Vietnam, and that "we are going to win." *Credit: Photo by Yoichi R. Okamoto, Photograph A-2710-18, LBJ Library Collection.*

The failed Viet Cong assault on the U.S. Embassy in Saigon was a minor part of the communist attack plan but probably received as much press attention as the rest of the first Tet attacks combined. *Credits: (top) Photo by SP6 Samuel L. Swain, Photograph VA035387, Jan. 31, 1968, Peter Braestrup Collection, The Vietnam Archive, Texas Tech University; (bottom left) Photo by SP5 Edgar Price, Photograph VA030812, Jan. 31, 1968, Donald Jellema Collection, The Vietnam Archive, Texas Tech University; (bottom right) Photo by SP5 Edgar Price, Photograph VA030824, Jan. 31, 1968, Donald Jellema Collection, The Vietnam Archive, Texas Tech University.*

Eddie Adams' Pulitzer Prize-winning photograph of General Nguyen Ngoc Loan summarily executing VC assassin Bay Lop became the best known, most notorious, and least understood image of the war. *Credit: AP Photo/Eddie Adams, Feb. 1, 1968.*

Viet Cong atrocities, including deliberately killing women and children, received far less attention from the press. Left, a South Vietnamese officer returned from fighting in Saigon to find his family massacred; right, three year old Dieu Do was severely wounded in a Viet Cong flamethrower-backed "vengeance attack" that destroyed the hamlet of Dak Son in December 1967. 252 people were killed. *Credits: (bottom left) AP Photo, Feb. 1, 1968; (bottom right) USIA National Archives file # 3306-MVP-4-11, Dec. 6, 1967.*

The Battle of Hue was an important victory for the US Marines and South Vietnamese forces, but reports characterized the outcome as either a draw or an allied defeat. Top, a U.S. Marine machine gunner fires on communists positions across the Perfume River; bottom, Marines of "D" Company, 1st Battalion Fifth Marines, in the streets of Hue's old city, late in the fight. *Credits: (top) Photograph VA006864, No Date, Douglas Pike Photograph Collection, The Vietnam Archive, Texas Tech University; (bottom) Defense Dept. Photo (Marine Corps) rfs A190565, Photograph VA035338, Feb. 24, 1968, Peter Braestrup Collection, The Vietnam Archive, Texas Tech University.*

"In a tone beyond bitterness, the people there will tell you that the world does not know what happened in Hue or, if it does, does not care." *Credit: Photograph VA006889, No Date, Douglas Pike Photograph Collection, The Vietnam Archive, Texas Tech University.*

Communists systematically massacred as many as 6,000 people during their occupation of Hue. The atrocity was overshadowed by reportage of the killing at My Lai by U.S. Soldiers. Left, women reacting to finds at a mass burial site near Hue; right, a woman mourns her missing husband at a memorial service in Hue, October 1968. *Credits: (bottom left) Slide 10 from a December 8, 1969 Congressional briefing, US Army Military History Institute; (bottom right) National Archives file # 306-MVP-4(8).*

The defense of Khe Sanh produced images such as this burning aircraft that conveyed a sense of American defeat even as the battle was being won. *Credit: United States Marine Corps photo by David D. Duncan from* The Battle for Khe Sahn, *History and Museums Division, HQ USMC, 1969, p. 77.*

Washington Post Saigon bureau chief Peter Braestrup said "There were a lot of incentives journalistically to make [Khe Sanh] a bigger story than it turned out to be." A U.S. Marine recycled a quote from a *Newsweek* article on his flak jacket. *Credit: AP Photo/ Rick Merron, Feb. 21, 1968.*

Walter Cronkite's reports from South Vietnam conveyed a sense of defeat, though most Americans wanted to escalate the war and finish the job. *Credit: Photo by Lt. Cumins, USMC, National Archives file # 127-GVB-306, Feb. 20, 1968.*

"If I've lost Cronkite I've lost Middle America," President Johnson reportedly said. His March 31, 1968 speech in which he announced his decision not to run for reelection (pictured) was the biggest surprise move of the war, and was seen by many as an act of unilateral surrender. Said advisor John P. Roche, "I've never been so heartsick in my life as I was that night." *Credit: Photo by Yoichi R. Okamoto, Photograph C9284-35, LBJ Library Collection.*

talion for three weeks. Overcast skies and rainy weather made it difficult to provide air close air support and to evacuate casualties, a task that fell to ground troops, who were harried by enemy snipers and mortar teams. The situation improved on February 1, when ARVN airborne and cavalry units recaptured the airfield, but fog and rain still masked the movement of enemy supplies and reinforcements in and out of the citadel.

Meanwhile, Group 5 had occupied almost all of the new city on the south side of the river. The MACV headquarters had been taken, but the enemy did not seize the American military compound. This was consistent with Communist orders to avoid engaging the Americans, but it proved to be a major tactical oversight, since the compound became the focal point of the initial American response. By the end of the first day two companies, A of 1st Battalion 1st Marine Regiment and G of 2nd Battalion 5th Marine Regiment, plus four tanks, had fought their way to the MACV compound. They were ordered to link up with the isolated 1st ARVN Division headquarters defenders, a clearly impossible order, revealing that the commanders in Da Nang did not yet appreciate the gravity of the situation. Nevertheless, G Company, with the assistance of two ARVN tanks, seized the bridge over the Perfume River after a two-hour firefight and held it for another three hours before retiring in the face of growing enemy fire.

The American units near Hue were part of Task Force X-Ray, which was a subdivision of the 1st Marine Division (Forward), commanded by Brigadier General Foster C. LaHue, headquartered at Phu Bai. His command included the 1st and 5th Marine Regiments, each with two battalions. Their mission was to provide combat action platoons to nearby villages to gain support of local inhabitants by securing their safety. This was in accordance with I Corps commander General Cushman's view that the VC forces were the operational center of gravity and the population had to be kept separate from the insurgents; this premise was the basis for the successful Combined Action Program (CAP) the Marines implemented in I Corps. Consequently, U.S. troops were widely dispersed before the battle, and only the two companies mentioned above were ready for immediate movement. As

U.S. forces began to concentrate on Hue, enemy troops moved to block U.S. and ARVN reinforcements from the north and south. Throughout the battle, the enemy's blocking forces slowed road movements with rifle and mortar fire.

Meanwhile, a drama was developing a mile from the American compound at the Armed Forces Vietnam Network building. Nine members of a television crew called Detachment Five holed up inside their living quarters in the AFVN building as the attack swirled around them. "It was like watching a movie and we had front-row seats," Marine Lieutenant James V. DiBernardo said. "Our aircraft came in at treetop levels to bomb and strafe buildings directly behind us. We were shot at by American gunships, who mistook us for the enemy. We were tear-gassed. We had no gas masks."[4] DiBernardo had been in Hue since October; he had heard the rumors of an impending attack but hadn't believed them. But now the war had come to them.

The men in the station were mostly overlooked for a few days, facing only random sniper fire. But on February 4 a seven-man NVA force attacked the building, the lead man carrying a satchel charge. DiBernardo shot the leader, and the satchel charge detonated. The Communist trooper disintegrated. A 16-hour battle commenced, lasting through the night. Sergeant Thomas Franklin Young was killed by small arms fire during the battle. By morning the men were low on ammunition and provisions. The enemy then fired B-40 rockets, setting the building ablaze, and the crew darted out the back into a rice paddy.

The Americans tried to make it to the MACV compound a mile away. Master Sergeant John T. Anderson took a round to the chest, but it did not kill him. When he regained consciousness he saw a North Vietnamese soldier pointing a rifle at his head. "I had just 23 days left 'in country,'" he thought, "and now I've got three bullet wounds."[5] E4 John A. Deering, USMC, director of the TV station, received shrapnel wounds in the hands and feet before he was captured. Lieutenant DiBernardo was shot in the arm as he made his break and suffered shrapnel wounds from grenades as the North Vietnamese swarmed across the rice paddy. He was captured there. Master Sergeant Donat J. Gouin, chief engineer for the station, was also captured. Specialist 4 John Bagwell of the 1st Cavalry Division had been attached to AFVN Hue as an announcer to start a radio service for his unit. He found his way to a Catholic church, where a priest hid him. He later snuck back to the American lines. Specialist 5 Steven J. Stroub, also attached to AFVN from the 1st Cavalry, was not as lucky. He was captured, led into the street, and summarily executed. Courtney Niles of NBC International, who was serving as a media adviser for Armed Forces Vietnam Network, was wounded in both legs and fell to the street. A Communist soldier came up and shot him in the head. Niles was a ten-year Army veteran and had fought well during the brief siege, taking out several enemy soldiers. Sergeant First Class Harry Lawrence Ettmueller, who witnessed the killing and was himself captured, said that it was "too bad [Niles's] name is not on The Wall, but he deserves to be recognized." In all, three AFVN members were killed, one escaped, and five became POWs. The prisoners were held until March 1973. In 2007 the detachment was inducted into the Army Public Affairs Hall of Fame with a ceremony in the Pentagon. Sergeant Ettmueller presented his prison sandals to the Chief of Public Affairs and the tattered Detachment Five flag that he had taken from Hue and kept hidden throughout his prison ordeal.

URBAN WARFARE

On the second day of fighting two companies of Marines made it to the American compound, one overland and another by the Perfume River. Fighting was fierce entering the city, although resistance was lighter closer to the MACV compound. But fighting raged in the north. Attacks by ARVN units from outside the city were repulsed, while inside the citadel the 1st Division headquarters defenders continued to hold out despite concerted attacks by the enemy.

On the fourth day Colonel Stanley S. Hughes, commander of the 1st Marine Regiment, arrived at the compound to take command of all U.S. Marine forces in Hue. Hughes was a former enlisted Marine who had risen through the ranks, and he was awarded the Navy Cross and Silver Star during the Second World War. Hughes gave order and direction to what had been an ad hoc battle. He meant to secure the city and told Lieutenant Colonel Ernest C. Cheatham, a former professional football player who commanded 2nd Battalion 5th Marine Regiment, "You do it any way you want to. Use whatever you have to use."

The next day Marines began clearing the south side, moving west from the compound parallel to the Perfume River. The available ARVN troops in the new city moved behind the Marines, engaging pockets of resistance and snipers and tending to the crowds of displaced civilians. Unfamiliarity with the city streets forced the Marines to use maps from a local gas station and the police headquarters. Meanwhile, the 2nd Battalion 12th Air Cavalry, which had been deployed north just prior to Tet, assumed blocking positions 18 miles northeast and northwest of the city along with ARVN units. On day seven, the day the original Tet ceasefire was supposed to have ended, the Marines in Hue moved west, clearing the city block by block with massive firepower. That same day NVA sappers blew the remaining span of the Nguyen Hoang Bridge, the last link between the north and south city.

The enemy would disappear as Marines seized parts of the city, then reappear in the cleared areas at night. Most Marines had not been trained for or experienced urban combat. Casualties were highest in the first few days as they learned and adapted. The enemy was well emplaced, and it was hard to bring superiority of numbers to bear because of the limited frontages. Cheatham, known affectionately as "Big Ernie," described the combat on the south side. "It's an intimate type of fighting," he said. "We have three companies, more than three hundred men fighting house to house, but maybe only thirty-five or forty are engaged at any time. You can't get any more Marines that close to them at one time."[6]

Infantry teams blew holes in walls and buildings with M48A3 tanks and 106mm recoilless rifles. Mortar teams supplied quick responding indirect fire, and M42 40mm self-propelled antiaircraft weapons, with no NVA aircraft to engage, supported the infantry with devastating effect. U.S. forces attempted to minimize civilian casualties, a task made imperative by the watchful press. In many cases, the enemy used civilians as human shields, and the Marines countered with E-8 tear gas launchers that effectively flushed enemy troops into the open from buildings and underground tunnels. But there were limited numbers of these launchers, and civilians often bore the brunt of the fighting.

Marines took the imposing Thua Tien Provincial Headquarters on February 6 after a hard fight. Marine Captain Ron Christmas described the breakthrough after several attacks had been beaten back:

> The men smashed into the building, cupping tear gas grenades in their hands. One Marine was shot and killed on the stairway, and two others were wounded, but the assault continued. They cleaned out the building, room by room, until it was theirs.[7]

Christmas notified Lieutenant Colonel Cheatham of their success. "We have the building, sir," he said. "We are going to run up the American flag." A large NLF banner had flown from the building for the past week. U.S. troops were not authorized to fly the stars and stripes from South Vietnamese buildings, but Cheatham said, "Go ahead and run it up before anyone tells us not to. We are doing the fighting. We may as well have our guys get the credit." He also wanted to let the Communists in the old city know that one of their bastions had fallen. Christmas, along with Gunnery Sergeant Frank A. Thomas, PFC Walter A. Kaczmarek, and PFC Alan V. McDonald, pulled down the NLF banner and raised an American flag. "When the Stars and Stripes reached the top of the pole, the gunny looked up and then burst into tears," Christmas recalled. "From their positions in the building and the courtyard the men in the company began to cheer. I was truly moved by the experience; there were tears in my eyes." Meanwhile Cheatham radioed regimental headquarters that his men had taken the provincial headquarters and that "somehow or other an American flag is flying over there."[8]

Further progress was slow but steady, and on February 10 Colonel Hughes declared the south side of the city secure, although sniping continued for several more days. On February 11 the U.S. took the battle north. A company from 1st Battalion 5th Marines with five tanks moved upriver and with some heliborne troops relieved the besieged troops at the ARVN 1st Division headquarters. The next day a Marine company crossed the river at Bao Vinh and entered the citadel through the Cua Hau gate.

South Vietnamese troops had been bitterly contesting the enemy occupation of the walled city since the first day. They had recaptured the An Hoa gate on February 4 and moved toward the imperial palace. A series of assaults on other parts of the imposing fortress were repulsed, usually with heavy losses. The enemy was dug in solidly behind the thick citadel walls, and maintained some positions outside. At this point the NVA held half the northeast wall, the southeast wall, and the imperial palace. Marines relieved the ARVN forces along the part of the northeast wall they had secured, and the South Vietnamese concentrated on retaking the area around the palace. The Marines encountered a well dug in enemy, with defensive positions with interlocking fields of fire and countless snipers.

The street fighting in the old city was as punishing as it had been in the new. "The battle went on unceasingly from house to house," an eyewitness wrote. "In each garden, from street to street, everywhere—manholes, walls, or anything that was somewhat a good place to hide—contained soldiers."[9]

"We had to blow our way though every wall of every house," Lieutenant Colonel Cheatham said. "It's a shame we have to damage such a beautiful city. In this kind of fighting, we're like a football team. . . . Four men cover the exits of a building, two men rush the building with grenades, while two men cover them with rifle fire. We hope to kill them inside or flush them out for the four men watching the exits. Then taking the next building, two other men assume the hairy job of rushing the front. It sounds simple, but the timing has to be just as good as a football play."[10]

Both ARVN and U.S. units were trying to minimize damage to the historic city as they fought through it. In the first two weeks of the battle the American rules of engagement were more restrictive than those of the South Vietnamese, and the U.S. had banned the use of artillery, naval gunfire, aerial bombs, and napalm. Marines were also forbidden from engaging enemy forces in religious or historic structures without special permission. In one case, Marines encountered a squad of enemy troops holed up in a pagoda and sent word to headquarters they would like to attack them. The response from II MAF in Da Nang took two hours to reach the Marines, by which point the NVA had withdrawn.[11]

Given the tougher resistance in the northern part of the city, and with the pressure of time, Colonel Hughes was able to convince higher command to ease the restrictive rules. Marines were then able to call on tactical air support, 155mm howitzers, and six-inch naval guns. Hard points were taken out by M48A3 tanks and ONTOS vehicles that mounted six 106mm recoilless rifles. When the weather cleared after two weeks, the Americans wanted to call in artillery and air support. President Thieu resisted, since he felt such force would be too damaging to the city. But eventually he relented, and U.S. air assets were deployed. Three days of bombardment followed, coupled with concerted clearing operations on the ground.

Another shift in the rules of engagement occurred on February 16, when, with the prospect of more NVA reinforcements moving in from the west, U.S. forces were given the right, under an agreement by Deputy Theater Commander General Creighton Abrams and Vice President Ky, to immediately engage enemy forces fighting from pagodas, churches, and other structures previously off-limits.

The NVA troops were hard to dislodge. Bombing missions reduced whole sections of the city to rubble. Napalm attacks burned out whole neighborhoods. William Tuohy described the north bank. "The scene looked like something from the western front in World War I—tangled barbed wire, shell holes, crumpled masonry, shattered trees, a riddled flare parachute, tin roofing, and hundreds of shell casings and C ration cans. 'The neighborhood is deteriorating,' cracked one Marine, 'I'd like to move out.'"[12]

But the battle was well defined along a sharp edge. "This is a funny kind of war," Lieutenant Colonel Cheatham told William Tuohy as he puffed on a cigar. "A block in front of us Marines are getting shot. Six blocks behind us they are buying cigars and cigarettes at the PX in the Army compound."[13] Fighting generally began early in the morning and ended at night.

Marines secured the citadel's northeast wall by February 21, but ARVN forces had not made similar progress. The battered Marines redeployed to assist the ARVN against the last NVA holdouts. But the decisive stroke came not inside the city but a few miles to the west. The NVA had a major supply depot in the La Chu Woods that had been relatively untouched throughout the battle. As the Marines were clearing the northeast wall, four battalions of the 1st Cavalry Division made a devastating strike on the NVA supply hub and cut their lines of communication. This action convinced the commanders of the 6th NVA Regiment that continued resistance was futile, and the Communists ordered their men to withdraw. Top officers departed first, followed by all but 400 troops left behind to continue the fight, by then vastly outnumbered. The withdrawing forces were hunted by American air cavalry, although many escaped.

On the morning of February 24, the Communist flag that had flown over the citadel for 24 days was torn down and the South Vietnamese flag raised. But the fight was not yet over. There was a bloody contest at the Nha Do gate and the west side of the citadel, an area called Nam Dai, where the enemy had strong earthwork defenses. The 2nd Battalion 3rd ARVN Regiment and the Hac Bao Company were given the task of recapturing the imperial palace. That afternoon the Black Panthers slipped into the building one by one before mounting a surprise assault. The attack began at 1515 and was over by 1700. The 80 enemy defenders had fought in their positions until killed. At the Nha Do gate the fighting was reduced to hand to hand, and 73 enemy troops died. The next day President Thieu, who at one time had commanded the ARVN 1st Division, flew to Hue to congratulate General Truong on his victory.

Although the North Vietnamese made their best showing in Hue, the battle also underscored the central flaws in their strategy. Hue was the city thought most likely to see the predicted and necessary general uprising. It did not. Once the uprising failed to materialize, the Communists should have retreated. Instead, they chose to hold the terrain they'd seized and conduct an urban defense. Once committed to this course of action, the Communists sacrificed their primary strength, mobility, to engage the primary allied strength, firepower. They were pinned down, outnumbered and outgunned. The city was effectively surrounded, if not sealed, and the Communists could not expect to receive the stream of reinforcements and supplies they would need to make their defense tenable.

Given their situation, the Communists sought to inflict as much damage as they could, but it came at the cost of massive casualties among their own forces. Americans lost 216 killed and 1,364 wounded, with South Vietnamese dead numbering 384 and wounded 1,830. Enemy casualties in and around the city were estimated at 5,000, of which 1,959 were killed. The enemy's only achievement was keeping the fighting in the news.

Urban war fighting is a high-casualty affair for both attackers and defenders, but insurgents are less able to afford them. There was no question in Hue that the Communists would prevail, absent some external intervention, and the city became a trap for the defenders. It is always a mistake for insurgents to take a stand in a city against a motivated conventional force with superior numbers. Operation Phantom Fury, the November 2004 battle to retake the Iraqi city of Fallujah, was a similar situation, and resulted in the deaths of over 1,300 insurgents. The lesser-noted seizure of Grozny in 1996 by Chechen fighters was an example of a battle that worked the way Tet was supposed to. The Chechens were able to negotiate a political settlement with a weakened Russian government lacking the political will to retake the city, as it had the previous year. But this victory was short-lived; when power passed to Vladimir Putin he showed more backbone than Boris Yeltsin. Russian troops returned to Grozny in 2000 and flattened the city.[14]

As with Grozny, the imperial city itself was the greatest casualty. By the end of the battle it was desolate. The historic structures were damaged or destroyed, their contents either destroyed in the fighting or looted. Of the 135,000 residents of Hue, 110,000 were homeless. What remained of the ancient capital was "ruins divided by a river."[15] Nguyen Van Chu, a 24-year-old medical student in Hue Civilian Hospital, said, "Hue has nothing now, nothing. It is not only the loss of our buildings and monuments, it is the loss of our spirit. It is gone."[16]

But the ultimate cost of the battle of Hue was yet to be discovered.

XII.

HUE
AND MY LAI

In late March 1969, a farmer tripped over a length of wire while walking among the grass-tufted sand dunes in the Phu Tu district near the South China Sea coast, about eight miles southeast of Hue. He yanked the end of the wire, and after a few tugs a bony hand and the remains of an arm emerged from the sand. The farmer had found the first of 809 bodies eventually unearthed from three separate sites in Phu Tu. Forensics showed that the victims had been bound in groups of ten to twenty, lined up next to pits and cut down with Russian-made submachine guns. There were three to four layers of bodies per pit. Almost all of the victims were noncombatants.

> What actually happened at Hue is truly beyond human description, but needs to be told.
>
> —ALJE VENNEMA

The discovery at Phu Tu was one of many that took place in the vicinity of Hue in the months and years following the Tet Offensive. Peasants seeking wood near Da Mai Creek returned with armfuls of bleached white bones. Abnormally bright green patches of grass scattered in fields around Hue pinpointed mass graves. Rainfall washed away sand, leaving protruding arms, legs, and skulls. One grave was found five miles east of Hue when an American soldier spotted a hand seemingly reaching to him from out of the ground. Eventually, around 2,800 bodies were uncovered. They told a tragic story of the functional brutality of the Communist system. Government officials, businessmen, Catholics, intellectuals, and others deemed socially undesirable or simply in the wrong place at the wrong time were shot down in trenches dug in the city parks, clubbed to death in makeshift prisons, or led away in the countryside to be murdered and thrown into pits. "Americans tend to remember the Vietnam War through images depicting the massacre of innocent civilians by American troops," said Dr. Toan Truong, who was a child in South Vietnam and came to the U.S. with the first wave of refugees. "What is chiseled in my own mind is footage of Vietnamese wailing over bodies of loved ones who were buried alive, in huge mass graves by the Viet Cong, during the Tet Offensive, in 1968."[1] Despite its scale and brutality, the Hue Massacre was virtually unnoticed in the United States at the time and is now largely forgotten.

THE HUE MASSACRE

The Hue Massacre was a natural expression of Communist revolutionary doctrine, the type of incident common in totalitarian systems. The NLF, acting under specific orders from Hanoi, sought to jump-start the revolution by physically eliminating the "ruling class" at one stroke. "The former imperial capital was regarded as a nest of feudalism, a den of enemy thugs," Bui Tin said. "Special units had to be set up to detain all these prisoners as well as the many Saigon troops who were captured."[2] A document captured in Quang Ngai Province described the systematic nature of the VC program. "The destruction of Nationalist Party reactionaries

196

is not a one-shot affair," it said. "It is a continuous process. We must destroy them by every means available."[3] An enemy planning document dated January 26, 1968, noted under the first general mission to "destroy and disorganize the enemy's restrictive administrative machinery from the province and district level to city wards, streets and wharves" and to "pursue until the end" spies and reactionaries.[4]

An important witness to the events at Hue was Alje Vennema, a Dutch citizen who was the director of Canadian Medical Assistance to Vietnam during Tet and who had been doing humanitarian work in the country since 1962. He was an outspoken activist who had pro-NLF leanings, saw the Saigon government as corrupt, and believed that the United States should leave Vietnam because the war was undermining U.S. values. Vennema was present in Hue during the battle and its aftermath. When word of the mass killings began to emerge, he was approached by the *New York Review of Books* to write an article "disclaiming the allegations of the South Vietnamese government that an efficient slaughter had taken place."[5] Presumably the *Review* felt that given Vennema's political leanings he was ideologically reliable. But once Vennema began writing, he realized that he could not complete the essay following the *Review's* story line. He could not deny what he had seen; truth overcame political correctness. "The events of Hue rested on my conscience," he wrote, "and would not let go. . . . What actually happened at Hue is truly beyond human description, but needs to be told."[6]

The NLF was given the task of organizing the liberated zones in Hue while the North Vietnamese Army conducted the defense of the city. An operations plan states that by day three the Front should "begin to establish the revolutionary machinery in the city."[7] The NLF immediately set up committees, held mass indoctrination sessions, and visited each house to register all the inhabitants and compile special lists. They collected radios and weapons, and imposed food rationing. The NLF cadre told the people of Hue that the entire country was under Communist control, so there was no point in trying to resist. Citizens were required to attend Party meetings, dig trenches, bury the dead, haul ammunition and supplies, or whatever the NLF needed done. The Communists asked all civil servants and members of the military to register. Those who did were issued special cards and allowed to go home. A few days later they all disappeared; word was that they were being "re-educated."

Tribunals were immediately established to process people on NLF lists. Many NLF cadres were locals who had been underground or who had returned with the NVA forces, and they had grudges to settle. "Often before the lists were prepared, the locals already knew whom they wanted," Vennema wrote. "Systematically, civil servants, military men, students, those having nationalistic feelings, opposition politicians, anyone who showed natural leadership qualities and presented a threat was being marked. The lists were endless."[8] At the tribunals, "menacing words often mixed with propaganda slogans, accusations, threats and warnings were commonplace. Most of those who were dragged before the tribunals were convicted for unknown reasons. All were sentenced, some to die immediately."[9]

The tribunal period lasted about two days until the initial lists were exhausted. Guidance from Hanoi stated that should the city not be secured by then the remaining prisoners should be forced "to write a statement of surrender, to denounce the U.S. imperialists' crimes, and to reveal their friends before we kill them on the spot." The order cautioned, however, that "we must not take this opportunity to kill them indiscriminately," although this caveat appears to have applied only to "the province chief, his assistant, or American officers."[10] For those outside this elite circle formalities were frequently dispensed with, and people were summarily executed for a variety of trivial crimes against the new regime. "A man who had not turned in his radio got shot in the open to serve as a precedent," Vennema noted, "another, a student, was openly executed for failing to attend a training session."[11] Others were rounded up because they had been termed "social negatives," members of social classes or occupational groups deemed detrimental to the new social order.

In the first weeks of the battle the NLF may have believed that Communist forces could hold the city. Communiqués and newspapers from the North reinforced this notion with claims of nationwide victories. But when it became clear that Hue would fall, the NLF commenced the third phase of killings, eliminating the witnesses to the crimes of the occupation. Underground NLF cadres would not be able to blend back into their covert lives while those who knew them lived. Bui Tin, who claimed that some deaths outside the city were the result of collateral damage from American bombers attacking the enemy columns, nevertheless acknowledged that "many other detainees who could not be evacuated in the confusion of the withdrawal were massacred in an attempt to cover up the reality of what had happened in Hue during our temporary occupation of the city."[12]

"In the last few days the Vietcong lost their heads and did nothing but make reprisals, kill, punish," Oriana Fallaci wrote. "They compiled new lists of those accused of even the most trivial slights. Two accusations meant death. Sometimes individuals were killed, sometimes whole families vanished. A house would be marked with red paint, and that night everyone inside would be wiped out."[13] The killers were thorough; in one case a Communist death squad invaded a community leader's home and killed everyone within, including his wife and children, servants and their baby, then strangled the family cat, bludgeoned their dog, and tossed their goldfish onto the floor.[14] In the Tang Quang To pagoda, 67 people were killed over the course of two weeks, shot by pistol or rifle and buried in the plowed fields behind the structure. A monk in the pagoda heard the nightly ritual of the arrival of the executioners, the pleas of the victims for mercy, and the gunshots that ended the matter. When the NLF finally departed the city they took hundreds of prisoners off into the jungle, who were never seen alive again. This was consistent with operational guidance for "cruel tyrants, reactionary elements and the allies" that "when it is convenient, we should move them out of the city to exploit and punish them."[15]

The first signs of the scope of the massacre were evident as the battle subsided. Many corpses were simply left out in the open. Fallaci, who was in Hue in the immediate aftermath of the battle, while the carnage was still fresh, saw bodies strewn all over the city, some the victims of combat, others the product of Communist executions, piled in ditches, in warehouses, heaped at the foot of walls where they were shot down. "We seem to be looking at Mathausen, Dachau, the Ardeatine ditches," she wrote.[16] South Vietnamese government officials immediately began to assess the scope of the carnage. By March 1, 1968, 250 people were known to have been killed by the NLF, but thousands more were listed as missing. Two months later the figure was revised upward to 900 executed, with 5,000 still unaccounted for.

By then the mass graves were being uncovered, a process that became a rolling horror over many months. The first site was found at the Gia Hoi Secondary School, which had served as a seat for one of the NLF tribunals. It was excavated by South Vietnamese Marines starting on February 26, 1968. Fourteen trenches were found in front of the school holding 101 bodies. Later finds raised the total to 203.

With every victim came a story. Here was 26-year-old Hoang Thi Tam Tuy, a pretty market vendor who was taken from her home on February 22 for no clear reason. She was found with her hands and legs tied, a rag stuffed in her mouth, and no obvious signs of wounds. She had been buried alive. There was 48-year-old Mrs. Nguyen Thi Lao, a street vendor, who met the same fate. Mr. Tran Dinh Trong was a newlywed student at the technical school, taken from his bride for unknown reasons and killed. Police officer Le Van Phu, 47, was dragged from his home on February 8 as his wife and children begged the VC to let him stay. He was shot in the head that evening. These were just a few of the victims of the Gia Hoi Tribunal. And there were thousands in other sites yet to be found.

When the first mass graves were discovered, "there was a tremendous outcry both in the South and internationally," Bui Tin said. "Even the leadership in Hanoi had to pay attention." General Tran Van Quang, who commanded the Hue attack, and some of his senior officers were criticized, but were not severely disciplined.[17] Initially NLF sympathizers promulgated the line that a few Front members had gotten out of hand at Hue and killed more people than the limited number the Communists had intended to execute. NLF Minister of Justice Truong Nhu Trang wrote that "discipline in Hue was seriously inadequate" and "fanatic young soldiers had indiscriminately shot people." He called it "one of those terrible spontaneous tragedies that inevitably accompany war."[18] This was in the tradition of Stalin's 1930 essay "Dizzy with Success," in which the collectivization effort had become so damaging and caused so many deaths that it had to be temporarily halted.[19] Yet the after-action report from one regiment noted laconically, "With the help of our local [agents] we killed 1,000 local administrative personnel, spies and cruel tyrants," the tone suggesting that it was all part of the plan.[20]

The Communists soon recovered their composure and stood by the killings. On April 26, 1968, Radio Liberation declared that the victims were "hooligan lackeys who had incurred blood debts to the Hue compatriots and who were annihilated by the southern armed forces and people in early spring."[21] When the South Vietnamese government sentenced a single Viet Cong collaborator, Mai Ngu, to death by firing squad for his role in the Hue killings, the U.S. State Department sought to intervene on the possibility that a reprisal execution would be taken against an American POW.[22]

Meanwhile the grim discoveries went on. Bodies turned up for months near the imperial tombs south of the city. Most were bound together in groups of ten to fifteen and buried alive. There lay French priest Father Urbain, 52, from the Benedictine Monastery of Thien An, six kilometers south of Hue. His monastery had become a haven for refugees until the VC arrived. Operational guidance singled out Catholics for special treatment, noting that "Priests and vicars who protect and conceal the enemy should be arrested immediately." Buddhist monks, on the other hand, were seen as potential allies and generally were not to be harmed.[23] Father Urbain was found at the Dong Khanh tomb, hog-tied with ten others before being buried. In his last moments he had called the actions of the VC an "abomination against God." Another priest, Father Guy, 48, was forced to kneel and was shot in the head. A third priest who survived the ordeal was driven mad by what he witnessed.

As the search widened, more massacre sites were found. "As people, mainly relatives of the missing, continued to look they discovered many trenches scattered everywhere in the environs," Vennema noted. "Led by people who lived in the neighborhood and others who had witnessed the burials, more and more discoveries were made and a picture of horror was disclosed. Later on, protruding arms or the stench of decaying flesh would give the place away. The spectacle was one of extreme tragedy, wailing and howling, digging and identifying."[24] The excavations were done systematically and with great care, using archaeological techniques to preserve all possible evidence. Each body required six man-hours of effort. The corpses were registered and their identifying features noted. They were then sent to a clearing station, where relatives might be able to identify the remains.[25]

In the first seven months of 1969 there was a cluster of new discoveries, including the sand dunes of the Phu Thu district, which yielded new trenches full of bodies into the winter. In September 1969 came the discovery at remote Da Mai Creek. The creek bed was filled with loose bones, even whole skeletons. Five hundred skulls were counted, caved in at the front, showing signs of being clubbed. The NLF and American apologists promulgated a line that these were the remains of VC killed in a B-52 strike, but there were no such operations in that area; the pattern of trauma to the skulls suggested systematic killing; and eyewitnesses emerged who confirmed the massacre.[26] As late as May 1972 a grave containing 200 bodies was discovered in front of a Phu Thu district elementary school by a third-grader pursuing a cricket ball.

In all, over 2,800 bodies were excavated from the pits. An additional nearly 2,000 people remained unaccounted for.

The scope of the killings at Hue was inconceivable. Bodies were found in the city and outside it.

They were buried in schoolyards, pagodas, seminaries, parks, under bridges, in fields, in swamps, beside streams.

Some had been given perfunctory trials, some not.

Some had been forced to dig pits for those executed before them, and then were thrown in themselves.

They were tied with rope, with twine, with barbed wire.

They were shot, bludgeoned to death, or buried alive.

They were civil servants, soldiers, police, politicians, monks, priests, doctors, students, homemakers, merchants, teachers, and laborers.

They were Vietnamese, American, Filipino, French, and German.

They were men and women, young and old, husbands and wives, grandparents, parents, and children.

PRESS COVERAGE

The cover of the December 5, 1969, issue of *Life* magazine announced: "VIETNAM MASSACRE: Exclusive color pictures and interviews with soldiers who were there." The story was not about the slaughter at Hue, but revelations about killings at the South Vietnamese village of My Lai 4, also known as Pinkville. On March 16, 1968, U.S. troops brutally shot and stabbed to death 347 South Vietnamese civilians in this small hamlet, until stopped by other American soldiers who came upon the scene and threatened to open fire if the men did not cease.[27]

The My Lai incident was brought to the attention of high-level officials in March 1969, when a soldier named Ronald Ridenhour, who had not been present at My Lai but who had spoken to many soldiers who had been, sent a letter to the President, the Joint Chiefs, the Secretaries of State and Defense, and 30 members of Congress detailing what he had learned and asking for an investigation. "I have considered sending this to newspapers, magazines and broadcasting companies, but I somehow feel that investigation and action by the Congress of the United States is the appropriate procedure," Ridenhour wrote, "and as a conscientious citizen I have no desire to further besmirch the image of the American serviceman in the eyes of the world. I feel that this action, while probably it would promote attention, would not bring about the constructive actions that the direct actions of the Congress of the United States would." The Army began to investigate the incident in April. In September Second Lieutenant William

Calley was charged with several counts of premeditated murder, and later charges were brought against 25 other soldiers.

The My Lai story broke in the *Detroit News* on November 12, 1969, followed the next day by Seymour Hersh's reporting in the *St. Louis Post Dispatch*. Hersh had been tipped off in October, and although he has been given the lion's share of credit, there were several news organizations working the My Lai beat. The timing of the stories coincided with the massive antiwar "Moratorium" demonstration in Washington, D.C., on Saturday, November 15, 1969, the largest such demonstration ever in Washington, with over 250,000 participants. My Lai was an instant media and cultural sensation. As Ridenhour had predicted, the incident became a continuous and inescapable moral indictment of the United States, its military, and its effort in South Vietnam. It was red meat for the antiwar activists, who were never short on sanctimony; but the same people who drew My Lai like a gun had never heard of Hue and would not care if they had.

Some people tried to lend context as the My Lai story began to take off. In late November 1969 MACV released a captured enemy document revealing that 2,900 Vietnamese had been killed by the Communists during their occupation of Hue.[28] On December 3, 1969, Richard H. Ichord (D-MO), the Chairman of the House Committee on Internal Security, addressed the House on the issue of the one-sided publicity given to massacres in Vietnam. "It is regrettable, to say the least" he said, "that the world media, including that of the United States, has not given Communist atrocities in Vietnam the same intense degree of news coverage now being given the events that transpired at [My Lai]."[29] On December 8 Ichord held an information briefing on Communist atrocities in Vietnam and the Hue Massacre in particular. The briefing was prepared by the Army Operations Center at Representative Ichord's request.[30] Around 75 people attended, and although Ichord had invited every member of Congress to attend, only three showed up. The session covered the facts as they were then known, the enormity and barbarity of the Hue Massacre, and other atrocities committed by the VC through the course of the war. Mr. Ichord noted afterward the disproportionate attention being paid to My Lai and stated that "the world press is severely challenged to place this whole matter in proper perspective. To fail to do so might well result in the perpetuation of the biggest lie in history."

One impediment to placing the Hue Massacre in perspective was the lack of sufficiently compelling pictures. The issue of *Life* on the newsstands at the time of the Ichord briefing featured a ten-page photospread of My Lai with pictures by Army photographer Ronald Haeberle, extremely graphic color photos of dead men, women, children, and babies, in grotesque poses and covered in blood. Mr. Ichord pointedly asked why the Army officers at his briefing had shown only two black-and-white photos from Hue. Lieutenant Colonel Arno L. Ponder replied, "I don't know of any more." The *Washington Post* found the absence of photos at the briefing more compelling than the fact of the massacre.[31]

Most pictures of the Hue killings lack the drama of the Army pictures of My Lai, but this was not for lack of effort. John Roche recalled that once bodies began to be unearthed, the White House tried to have the events documented and get the images out.

> We get USIA camera people up to Hue and get the pictures.
> I'm screaming my head off about this to the press—AP, UPI,
> the *Times,* et al.—to go up and take pictures. None of them
> did. I think maybe AFP did, I think maybe in France there was
> some coverage. So we ended with only pictures taken by the
> USIA which by law could not be distributed within the United
> States. The press showed absolutely no interest in this at all.[32]

The visceral impact of images cannot be overestimated. With My Lai, as well as the photograph of General Loan executing Bay Lop and other photos, the war was contextualized visually in a way that swept away nuance. Hue might have been remembered more vividly had the memory been set with a defining image. And the need for compelling visuals is not lost on contemporary terrorists, insurgents, and state adversaries.

Most of the photos taken at Hue were of people mourning. Funerals were incessant. The identified victims were placed in ancestral plots, and the unknown victims were honored with a new tomb, Nui Ba Vanh, to join those of Hue's emperors. The massacre may have been forgotten in the United States, but inside South Vietnam it had a lasting impact. Author James Jones, who visited South Vietnam in 1973, wrote that "whatever else they accomplished, the Hue massacres effectively turned the bulk of the South Vietnamese against the Northern Communists. In South Vietnam, wherever one went . . . the 1968 Tet massacres were still being talked about in 1973."[33] But what transpired at Hue, a massacre greater than any perpetrated in the Vietnam War and among the greatest such massacres in military history, faded from international view almost immediately. In February 1970 Douglas Pike wrote, "In a tone beyond bitterness, the people there will tell you that the world does not know what happened in Hue or, if it does, does not care."[34]

There were some attempts to keep the memory of Hue alive. On September 11, 1973, Aleksandr Solzhenitsyn published a 3,000-word letter in the Norwegian newspaper *Aftenposten*, soon reprinted in the *New York Times*, castigating Western liberals for their persistent moral relativism, highly selective outrage, and hypocritical tendency to ignore blatant Communist iniquity. One of his examples was the lack of outcry over the Hue Massacre.

> The bestial mass killings in Hue, though reliably proved, were only lightly noticed and almost immediately forgiven because the sympathy of society was on the other side, and the inertia could not be disturbed. It was just too bad that the information did seep into the free press and for a time (very briefly) cause embarrassment (just a tiny bit) to the passionate defenders of that other social system.[35]

Solzhenitsyn, who had been awarded the Nobel Prize for Literature in 1970 "for the ethical force with which he has pursued the indispensable traditions of Russian literature," was an established moral voice whose charges could not easily be ignored. Eric Sevareid of CBS News felt compelled to rebut Solzhenitsyn's assertions on the air on September 12, 1973:

[Solzhenitsyn] is saying that in general Western liberals tend to excuse the profound inhumanity of communist regimes. Some do. But . . . the Hue massacres were heavily reported. Many other brutalities by the North were missed or reported sketchily at second hand, simply because we could have no reporters or cameras with the enemy forces.

What constitutes being "heavily reported" is open to question, but Sevareid's statement is difficult to defend, particularly when compared to the tidal wave of coverage given My Lai, which of course was Solzhenitsyn's point. The problem was that there was no play to the Hue story. As James Jones noted in the *New York Times Magazine* after visiting the city in 1973, "Anti-U.S. feeling was high at home. Why buck it in the cause of unpopular truths? Much better to concentrate on our own rottenness at My Lai." Jones noted that the liberal view chose not to admit that the Communists had really committed any significant crimes. "By applying our Western-film mentality, if we were the bad guys, then the other side must be the good guys," he said. The Hue killings "had not really happened, not as far as liberal America was concerned."[36] These same critics also ignored the thousands of documented targeted political killings that had taken place on a daily basis in Vietnam over decades.

The moral decrepitude of the antiwar faction was exemplified by its attempts to minimize Hue and in effect serve as apologists for the North Vietnamese. When Richard Nixon referred to the massacre in a November 1969 speech as an example of why the United States should not undertake a precipitous withdrawal from Vietnam lest a bloodbath follow, the antiwar left howled. In a typical response, D. Gareth Porter and Len E. Ackland argued that most of the Hue killings took place in the latter stages of the occupation, when the NLF and NVA were under pressure and being forced to retreat, and were largely the actions of angry soldiers pursuing vendettas or under the strain of circumstances.[37] That the enemy troops could have chosen not to bury innocent people alive was an option whose moral implications the authors elected not to discuss. As late as the spring of 1975, with the U.S.

having abandoned its South Vietnamese allies to their fate, Senator George McGovern found it necessary to insert his view into the *Congressional Record* that the accounts of Hue were largely mythical, a claim he backed citing Porter, who made something of a career by knocking down the straw man of an anticipated bloodbath when the Communists took power.[38]

OUR MISTAKES VERSUS THEIR BARBARISM

My Lai was a Pulitzer Prize-winning story, and was compared to every act of brutality during war that could be remembered. Oriana Fallaci said, "The massacre of My Lai is the same as the massacre of Sant' Anna, of Marzabotto, of Lidice, of Babi Yar, of Hue, of the Ardeatine ditches."[39] Max Lerner added Malmedy and the Katyn Forest.[40] Some argue that for Americans My Lai was more important than Hue because My Lai was a product of American arms, and Hue was perpetrated by the enemy. Hue was the kind of thing one would expect from the Communists, while My Lai destroyed the moral basis for the entire war effort. At best this approach placed the U.S. on the same moral plane as the enemy; at worst it exposed the war as a grand hypocrisy.

But this line of argument ignores the most important distinguishing characteristics of the two events. My Lai was an indiscriminate, illegal act on the part of a small group of Americans, and it was halted by American soldiers who recognized it as a crime. When the events of My Lai came to light, charges were brought against 26 officers and enlisted men. Americal Division commander Major General Samuel W. Koster was censured, stripped of a Distinguished Service Medal, demoted to Brigadier General, and relieved of his post as Superintendent of the U.S. Military Academy at West Point for conducting an inadequate investigation. Forty years later My Lai is taught to officers in professional military education programs as a case study in the failure of ethical leadership.

In contrast, Hue was not a spontaneous act of excess but the cold-blooded implementation of North Vietnamese policy. Those who committed the crimes were doing the bidding of their superiors, and had the Tet Offensive turned out the way the North Vietnamese leadership had expected, they would have been hailed as heroes. In short, we regard My Lai as an atrocity; the enemy regarded Hue as a job well done.

The belief grew that civilian killings like those at My Lai were commonplace in Vietnam, even routine. In 1970 lawyer Mark Lane, previously known for writing sensationalistic books promoting Kennedy assassination conspiracy theories, published *Conversations with Americans*, which was billed as "one of the most shocking, eye-opening books ever encountered in the annals of wartime reporting." The book was based on interviews with American troops, and contained a number of confessions by Vietnam veterans who had participated in a variety of gruesome activities, vividly portrayed. Lane worked with the Vietnam Veterans Against the War to organize the "Winter Soldier Investigations," a media event held in Detroit January 31-February 2, 1971, to publicize alleged war crimes and atrocities perpetrated by the U.S. military. 109 veterans and 16 civilians gathered in a Detroit hotel to tell similar tales of brutality and barbarity. This event led to hearings before the Senate Committee on Foreign Relations that April, during which VVAW member John Kerry gave emotional testimony that brought him to national prominence and launched his political career. Other groups, such as the Committee of Concerned Asia Scholars, prominently represented by Noam Chomsky, trumpeted war crimes allegations at every turn. American troops were called baby killers and people spat on them. The entire conflict was delegitimized, and by 1975 it was easy enough to blank out South Vietnam when the country was in its death throes. By then the popular image of the Vietnam veteran was that of a shell-shocked, alcoholic, homeless misfit driven to despair by his participation in an unjust war.

However, the confessions in *Conversations with Americans* were largely if not wholly fabricated. Lane was dubbed a charlatan, and his book a sham. Pulitzer Prize-winning Vietnam War reporter Neil Sheehan, who had substantial antiwar credentials, savaged Lane's work in the *New York Times Book Review*, demonstrating that Lane did not do even the most basic research to substantiate the claims of his witnesses, none of whom came across as legitimate. A recalcitrant Lane stated flatly that the book was written with "antiwar motives" and that he was unconcerned with its glaring inaccuracies, since his purpose was righteous. Sheehan disagreed but thought that it might indirectly do some good. "This book is so irresponsible that it may help to provoke a responsible inquiry into the question of war crimes and atrocities in Vietnam," Sheehan wrote. "*Conversations with Americans* is a lesson in what happens when a society shuns the examination of a pressing, emotional issue and leaves the answers to a Mark Lane."[41]

The practice of inventing atrocities continued after Vietnam. The media are spring-loaded to report atrocity tales from members of the military, and there has been a spate of them in recent years. Jesse MacBeth claimed to be an Army Ranger, admitted to having executed children while interrogating their parents, shot down rock-throwing protesters, and slaughtered hundreds of worshippers in a mosque. None of that was true.[42] Former Marine Jimmy Massey said he either killed children and civilians personally, witnessed the killings, or heard about them, depending on which version of the story he was telling at the moment. Korean War Veteran Edward Lee Daily came forward in the 1990s claiming to be present at the killings at No Gun Ri, as well as being a lieutenant, a POW, and wounded by shrapnel, all of which were lies.[43] And Scott Thomas Beauchamp's highly questionable war stories were featured prominently in *The New Republic*, and told of such crimes as running over dogs in an armored fighting vehicle and mocking the severely wounded.[44]

It is an indictment of American culture that any members of the U.S. military might believe it morally cleansing to falsify personal participation in atrocities, to tell bogus war stories not as false braggadocio but *faux* confession. In the process they blemish themselves and their comrades, their service, and their country. Lying about atrocities is a perverse bid for attention. It fills a complex psychological need to be seen as both victimizer and victim, to be acclaimed for confessing and thus be absolved of the crime. Those who publicly own up to these imagined great sins are praised for having the nerve to come forward rather than condemned for the offense itself, which is blamed instead on the senior military leadership, government policymakers, or both. There is no shame in it; in America's "victimization" culture individuals are not responsible for what they do. Atrocities are a product of the "brutalization of war," and a person claiming to have committed them is a casualty of the people who sent him to war in the first place. This line of argument was more effective in the days when the United States had conscription.

The reward for this act of bravery is fame, travel, maybe a book contract. Professional left-wing activists and politicians are ready to help, since these kinds of stories serve their interests. Meanwhile accounts of valor and charity, of service and sacrifice, are rarely told and not remembered. For every exaggerated tale of the brutal or bizarre, there are a hundred true accounts of bravery and benevolence that more clearly and accurately represent the spirit of our fighting forces. That is not news, but it should be.

Meanwhile, actual atrocities are ignored. Atrocity stories have had a mixed history as motivators, particularly as people have learned how such stories have been and can be exaggerated and manipulated. This was demonstrated after the First World War, when many of the most famous tales of "Hun brutality" were exposed as exaggerated or invented propaganda tales. Skepticism born of this experience continued into the next war. In January 1944, the *New York Times Magazine* published an essay by Arthur Koestler entitled "On Disbelieving Atrocities." It conveyed his frustration at trying to communicate the barbarities he and others had seen taking place in Nazi-dominated Europe. The events that came to be known as the Holocaust were being revealed by this time, but they were not widely accepted as true. "I have been lecturing now for three years to the troops and their attitude is the same," he wrote. "They don't believe in concentration camps, they don't believe in the starved children of Greece, in the shot hostages of France, in the mass-graves of Poland; they have never heard of Lidice, Treblinka or Belzec; you can convince them for an hour, then they shake themselves, their mental self-defence begins to work and in a week the shrug of incredulity has returned like a reflex temporarily weakened by a shock."[45] Even late in the war, when most people believed there was some truth behind the stories, few grasped the scope of the tragedy then underway. This all changed when the death camps were liberated and photographs and newsreels brought home the enormity of what had happened. Incredulity and dismissiveness were replaced with outrage and shame. It turned out that sometimes atrocities are real.

Today cynicism has returned, and the disillusionment of the Vietnam era seems to have left people numb to genuine atrocities. We have witnessed the discovery of mass graves in Iraq, ethnic cleansing in the Balkans and Africa, wide-scale execution and repression in Iran, and a human rights nightmare in North Korea. We have seen the predations of terrorists attacking innocents. It is not necessary to stigmatize an enemy like al Qaeda through propaganda; its principal war-fighting method is to either kill noncombatants en masse or to kidnap individuals, videotape its acts of torture and brutality, behead the victims, and post the images on the Web.

But any blunder by the United States or its allies is immediately raised to the level of Auschwitz or the Gulag by radicals, lazy intellectuals, and a politically biased media seeking a story line. They use controversies such as Abu Ghraib and Guantánamo to level the playing field with insurgents and terrorists, utilizing such events to indict that which they already opposed. The direct beneficiaries of this tendency are the terrorists, whose ongoing, brutal, intentional, and directed atrocities are seen at worst as morally equivalent to the mistakes of the United States and its allies, and at best taken for granted and ignored. U.S. actions undertaken by individuals violating policy are portrayed as great crimes that delegitimize the whole effort. This is a powerful advantage for the enemy, which only has to wait until the inevitable human failings present it with an opportunity. In the meantime, it can commit atrocities at will.

Twenty-eight years to the day before the 9/11 attacks, Aleksandr Solzhenitsyn declaimed the unwillingness of the United Nations to offer a moral condemnation of terrorism, instead being preoccupied with asking "whether any form of terrorism was, in fact harmful, and what is the definition of terrorism anyway?" He wrote that the U.N. refused "to regard as terrorism a treacherous attack in a peaceful setting, on peaceful people, by military men carrying concealed weapons and often dressed in plain clothes. They demand instead that we study the aims of terrorist groups, their bases of support and their ideology, and then perhaps acknowledge them to be sacred 'guerillas.'"[46] The mark of decrepitude in the West was its unwillingness to declare and adhere to objective standards of judgment regarding freedom's enemies. This is why My Lai has become a byword for brutality while Hue is a footnote. By rights these incidents should demonstrate that Americans are morally superior to their enemies; we recognize and punish atrocities, while the enemy uses them as instruments of policy. We are civilized; they are barbarians. We fight for objectives that are realistically superior to what they are fighting for. Our struggle is legitimate; theirs is not. There is no room for moral relativism in war. We should take fanaticism at face value. Those jihadists who view torture and beheading as acts of piety certainly have no problem seeing the current conflict as a struggle of good against evil, with themselves acting as the agents of God and the horrors of Hue awaiting those who fall into their hands.

XIII.

KHE SANH

Always in the background of Tet was Khe Sanh. The 77-day siege, also known as Operation Scotland, began a week before Tet and ended over a month after the last major fighting in Hue. Whether Khe Sanh was an integral part of the offensive or a strategic deception is a continuing source of debate, but the battle left an indelible negative impression on Tet and the Vietnam War.[1]

The Khe Sanh combat base was located in a hilly, beautiful part of South Vietnam, reminiscent some said of the hills of Tuscany, though with man-killing tigers roaming the slopes. In more peaceful times the area was dotted

> Flower power ain't gonna stop no incoming.
>
> —U.S. NAVY SEABEE AT KHE SANH

with French coffee plantations, some of which were still operating in the late 1960s. U.S. forces established a presence near Khe Sanh village in 1962, when a Special Forces camp was constructed near an old French fort to support observation and interdiction missions along the Ho Chi Minh Trail. The Special Forces later moved to the Xom Cham Plateau in the Rao Quan River valley, where the Khe Sanh base would eventually be built. The first Marine combat troops arrived in April 1966, and in January 1967 the Special Forces left for their new camp at Lang Vei, five and a half miles west along Route 9, closer to the border with Laos. Khe Sanh was improved and expanded, a runway was added, and two fire support bases were established 17 miles away at Camps Carroll and Rockpile.

U.S. planners had long expected a major Communist attack in the north because it made military sense; enemy troops would be better able to sustain a conventional assault there since they were close to the DMZ and to bases of supply. Of the possible targets in I Corps, Khe Sanh was ideal; it was in the northeast corner of the country, 14 miles from the border with the North, seven miles east of enemy sanctuaries in Laos. American planners thought it was the perfect target from the enemy's perspective. General Westmoreland wanted to further build up the position at Khe Sanh, but III MAF Commander Marine General Lewis W. Walt objected, believing the plan to be a waste of manpower that could more profitably be used protecting the South Vietnamese people. Brigadier General Lowell English, assistant commander of the 3rd Marine Division, felt that it made no sense to take a stand at Khe Sanh, because the only object of military significance in the area was the base itself. "When you're at Khe Sanh, you're not really anywhere," he said. "You could lose it and you really haven't lost a damn thing."[2]

But to Westmoreland Khe Sanh was strategically significant. "Khe Sanh could serve as a patrol base for blocking enemy infiltration from Laos along Route 9," he later wrote, "as a base for SOG operations to harass the enemy in Laos, as an airstrip for reconnaissance planes surveying the Ho Chi Minh Trail, as the western anchor for defenses south of the DMZ, and as an eventual jump-off point for ground operations to cut the Ho Chi Minh Trail."[3] The last point was particularly important because the Joint Staff had developed an ambitious concept to respond to enemy provocation in the area—strike west into Laos, cut the Ho Chi Minh Trail, then move north into southern North Vietnam. Westmoreland had sketched a number of proposed operations involving large-scale moves against the enemy in Laos, among them Operation Full Cry in 1966, Operations Southpaw and High Port in 1967, and Operation El Paso in 1968.[4] Furthermore, Khe Sanh was tempting bait; if the enemy massed to mount an attack it would face the full force of American firepower.

The strategic heights northwest of Khe Sanh, Hills 881N, 881S, 861, 861A, and 558, had to be occupied to prevent them from being used as firing platforms for possible enemy attacks. Marines pushed out onto the heights and soon made contact. In April 1967 two PAVN regiments attacked a patrol from Bravo Company, 1st Battalion 9th Marines, on Hill 861. It should have been an easy victory for the Communists, but a combination of tenacity, terrain advantage, and superior firepower allowed the Marines to hold out for 12 days before the enemy withdrew. The "Hill Fights" in late April pitted two battalions of the 3rd Marine Regiment against much larger enemy forces, but the Marines were able to seize and hold the critical heights on hills 861, 881N, and 881S after a hard contest with the PAVN.[5] Company-sized units held the hills throughout the siege except for 881N, the northernmost and farthest from Khe Sanh, which was not deemed critical and abandoned. Other battles were fought near Khe Sanh and along Route 9 through October. Because supply convoys were subject to ambush, Khe Sanh began to be supplied by air months before the major attack began in January 1968.

By the end of 1967 the enemy showed signs of taking a more serious interest in Khe Sanh. In November 1967, 20,000 PAVN began to converge on the base, and the next month two more PAVN divisions moved toward the base, the 325C and the elite 304th Division, which had been present at Dien Bien Phu. There were an additional 12,000–14,000 PAVN troops in support positions. Ultimately the Communists would have up to 40,000

40,000 → 6,000

4,000

troops around the base, facing about 6,000 troops, primarily from the 26th Marine Regiment, commanded by Colonel David E. Lownds, a cigar-chomping, mustachioed veteran of three wars who had been a platoon leader at Saipan and Iwo Jima. Lownds was a natural leader with a steady presence under fire and was greatly respected by his men. He had taken command of the 26th Marine Regiment in August 1967 and by January the entire unit was at Khe Sanh.

The enemy had attempted to use the monsoon season to cover its movements toward the base, but the actions did not elude U.S. intelligence, who tracked them closely. The prospective attack fit the model of what the Americans expected the enemy to do, and as the Communists conducted their buildup the Marines dug in. Excavation was incessant; Colonel Lownds joked, "Dig another foot and we're into China."[6] While the enemy troops massed around Khe Sanh, General Westmoreland planned ways to take advantage of the growing target-rich environment. He instituted Operation Niagara I, an intelligence collection effort using CIA assets and aerial reconnaissance to pinpoint the assembly areas, routes of march, and headquarters of the PAVN force, with a view toward using airpower to take them out.

The enemy attack was planned to open just after midnight on January 21, but a lucky break ruined the chance for achieving tactical surprise. On the afternoon of January 20 a North Vietnamese defector walked onto the base; as Westmoreland put it, he "appeared off one end of the airstrip at Khe Sanh, an AK-47 rifle in one hand, a white flag in the other."[7] Senior Lieutenant La Thanh Tonc of the 14th Antiaircraft Company, 325 C Division was a disgruntled soldier who had been passed over for promotion, and he defected as payback. He warned the Americans of an imminent attack on hills 861 and 881S by two divisions, his and the 304th. The plan was to take the hills, sweep down on the main base at Khe Sanh, then move on to Hue in a pincer movement with forces scheduled to attack there on January 31. He claimed that the attack was a prelude to overrunning all of Quang Tri Province and that General Giap was personally directing the initiative.[8]

As Lieutenant Tonc predicted, the PAVN attack began at 0030 hours on January 21. Approximately 300 North Vietnamese hit Hill 861. The hill fight was particularly fierce, and it became a vicious hand-to-hand struggle after some enemy soldiers penetrated the outpost's perimeter. Meanwhile, the PAVN shelled the main base with mortars and 122mm rockets, some of which were based over the Laotian border. The enemy fired around 300 rounds on the first day, an intense bombardment by North Vietnamese standards but less so compared with other wars. (For example, at the height of the fighting in Grozny, Chechnya, in January 1995 the Russian attackers fired 300 rounds every five minutes.) One shell hit the Khe Sanh ammo dump at the eastern end of the runway, causing a massive explosion that shook the base. Ammo and fuel cooked off, and clouds wafted up from broken tear gas shells. A secondary explosion caused by the fire was even more severe. Ninety percent of the Marines' ammunition was lost, and resupply flights began to stream in, a few of which fell victim to enemy fire and other mishaps. The larger C-130 transports had trouble negotiating the runway, and one of them crashed, whereupon the resupply task fell to the lighter C-123s, requiring more flights. This unlucky series of events heightened the sense of danger at Khe Sanh, and the ammo dump explosion became a huge news item that focused national attention and concern.

After a day of fighting, nine Marines were dead and 75 wounded. Half of the wounded were not severely hurt and were still in the battle. Casualties were light despite the intensity of the fight. Khe Sanh village had been overrun, however, and Special Forces, Marines, and Montagnard members of the Civilian Irregular Defense Group pulled back to Forward Operating Base 3 adjacent to the main base. Reinforcements were rushed to Khe Sanh—a battalion of the 9th Marines and the 37th ARVN Ranger Battalion. The 6,000-man force remained the basic lineup at Khe Sanh until the end of the battle on April 8, with about half of the defenders on the hills outside the main base.

The American response to the attack was immediate and devastating. Westmoreland launched Operation Niagara II, the planned large-scale aerial bombardment. The attacks continued throughout the siege. On average, 60 B-52 bombers, 350 tactical fighter bombers, and 30 light reconnaissance aircraft were operating daily near Khe Sanh as part of Niagara II. Seismic and acoustic sensors were dropped in the area as part of Operation Igloo White, which allowed for precise targeting even through the persistent clouds and fog. American aircraft pummeled the enemy with high explosives and scorched the surrounding area with napalm. The joint campaign involved Air Force aircraft and Navy and Marine Air Wings, which caused some difficulties with air command and control, since there were significant doctrinal differences, particularly between the Air Force and the Marine Corps. But the air campaign was a stunning achievement that made full use of American firepower dominance. Lownds said the B-52 strikes were "a godsend, a miraculous thing. It's almost scary when you think about it."[9]

Niagara II dealt the enemy a critical blow. B-52s struck a target identified as the main headquarters for the North Vietnamese forces at Khe Sanh, throwing the enemy into disarray. The North Vietnamese were still able to conduct some operations—on January 24 there was a large bombardment by enemy 100mm and 152mm guns—but their more extensive attack plans were disrupted, and radio traffic from the PAVN headquarters ceased for almost two weeks.

When the Tet Offensive kicked off a week later, the Khe Sanh sector was relatively quiet. The lack of a coordinated major effort may have been due to the impact of Niagara II, although it has also been argued that the enemy was waiting to see the effects of the expected mass popular uprising and potentially to use Khe Sanh units to reinforce the lowlands. Later some units were shifted to the fight in Hue, for example.

Failing to press the assault at Khe Sanh while the United States was focused on the nationwide urban attacks seems militarily unsound in retrospect, but it ties into the debate over why the North Vietnamese attacked Khe Sanh and what their objectives were. Attacking a week before the nationwide assault indicates that Khe Sanh was initially a way to draw U.S. attention away from the urban areas, particularly Hue, Da Nang, and other cities in I Corps. But after the initial strikes in January there was a lull until days after the first wave of Tet attacks. When action at Khe Sanh resumed in earnest, it may have been a way to draw U.S. forces from assisting the ARVN with the fighting elsewhere, consistent with the North Vietnamese policy not to become decisively engaged with U.S. forces in the city fights. But by that time it was a week into the fighting, and there was no sign of popular uprising or any hints of even small-scale victory outside Hue, so the intensified attack on Khe Sanh had something of a "too little too late" quality.

The timeline makes more sense in light of what the enemy expected rather than what it had achieved. The North Vietnamese campaign plan may have assumed that after the first week of the Tet attacks the base would be vulnerable, its supply lines harried and reinforcements uncertain. The ideal scenario was the one disclosed by the defector Lieutenant Tonc: the U.S. would become committed to the Khe Sanh fight, keep reinforcing failure, and ultimately collapse. The enemy could then move along Route 9 northeast to Dong Ha and south on Route 1 to Quang Tri and Hue. From there the enemy forces would spill out into the plains and take control of all of I Corps. At the very least, the relative Communist success at Hue meant that it was important to keep the Americans occupied in the north.

This was fine from Westmoreland's point of view. Khe Sanh was both the battle he expected and the battle he wanted. By massing in a set location to attack a known objective over a long period of time, the enemy lost its traditional advantages of mobility, surprise, and stealth. U.S. and allied forces had the advantage of being on the tactical defensive and were able effectively to utilize the essentially unlimited fires at their disposal. Khe Sanh was a more conventional form of warfare, the kind that appealed to the American military. There were no hearts and minds involved, just firepower. Westmoreland said that he had "a desire to fight the enemy away from the populated areas."[10] Hence the code name "Niagara," which Westmoreland envisaged as a Niagara Falls of munitions raining down on the enemy without the restrictions faced in other, more densely populated areas. The 1,200 civilians who had lived in Khe Sanh village were evacuated on January 31 so that they could be cared for elsewhere; the Bru villagers shouldn't be caught in the crossfire, and the base shouldn't add supporting a refugee population to its supply challenges. Press reports, however, cast this humanitarian evacuation as something of a defeat, that the United States moved the noncombatants because it could not defend them. Yet the reporters missed the point. The best way to defend the civilians was to get them out of the line of fire. The Americans put the villagers out of harm's way better to perfect the Khe Sanh killing zone.

"DINBINPHOO"

The January 21 attack at Khe Sanh seemed to confirm what many analysts believed the enemy had been planning to do. It was a moment of high drama. It seemed to signal that the decisive battle of the war had begun. "The eyes of the nation, the eye of the entire world, are on that brave little band of defenders who hold the pass at Khe Sanh," Johnson said shortly after the attack commenced, apparently invoking the image of Thermopylae, or perhaps the Alamo.[11] The President was fixated on the battle. He had a 1/50,000th scale terrain model of Khe Sanh erected in the White House basement situation room, the only such model he asked for during the war. Throughout the siege he received daily updates cabled from Westmoreland personally. On January 29 he took the unusual step of making the Chiefs sign "in blood" a document promising that the base would be held.[12] None of the Chiefs or Westmoreland believed the place could possibly fall, but Johnson was adamant. "I don't want any damn Dinbinphoo," he said.[13]

The French base at Dien Bien Phu fell to the Viet Minh on May 7, 1954, after a 56-day siege, one day before the scheduled Geneva peace talks. The loss there heavily influenced the course of the talks and led directly to the agreement that divided Vietnam and contributed to the collapse of French Prime Minister Joseph Laniel's government. Bernard Fall's account of the French experience, *Hell in a Very Small Place,* came out in the summer of

1966 and became a must read among journalists and the military alike.[14] Also popular was the 1965 book *The Battle of Dienbienphu* by Jules Roy, a Frenchman who had survived the battle. The press instantly picked up this story line with built-in drama. Journalist Michael Herr wrote,

> As the first Marine briefings on Khe Sanh took place in
> Marine Headquarters at Da Nang or Dong Ha, the name Dien
> Bien Phu insinuated itself like some tasteless ghost hawking
> bad news. Marines who had to talk to the press found refer-
> ences to the old French disaster irritating and even insulting.
> Most were not interested in fielding questions about it, and the
> rest were underequipped. The more irritated they became, the
> more the press would flaunt the irritant. For a while it looked
> like nothing that had happened on the ground during those
> weeks seemed as thrilling and sinister as the recollections of
> Dien Bien Phu. And it had to be admitted, the parallels with
> Khe Sanh were irresistible.[15]

Dien Bien Phu had been used as an emblem of unexpected defeat long before Khe Sanh. References to the battle were fairly common in a variety of contexts. Karl E. Meyer referred to the battle in 1962 when reflecting on the fourth game of the 1941 World Series: "What should have been the last out in the ninth and a Dodger victory tying the Series turned into a baseball Dienbienphu when Mickey Owen dropped the third strike."[16] General Westmoreland himself had raised the analogy during the Battle of Con Thien in October 1967, saying the North Vietnamese "tried to make another Dienbienphu of Con Thien. Instead we made it a Dienbienphu in reverse."[17]

But with Khe Sanh the analogy truly came into its own. "The parallels are plain for all to see," Walter Cronkite declared on January 26. Like Dien Bien Phu, Khe Sanh was a remote outpost in the hilly frontier country. It was being attacked by North Vietnamese regulars, including units that had stormed the French base. General Giap, the mastermind of Dien Bien Phu who wore the victory like a cloak of invincibility, was commanding the North

Vietnamese forces, and some said he was personally directing the Khe Sanh battle, although he was not on site. But what made the comparison most compelling was the sense of doom attached to the potential outcome. Dien Bien Phu was the French gravestone in Indochina. The implicit notion was that should Khe Sanh fall it would mean the United States had lost the war. This was why Dien Bien Phu became an idée fixe for President Johnson and the press corps alike.

Yet what was obvious to the press corps was more nuanced to the military. High-ranking officers were well aware of the lessons learned from that battle. General Westmoreland had commissioned a staff study of Dien Bien Phu and discussed it in detail with one of the former French commanders. He understood the points of comparison, but also the significant differences, most of which were under his control. The most important difference was the availability of much greater fire support than the French could command, both from artillery and aircraft. The latter was crucial. Even Bernard Fall had concluded that had the United States lent France sufficient airpower—he estimated 100 American planes—Dien Bien Phu would have been saved. Khe Sanh also had more reliable supply lines, another area in which airpower played the key role. Also, unlike the French at Dien Bien Phu, the Marines held the high ground overlooking the base, and it would be impossible for the enemy to take Khe Sanh as long as the hills were in friendly hands. Furthermore, the U.S. force commitment at Khe Sanh was not as great; the almost 11,000 troops at Dien Bien Phu comprised 10% of the total French manpower in Indochina, while the 6,000 U.S. troops at Khe Sanh were slightly over 1% of U.S. strength in Vietnam. Thus there were more forces available for reinforcement if necessary, and a loss would not have been as significant to the conduct of the overall war effort.

In time, even the press began to question the analogy after its use became so widespread that it became a news story itself. On February 10, 1968, the *Washington Post* ran a piece addressing the analogy, calling it "inevitable" but noting the many differences between the 1954 and 1968 battles, such as greater U.S. firepower, ability to resupply and reinforce, and a very different overall situation inside the country.[18] Nevertheless, the Dien Bien Phu story line was inescapable and persisted throughout the battle. "Every new reporter who came up tried to equate [Khe Sanh] with Dien Bien Phu," Colonel Lownds later said, "and I kept trying to tell them . . . that the comparison is not good."[19]

LANG VEI

As the siege settled in at Khe Sanh, another drama was played out not far to the west. The Special Forces camp at Lang Vei was located a few miles from the Laotian border, set before a gap in the mountains through which Route 9 wended toward Khe Sanh. From the American perspective it was a useful base for operations against North Vietnamese lines of communication. From the enemy perspective, Lang Vei guarded the "back door" to Khe Sanh.

Lang Vei was a hard-luck post. In March 1967 the Air Force accidentally napalmed the nearby village, killing and wounding almost 350 people and burning parts of the camp. A May 1967 Viet Cong raid wiped out the Special Forces command group in their bunker. When the Khe Sanh siege started, the camp was commanded by Captain Frank C. Willoughby of Company C, Detachment A-101, 12th Mobile Strike Force, 5th Special Forces. At the camp were 24 U.S. Special Forces troops, including members of Detachment A-113 Mobile Strike Force; 14 South Vietnamese Special Forces (LLDB); over 400 Bru and Vietnamese Civilian Irregular Defense Group troops (CIDG, or "sid-gee"), 6 interpreters, and a number of civilians. Lang Vei had been mortared on January 24 along with Khe Sanh, but for the next two weeks the area was relatively quiet.

Early in the battle hundreds of soldiers and dependents from the Kha tribal 33rd Laotian Volunteer Battalion streamed into Lang Vei from a military camp at Ban Houei Sane, just over the border. The Laotian troops said their camp had been attacked by North Vietnamese forces and overrun by tanks. Since the North Vietnamese had not used tanks in the war, and the presence of tanks had not been confirmed by intelligence sources, the Americans discounted the story. But the Laotian commander was adamant about his account of the attack. Furthermore, he outranked Captain Willoughby and did not want to take orders from him. The situation was reported to headquarters, and on February 6 Lieutenant Colonel Daniel F. Schungel arrived to supply the necessary rank to placate the Laotians.

Lang Vei came under mortar fire that evening, which was met with counterfire from the camp and from Khe Sanh. But this was not just another harassment attack. In the predawn hours of February 7, 12 Soviet-made PT-76 light tanks from the 202nd PAVN Armored Regiment assaulted Lang Vei, supported by infantry equipped with explosives and flamethrowers from elements of the 304th Division. Some men were caught outside the perimeter and overrun, but inside the camp the Americans rushed to prepare a defense.

The enemy fed the tanks in slowly, which gave the defenders a fighting chance. The two lead tanks approached from the south, and just inside the wire Sergeant First Class James W. Holt engaged them with a 106mm recoilless rifle. The PT-76 was a lightly armored 1950s-era Soviet amphibious reconnaissance tank, and the recoilless rifle was more than a match for it. Holt knocked two out in short order. Other tanks rolled into the camp, and Holt reloaded for another shot, aided by Staff Sergeant Peter Tiroch. The team took out a third tank and got off one more shot before having to flee in the face of fire from the 76.2mm guns and coaxial machine guns on the surviving vehicles.

Meanwhile, a team led by Lieutenant Colonel Schungel made a close assault attack on the tanks inside the perimeter, first with light antitank weapons, then with hand grenades, then themselves climbing on the tanks trying to shoot the crews. They managed to take out two of the vehicles before having to withdraw in the face of advancing PAVN infantry. The men scattered, and Lieutenant Colonel Schungel and Lieutenant Wilkins took cover under the camp dispensary.

Within 90 minutes the tanks and PAVN sappers had broken Lang Vei's perimeter and moved to the inner compound. Some survivors of the assault, Americans, South Vietnamese, and others, retreated to the main command bunker, a reinforced position at the center of the camp. The enemy threw satchel charges, hand grenades, and tear gas bombs down the air vents after them. Miraculously the men survived. The PAVN then announced that anyone voluntarily leaving the bunker would be spared but that the rest would be killed. The South Vietnamese Special Forces troops decided to take the offer and departed. A few minutes after they emerged, the men who had stayed behind heard massed gunfire as the PAVN shot down the prisoners in cold blood.

Captain Willoughby, Sergeant Nick Fragos, and six others remained in the bunker. The North Vietnamese tried to root them out for two hours, using grenades, satchel charges, tear gas, and phosphorous grenades. At one point an enemy soldier called down to the defenders in English.

"Are you there?"

"Yes, I'm here," Sergeant Fragos replied.

"Have you got a weapon?"

"Yep."

"Have you got ammunition?"

"I've got plenty for you." The fighting calmed until dawn, when the PAVN blew a hole in the wall of the bunker and threw in grenades, wounding Willoughby and most of the survivors.

Meanwhile, the fight continued outside. Scattered Americans outside the camp harassed the enemy near the command bunker with sporadic fire. Aircraft made strafing runs on roads and ravines outside the camp, and as the sun rose air strikes were called in on enemy positions and vehicles. Aircraft also made low-level passes to disorient the enemy troops and back them away from the command bunker. But while Lang Vei received some air support it got little else. A planned relief effort from Khe Sanh was canceled for fear that the Lang Vei attack was a diversion meant to draw the Marines out of the main base.

Special Forces troops outside the camp quickly took the initiative. One of these was Sergeant First Class Eugene Ashley, Jr., who served as intelligence sergeant. He was an 18-year Army veteran from Wilmington, N.C., who had served all over the world in positions as diverse as infantryman, ambulance driver, anti-aircraft ammunition handler, heavy weapons specialist, and parachute repairman. He had served in infantry, cavalry, armored, and airborne units before joining the Special Forces. During the initial part of the attack he manned a mortar and supported the camp with high explosive and illumination rounds. He also directed air strikes and artillery support. Later in the morning he assembled a team with two assistant medical specialists, Sergeant Richard H. Allen and Spec 4 Joel Johnson, plus 60 Laotian soldiers who had fled the camp. He led the force to Lang Vei and mounted a counterattack, which quickly failed when the Laotians retreated in the face of concerted PAVN fire.

Ashley was then joined by Sergeant First Class William T. Craig and Staff Sergeant Peter Tiroch, who had been hunting the PAVN tanks through the night. They rallied some of the fleeing troops and mounted more attacks on the camp. Sergeant Ashley led a total of five assaults that morning, each time being driven back by intense rifle and machine gun fire and grenade attacks. Between attacks he directed air strikes on enemy positions. On the fifth attack, with close air support, Ashley's team moved to within 30 yards of the beleaguered command bunker. At that point Ashley was critically wounded by a burst of enemy machine gun fire. One of his men was carrying the sergeant from the field when an enemy artillery round landed nearby, and Ashley was killed.

The repeated assaults and air strikes had a telling effect, and by afternoon the enemy began to pull back. Lieutenant Colonel Schungel and Lieutenant Wilkins, still lying low under the camp dispensary, were able to escape when the PAVN left the building. Captain Willoughby and the other wounded men in the command bunker received radio instructions to evacuate their position. While the enemy was distracted by aircraft buzzing the camp, the defenders made a break for a nearby landing zone. Meanwhile, Major George Quamo arrived with some Special Forces volunteers from Forward Operating base #3 at Khe Sanh and helped coordinate the evacuation of the survivors. By evening the camp was abandoned. The severely wounded were flown out by Marine helicopters, but most went toward Khe Sanh on foot, arriving early on the morning of February 8.[20]

Lang Vei had been overrun, but the enemy was not able to exploit the victory. The night the camp fell, some PAVN units moved down Route 9 to an outpost called Alpha-1 on the Khe Sanh perimeter but failed to take it and were pushed out the next day. The toll for the defenders was high. Fourteen of 24 Americans made it to Khe Sanh, only 60 of around 900 Montagnards, Laotians, and others. Three men, Sergeant First Class Harvey G. Brande, Staff Sergeant Dennis L. Thompson, and Spec 4 William G. McMurry, were captured. They were rushed from the area and eventually sent to North Vietnam as POWs, where they languished in prison until 1973. A total of 21 Silver Stars were awarded for the action, two Distinguished Service Crosses, and three Bronze Stars with V for valor. Special Forces Sergeant First Class Eugene Ashley, Jr., who had organized and led the most determined counterattacks and was killed in the process, was posthumously awarded the Medal of Honor.

The use of tanks in the battle caused a short-lived media frenzy. Newspapers initially misidentified the vehicles as World War II-era Soviet T-34s, the workhorse of the Red Army in defeating the German Panzers.[21] Visions of Red tanks in massed attacks combined with the loss of the Special Forces camp led to some ominous commentary in the first days after the battle, but the error was soon corrected.[22] Nevertheless, the combination of "firebase overrun" and "tanks" was irresistible to those seeking a dramatic story line. Of course, had heavier North Vietnamese tanks begun to roll down Route 9 toward Khe Sanh, they would have been pinned down and obliterated in short order, an easy target for massed air and artillery fires. As it was, the "tank assault" did not proceed through the mountain pass, but the PAVN fight at Lang Vei is still commemorated as the first victory of the Vietnamese armored force.

KHE SANH BESIEGED

Lang Vei was the only significant PAVN success during the 77-day battle. After that, Khe Sanh settled down into the traditional dynamics of a siege. The PAVN entrenched and moved on the

Marine works in classic style. Both sides made periodic attacks using fires, although the mismatch was dramatic. The North Vietnamese fired on average 150 rounds a day on the Marine positions. The United States averaged around 300 air strikes per day, or one bombardment every five minutes, plus regular saturation from the artillery support positions at Camps Carroll and Rockpile. The North Vietnamese were mostly helpless under the rain of fires, and only two American ground support aircraft were lost during the siege.

Colonel Lownds saw his mission in basic terms. "My job is to stay here," he said. "My job is to hold." Asked if he was worried about the much larger enemy force facing him, he replied, "Hell, no. I've got Marines. My confidence isn't shaken a bit."[23] The fighting at Dak To in November had demonstrated the costs of offensive operations in the hill country against dug-in North Vietnamese regulars. Lownds's men did conduct some operations outside the wire, although they were risky. On February 25 a patrol from Bravo Company 1st Battalion 26th Marines was ambushed by a PAVN battalion. The enemy killed nine and wounded 25; 19 went missing. The bodies of the men killed could not be immediately retrieved and lay outside the wire until the first week in April, when the siege was lifted.

Supplying the base was hampered by the monsoon weather and persistent cloud cover, not to mention the North Vietnamese habit of pouring antiaircraft fire on aircraft seeking to land or take off and periodically mortaring the tarmac. Consequently, most supplies for the main base were delivered by parachute, and Marines supplied the hilltop positions with massed groups of helicopters supported by A-4 Skyhawks.

Daily life in Khe Sanh was difficult. Eddie Adams, a veteran of 150 Vietnam operations, called Khe Sanh "probably the spookiest place."[24] The base was a labyrinth of trenches and bunkers, sandbags and wire, frequently wrapped in a damp, chilling mist. Enemy fire was random but always present, and men frequently had to rush for cover at the sound of enemy shells or gunfire. Journalist William Tuohy said that "in Khe Sanh happiness was a well constructed bunker," and the best of them were constructed by the Seabees.[25] Their primary duty was to repair damage from incoming enemy fire, but they also reinforced the existing defenses when possible. Tuohy noted that one of the sailors named Eshenaur, from Simi, California, had decorated his helmet cover with psychedelic script and the exclamation "Love!"

"I'm big on the flower-power movement," Eshenaur explained, laughing.

"Shit," another Seabee said, "Flower power ain't gonna stop no incoming."[26]

Khe Sahn's defenders dealt with conditions that would have been familiar to their grandfathers in the trenches of France during the First World War. Rats, dirt, the rumble of artillery, and the odd casualty were their everyday experience. Shelling sent the rats scurrying frantically, but the men got used to it. They spent hours hunkered down in bunkers, stacking sandbags, watching the enemy from observation points, and sometimes drawing the dangerous assignment of checking the perimeter wire. Trenches eroded from rain and from shelling and periodically had to be dug out. Meanwhile, the PAVN troops were active trying to snipe, machine gun, or mortar whatever Marines they spotted.

But the Marines were watching as well and shot any North Vietnamese who got too close to the wire or who happened to be out in the open and in range. When they spotted enemy troops at greater distances they would call in air or artillery strikes. One North Vietnamese soldier, nicknamed Luke the Gook, led a charmed life.

> "Old Luke is one tough hombre," said one Marine. "We watched him through our binoculars. He climbed out of his hole to take his morning constitutional. We called in an air strike. They hit him with napalm. He came out of the hole again to look around. The air hit him again. And afterward he came out again and started to dig some more. I just can't understand why we can't get that gutsy little bastard."[27]

The Khe Sanh battle followed a pattern that the defenders found tedious and somewhat frustrating. However, although the battle lacked movement, it did not want for drama. Khe Sanh was a magnet for reporters who wanted to be on hand for the moment of decision. Peter Braestrup, *Washington Post* Saigon bureau chief who went there himself, said that "it had all the ingredients, especially for television, of melodrama and impending doom . . . It had a certain irresistible appeal."[28] Khe Sanh was modern siege warfare as translated for the small screen. Press reports frequently emphasized the negative aspects of the conditions at the base because often there was little else to report. Stand-uppers were often narrated next to the ramp of aircraft loading casualties or body bags, or were filmed in the shadow of a KC-130 refueling aircraft that had crashed early in the battle but whose constant reappearance on the nation's television screen seemed to send a persistent message of failure.[29]

The mere duration of the battle kept Khe Sanh in the headlines, becoming a challenge in the war of perceptions. Press reports could not convey the damage being done to the enemy, and it was hard to generate an impression that the Americans had the upper hand when television viewers continually saw Marines running for bunkers and enemy shells exploding. There was no corresponding film of the devastation being wrought on the enemy. The continuing drama of the siege attracted coverage, and the staying power of the story gave it a journalistic momentum beyond what was actually happening day to day. The Khe Sanh update was a nightly news staple whether there was anything important to report or not.[30] "There were a lot of incentives journalistically to make it a bigger story than it turned out to be," Braestrup said.[31]

Back home the battle became fodder for critical commentary. Historian and Kennedy adviser Arthur Schlesinger, Jr., believed that the battle was not worth fighting and continued only because of Westmoreland's personal stubbornness. "We stay because Khe Sanh is the bastion, not of the American military position, but of General Westmoreland's military strategy," Schlesinger wrote, "his 'war of attrition,' which has been so tragic and spectacular a failure." Schlesinger counseled that "a humane or intelligent leadership would have arranged for the immediate evacuation" of the garrison.[32] Of course, evacuation would have been both a military and political disaster; it would have been trumpeted as a defeat following the Dien Bien Phu story line and done incalculable damage to the American war effort. Walter Cronkite also got Khe Sanh wrong. "Since Khe Sanh's usefulness as a roadblock and forward base has been so vastly diminished," he reported in mid-March, "it can be assumed that it is mostly a symbol. But of what? Pride? Morale? Bravery? Or administrative intransigence and military miscalculation? . . . I found very few people out there who really believe Khe Sanh could be held if the North Vietnamese are determined to take it."[33]

The North Vietnamese certainly seemed determined to take Khe Sanh, based on the commitment they had made to the siege. But Cronkite's comment is a good example of defining a battle in a way that favors the enemy, regardless of the facts. Saying "they could win if they wanted to" requires no evidence, cannot be disproved, and casts the enemy as possessing a boundless and inscrutable omnipotence. In Cronkite's view the Communists were toying with the Marines, allowing them to survive only for as long as they desired. Characterizing the battle that way made any meaningful victory impossible, because if the base fell it was a defeat and if it held it was not because of a dogged and well-executed defense but because the North Vietnamese simply chose not to take it.

A week after Cronkite's dour assessment the North Vietnamese made a final push. On the night of March 22–23 they subjected Khe Sanh to a ferocious bombardment, firing 1,100 shells into the base, and a final ground assault was expected that day. But punishing air strikes preempted the enemy attack, and intelligence later reported that some North Vietnamese units had already pulled back from Khe Sanh. The artillery barrage may just have been a parting shot.

On April 1, Westmoreland launched Operation Pegasus, a joint Army/Marine effort to reopen the land link to Khe Sanh. The 1st Cavalry supported an advance up Route 9 by the 2nd Battalion 1st Marines and 2nd Battalion 3rd Marines along with other units moving west ten miles from Landing Zone Stud at Ca Lu.

The cavalry was to move ahead of the column to seize key terrain along the route of march and hunt retreating enemy formations. General Cushman was incensed that Pegasus was being described as a "relief" operation, stating that Khe Sanh had never technically been besieged, since the aerial resupply link had always been open, and, anyway, the Marines did not need to be "rescued" by the Army's 1st Cavalry.

The operation succeeded against unexpectedly light resistance. The enemy had essentially abandoned the attack in the face of the determined defenders and the unprecedented volume of fires from aircraft and artillery. The Marines moving up Route 9 pushed aside minor resistance on April 6, and the first "relief" elements, from the 2nd Battalion 7th Cavalry, entered Khe Sanh on the morning of April 8. The Marines handed over the main base to the Army, and cavalry troopers erected a five-foot-high sign, "Khe Sanh—Under New Management." Route 9 was declared open on April 11. Westmoreland had wanted to conduct a hot pursuit of the retreating enemy into Laos, but this was overruled. Men from the 3rd Battalion 26th Marines drove the last enemy units from Hill 881N a week later.

The battle had lasted 11 weeks. Allied casualties of a force of 6,000 were 730 dead, 2,642 wounded, and seven missing. The Marines had been outnumbered four or five to one, and the enemy probably lost around half its force. Enemy casualties are difficult to determine with certainty; 1,602 bodies were found, but there was no way to count the enemy knocked out by Operation Niagara and other results of fires far outside the wire. Estimates range up to 10,000–15,000 PAVN dead, although these numbers remain speculative. During Pegasus the numbers were 92 Americans killed, 667 wounded, and five missing, plus 33 ARVN killed and 187 wounded. Enemy dead were estimated at over ten times allied dead. The North Vietnamese took their heaviest casualties of the war, many of them experienced troops they could not afford to lose, especially for no appreciable gain. Some argue that the siege was simply intended to tie down U.S. forces and was not an earnest attempt to take Khe Sanh, but it is hard to believe that the enemy would waste such large numbers of men for a purpose that could have been achieved with far less effort. And it is difficult to accept that they would deploy four divisions to the area if they did not intend to win, especially when troops were so desperately needed elsewhere.

The debate over the meaning of the battle had begun long before it was concluded, probably even before it began. Pegasus had the feel of the cavalry riding to rescue the settlers, a dramatic end to the siege but lacking a sense of decisive victory. It did not seem as though the United States had won so much as had avoided being defeated, which ironically was consistent with the strategic goals President Johnson enunciated in 1965. Yet Khe Sanh illustrated the futility of that approach. The United States sacrificed lives, resources, and its public image to hold a piece of ground useful only to bring on the fight that had just concluded. We won the battle by body count, but in retrospect the effort seemed a waste.

Had Operation Pegasus been more than a simple relief operation, much more could have been achieved. American forces could have made a bold stroke west into Laos, pursuing the wounded enemy, destroying his bases in Laos, disrupting the Ho Chi Minh Trail, and driving the PAVN back into the North. Such an effort, reinforced with fresh troops, would have made the question of victory indisputable. For an Administration that sought to use force as a means of sending signals, it overlooked the messages sent by failing to act decisively. Failure to seize the initiative, to not only win but also behave like a winner, threw the question of victory into the realm of speculation and debate. It allowed those who wanted to define Khe Sanh as a setback, and who already had been doing so for weeks, to hold their ground. There was nothing the Administration could point to that would prove them wrong.

On May 23 Secretary of the Navy Paul R. Ignatius presented Colonel Lownds with a Presidential Unit citation for the 26th Marines for their defense of Khe Sanh; Lownds was awarded the Navy Cross. Lownds said that he was satisfied with the outcome of the battle but added, "If I had my druthers I'd rather be out attacking."[34] At the same ceremony Marine Captain George Christmas was awarded the Navy Cross for his actions at the battle of Hue. Christmas was Lownds's son-in-law.

Khe Sanh's final chapter was written that summer. On June 10, 1968, General Creighton Abrams succeeded Westmoreland as head of MACV, and one of his first acts was to order Khe Sanh abandoned. The base was not going to be used for the strategic purposes Westmoreland had earlier envisaged; thus it was thought a drain on manpower. Abrams had a different vision for the war in Vietnam, relying more on South Vietnamese forces and tactics similar to the Marines' CAP program, which would ultimately prove highly successful in driving the Communists out of the villages.[35] Although leaving Khe Sanh may have made sense in logistical terms, it was a killing blow to the legacy of the battle. One reporter commented, "One of the hardest things for the U.S. command to explain now is why, if Khe Sanh is unnecessary in June, it was so vital in January when the siege began."[36] Journalists and commentators unearthed quotes from military and civilian leaders from earlier in the year discussing Khe Sanh's importance and indispensability. When the order came to leave Khe Sanh, the impression it left was that the entire battle had been a waste of time, a miscalculation, or plain stupidity.

Khe Sanh was dismantled starting June 20. On July 6 troops blew up the last two bunkers and withdrew under harassing sniper and mortar fire. On July 9 the NLF's National Liberation Radio announced that the "flag of the national liberation forces fluttered on the many hills and on Khe Sanh airstrip," claiming that the Viet Cong had taken the position, consistent with the fiction that the war in the South was a VC affair.[37] For the first five days after the American withdrawal North Vietnamese radio devoted 70% of its broadcast time in every Asian language to publicize America's "defeat" at Khe Sanh. They called it "proof of the inability of the United States to win the war." And in the end there was no escape from the analogy; Hanoi said that the defeat at Khe Sanh "spells doom for the American aggressors as Dien Bien Phu spelled doom for the French,"[38]

XIV.

THE WALTER CRONKITE MOMENT

The press is widely blamed—or credited—for the United States defeat in the Vietnam War. The case has been made both by those who believe that biased news organizations purposefully brought down the U.S. effort and by those who feel that reporters were able to cut through government secrets and deceptions to bring Americans the truth about the conflict. Neither case is definitive. But both analyses cite the Tet Offensive as the point at which the press went over to the other side and the public followed. North Vietnamese Colonel Bui Tin states the thesis explicitly: "Thanks to the media," he wrote, "which exaggerated the damage caused

Whose side are you on?

—SECRETARY OF STATE DEAN RUSK

by [the Tet] offensive, the American public was bedazzled, and under strong pressure the U.S. administration had to agree to negotiations in Paris."[1] In the Tet narrative the symbol of that switch is the "Walter Cronkite Moment."

If it can be isolated to a literal moment, it was when Cronkite seemingly spontaneously broke character on camera when the first reports of attacks were coming in and blurted out, "What the hell is going on? I thought we were winning this war." But the "moment" was actually a month of reporting, culminating with his February 27, 1968, hour-long special, "A Report from Vietnam," in which he called for a negotiated settlement and an end to the war. It was in response to this special that Lyndon Johnson allegedly said, "If I've lost Cronkite I've lost middle America."

The power that has been attributed to that moment has become legendary—the honest newsman as a bellwether of a nation, inducing despair in a President who understands that he has finally reached the end of the road.

It is no wonder that war critics have searched for another Walter Cronkite Moment. The search has been a staple of the Iraq war. The moment was invoked as early as July 2003, when Rupert Cornwell of the British *Independent* wrote that "Iraq has not had—and may never have—its 'Walter Cronkite moment,' when a modern day successor of the legendary CBS news anchor travels to Iraq to inspect the situation, as Mr. Cronkite did in Vietnam, and pronounces the war unwinnable."[2] But the war was just beginning in 2003, and the moment had yet to be declared. In June 2004, after a spate of insurgent attacks on Iraqi cities, former CIA analyst and antiwar activist Ray McGovern said, "It reminds me of Vietnam. And I don't know how many of your viewers would remember Vietnam. But there was a Tet Offensive that was in January and February of '68, and it turned the tide. It was the tipping point is what we would say today. And it—there was a Walter Cronkite moment when Walter Cronkite said the administration has been saying we've been making great progress and look what's happened."[3]

An August 2005 *Seattle Post-Intelligencer* article on antiwar activist Cindy Sheehan noted that "in Seattle, P-I readers, peace activists and callers to KUOW's 'Weekday' program have been saying lately that another Walter Cronkite moment is what's needed to tip an already tilting nation toward demanding an immediate withdrawal. Someone of fame and stature. Someone formerly neutral or even supportive of the invasion must speak out the way the father figure anchorman did in a watershed way during Vietnam. But, instead of someone famous, is it crazy to think that, this time, the grieving nobody mom of a young soldier killed in Iraq a little more than a year ago could be the catalyst?"[4] But Cindy Sheehan lacked the credentials to be the next Walter Cronkite. For the analogy to make sense, the invocation of doom had to come from a respected public figure, preferably someone who had favored the war at its outset. A Walter Cronkite Moment was declared when conservative godfather William F. Buckley expressed doubts about the course of the war in February 2006. Declarations also followed for conservative cable television personality Bill O'Reilly, former Secretary of State Henry Kissinger, and economist Thomas Friedman. The expression was deployed whenever anyone voiced a doubt who had not done so previously.

Michael Wolff, writing in *Vanity Fair,* gave a fawning nod to Bob Woodward, "the nation's most famous journalist—a wooden and sanctimonious television presence, as well as an author of books and a reporter for *The Washington Post*—is a reasonable equivalent of Cronkite. If he's going in another direction, the world has changed. He's the power barometer. And broker. If he's no longer sucking up to you, you better get out of town in a hurry."[5]

The "quest for the moment" became absurd at times. In 2006 MSNBC personality Keith Olbermann waxed rhapsodic on the decision by NBC News to refer to the war in Iraq as a civil war:

> It is civil war in Iraq, not says the State Department, not says the Iraqi government, but after long and painful consideration, it meets the technical standards for civil war, and we must call it that, says NBC News. Is this the Walter Cronkite moment of the Iraq War?[6]

The answer was clearly no. The "moment" could not be forced by Olbermann's self-conscious declaration. Don Imus, who also broadcast on MSNBC, called the news executives "nitwits" for trying to manufacture a Walter Cronkite Moment.[7] Fox News's Sean Hannity said, "They think that they're Walter Cronkite and they want to have an impact here. But they've never given the American public the story about all the success in Iraq."[8] In other words, Keith Olbermann, you're no Walter Cronkite. Contrast Olbermann with Katie Couric, who occupied Cronkite's anchor seat after Dan Rather. In 2007 she told Martin Kalb that she was not looking for a "Walter Cronkite moment" during a tour of Syria and Iraq. "Is it my job to go to Iraq and say this war is terrible and we should pull out?" she said. "I don't think that's the case."[9]

THE MEDIA AND THE MILITARY

The Vietnam War and the Cronkite legend inculcated a strong distrust of the media in the military establishment. The sentiment is that if the press can lose America's wars, it is something to be dealt with warily, if at all. But what comes across as bias is often the product of structural and unavoidable aspects of reporting. The primary role of the press is to expose and publicize information, while the military norm, based on the need for operational security, is to withhold and control information. General William T. Sherman stated this explicitly when he ejected Florus Plympton of the Cincinnati *Commercial* from his command in 1862. When the reporter protested that he had come only to learn the truth, Sherman replied, "We don't want the truth told about things here. We don't want the enemy any better informed than he is."[10]

For their part, journalists consider themselves watchdogs of the government, the presumptive "fourth estate," a necessary check on government power. This view lends a natural adversarial quality to reporting on the government. There is a working assumption that the government has something to hide and that every public statement emanating from official sources should not be taken at face value. Members of the military, on the other hand, have sworn an oath to defend the Constitution of the United

States and are instruments of government power. So while the journalistic ethic is one of "question authority," the military equivalent is "salute smartly."

There are also distinct differences in social class, education, and income between journalists and troops. They generally have different backgrounds and belief systems. They live fundamentally different lives, especially in the field. Robert Capa, the famed war photographer, summed it up: "I would say that the war correspondent gets more drinks, more girls, better pay and greater freedom than the soldier."[11] The two groups also have different perspectives on trust. A reporter is skeptical, probing, seeking to tease out information that the subject may not want known, and will say whatever he needs to say to get the scoop. But troops have to be able to trust one another instantly; it is vital to the conduct of operations. Hence the military expression "hand-con," knowing with a handshake that things are going to get done and that everyone is on the same team.

Journalists hold sacred the notion that their work is objective, which at the very least means that the reporter will attempt to report a story from a variety of points of view. In theory, the reporter does not take sides. Members of the military, on the other hand, are not objective- but mission-oriented and know what side they are on. The beliefs, attitudes, and feelings of the enemy are unimportant except to the extent they pertain to defeating him. The frustration that members of the military feel with press objectivity was summed up by CINCPAC Admiral Harry Felt in late 1962, when he was introduced to AP chief correspondent for Indochina Malcolm W. Browne. "So you're Browne," the Admiral said. "Why don't you get on the team?"[12]

The press fealty to the concept of objectivity can be taken to extremes that mystify members of the military. At an October 31, 1987, roundtable discussion of military ethics at Harvard University, moderator Professor Charles Ogletree, Jr., asked ABC News anchor Peter Jennings and Mike Wallace of CBS's "60 Minutes" if they would warn U.S. troops about to be ambushed by the enemy in a hypothetical war between the U.S. and "North Kosan." Jennings originally responded, "If I was with a North Kosanese unit that came upon Americans, I think I personally would do what I could to warn the Americans." But Wallace clucked that he and other reporters would "regard it simply as another story that they are there to cover," and stated, "I'm a little bit of a loss to understand why, because you are an American, you would not have covered that story."[13]

"Don't you have a higher duty as an American citizen," Ogletree asked, "to do all you can to save the lives of soldiers rather than this journalistic ethic of reporting fact?"

"No," Wallace responded, "you don't have higher duty . . . you're a reporter."

"I think he's right too," Jennings said. "I chickened out." When challenged by National Security Adviser Brent Scowcroft that "you're Americans first, and you're journalists second," Wallace asked, "What in the world is wrong with photographing this attack by North Kosanese on American soldiers?" General William Westmoreland, also on the panel, observed flatly that "it would be repugnant to the American listening public to see on film an ambush of an American platoon by our national enemy." Marine Colonel George Connell expressed "utter contempt" for the senior journalists:

> Two days later they're both walking off my hilltop, they're two hundred yards away and they get ambushed. And they're lying there wounded. And they're going to expect I'm going to send Marines up there to get them. They're just journalists, they're not Americans. . . . But I'll do it. And that's what makes me so contemptuous of them. And Marines will die, going to get a couple of journalists.[14]

In October 2001 Loren Jenkins, senior foreign editor of National Public Radio, who had been on one of the last helicopters out of the Saigon embassy compound before it was seized by the North Vietnamese in 1975, stated that his reporters were seeking and would report on American troops engaging in covert operations to find the whereabouts of Osama bin Laden.

In response to critics of this potential breach of security, Jenkins stated, "I don't represent the government. I represent history, information, what happened." He dismissed those who objected by saying, "They all blame the press for losing the war in Vietnam," a fairly simplistic analysis on his part, which has the benefit of being true. Similar attitudes are common in the cohort of the press corps that came of age during the Vietnam era, and they are reflected in the attitudes of many members of the military, who at times consider reporters akin to traitors. John Hart of CBS News took reportorial "objectivity" to new heights when he asserted that the Vietnam conflict was actually just a private affair of one branch of government that the press was misreporting as a "war":

> We, as a matter of course, refer to the North Vietnamese and
> the Communist guerrillas in South Vietnam as "the enemy"
> when they are in fact the enemy of the Saigon government
> and the American executive branch. The Congress of the
> United States has not declared war on North Vietnam, but we
> do. Millions of Americans do not consider the North Viet-
> namese *their* enemies, but we presume to speak for them
> [emphasis in original].[15]

But the relationship between the press and the military need not always be adversarial. Frederick Remington traveled extensively with military units, including the 10th Cavalry on the Geronimo campaign, and he recorded the late 19th century military experience in words, drawings, and paintings. James Creelman of the *New York Journal* advanced with U.S. troops on a Spanish blockhouse at the 1898 battle of El Caney in Cuba, and was wounded by enemy gunfire. Edward R. Murrow became famous with his dramatic coverage of the London Blitz in 1940 and later accompanied bomber crews on missions against Germany. And Ernie Pyle was a legendary and beloved World War Two journalist who lived with the soldiers he covered and, on the island of Ie Shima off Okinawa, died with them.

Joe Galloway flew into the Ia Drang Valley with the 1st Cavalry Division and risked his life along with the rest of the command. He believed a closer relationship between the military and the press can be beneficial for both. "I am here to argue for more openness, more contact, more freedom between your profession and mine," he said at an appearance at the U.S. Air Force's Air War College in 1996. "In this one instance I believe familiarity would breed not contempt but trust and respect." He recommended embedding reporters with troops and stated that "the experience of war will create bonds between them that cannot be broken; the young reporters will learn to love the soldiers and airmen just as you and your lieutenants have learned; and in the end 99% of the coverage that flows from this experience will be entirely positive."[16]

There is a significant difference between a Washington-based "national security correspondent" and a war reporter. Journalists who have spent their career on the Pentagon beat may have no idea what war entails, and some failed to see the humor when at the outbreak of the Gulf War a sign appeared in the DOD press room reading "Welcome temporary war experts." The practice of embedding reporters with units going to war in Iraq was devised as a useful way of giving reporters the necessary perspective to convey the reality of war, something that was previously outside the experience of most of them.

But critics of embedding and building trust between the two camps see the practice as a threat to the norm of objectivity. Reporter Jonathan Alter called embedding "subtly coercive," since it engenders loyalty between the reporter and the soldiers he is covering.[17] It introduces the paradox that those closest to the action and thus best informed will lack "objectivity" to report on it; that those who have lived an event are less qualified than outsiders to comment on it. It devalues the respect and admiration that a reporter might feel for American fighting forces once he has shared their hardships and seen them in action. These feelings could be more objective based on experience than the theoretical objectivity that casts both the United States and its enemies as morally equivalent. In short, a reporter in pursuit of the abstract norm of objectivity is less objective than those who are able to test their perspectives against experience. Reality informs the human condition more reliably than theory. One seldom hears negatives about Ernie Pyle.

MEDIA IN VIETNAM

An observer of the Vietnam War told Sir Philip Goodhart in the summer of 1967 "The Viet Cong can't beat us, but the *New York Times* and CBS Television can." The idea that the press would be decisive in deciding the conflict was current long before Tet.

During the Vietnam War reporters had a great deal of access to the front lines, and there were few restrictions on what, when, and how journalists would cover stories. Press agencies worked independently of the government and filed uncensored stories directly to their bureaus. It was the most unrestrained press environment since the Spanish American War. Criticism of war news being based on press releases and the canned briefings ridiculed as the "Five O'clock Follies" overlooks the fact that journalists were not restricted to official sources and frequently developed stories with a great deal of military assistance. "We had remarkable access to both the military and civilian folk," Peter Braestrup said, "particularly if you worked for a major news organization, remarkable access to senior officials, to junior officials in Saigon. If you wanted to work hard, you could find out a lot."[19]

Colonel Harry Summers has noted that much of the reporting from Vietnam was not particularly biased, and the reporters got a lot of it right. Barry Zorthian, former Marine and the top press spokesman at the U.S. embassy in Vietnam from 1964 to 1968, said that "most complaints about the press in Vietnam were misdirected. Only tactical military information was really censored by the U.S., and that never was a problem. I was there for four years, and I dealt with 2,000 journalists, and there was only one outright case of a journalist leaking tactical military information."[20] One analysis noted that the most conspicuous fact about the bulk of everyday Vietnam War reporting was its sameness. "For all the 'news' broadcast from 1965 to 1972 about the war," it concluded, "nothing of substance had changed. The same names on the same maps were being fought over. The same statistical measures were being cited. . . . The stories had fallen into a form letter."[21]

Reporters had to deal with the unconventional nature of the Vietnam War. Counterinsurgencies do not have the same sweeping troop movements and set-piece battles that define conventional wars. In conventional war, victory is achieved by dramatic events, such as defeating the enemy's forces, seizing its territory, and occupying its capital. In counterinsurgencies, victory—if the term is used at all—is defined in terms of promoting stability, reconstruction, training security forces, and other long-term pursuits that fundamentally lack drama. In these wars good news is seldom reported, because it does not attract readers. In essence it is not "news" as reporters define the term. The same could be said of coverage of Iraq, Afghanistan, or any other such conflict. Most of the good work done by coalition forces in education, medicine, construction, and other areas does not draw the attention of the national media because it lacks the dramatic value that makes something a news story. The truism "If it bleeds, it leads" still holds.

Technology also played a role in promoting drama. Vietnam was the "Living Room War," the first American conflict widely covered by television.[22] A fall 1969 survey showed that on a given weeknight under a quarter of Americans watched an evening newscast. Audience averages as of January 1967 were 17 million for NBC, 14 million for CBS, and 6 million for ABC.[23] The speed with which images of war could reach the country was unprecedented. Furthermore, unlike the Second World War, the government did not edit the footage. This task was left to network editors, who imposed some self-censorship, as we saw with NBC's reluctance to air the entire film of General Loan shooting Bay Lop. Generally speaking, the bloodiest and most gruesome scenes of devastation did not make the news. Despite the shock value of some of the footage aired, the American people were spared the full horror of war.

The impact of television had more to do with the nature of the medium. Images conveyed drama without context, and could be misleading. "The picture of a few flaming Saigon houses, presented by a gloomy-voiced telecaster as an instance of the destruction, caused in the capital," General Maxwell Taylor said, "created the inevitable impression that this was the way it was in all or most of Saigon. This human tendency to generalize from a single fact to a universal conclusion has always been a prime cause of the distorted views regarding Vietnam and certainly contributed to the pessimism in the United States after the Tet offensive in 1968."[24]

"TV was always worse," Peter Braestrup said. "The emotive demands of the medium and the commercial demands of holding an audience just worked against calm, dispassionate reporting. I shared a house in Saigon with Murray Fromson of CBS, a very able guy who'd been in *Stars and Stripes* in Korea, and a print guy originally. He was an old Asia hand. But his experience didn't matter a bit, all they wanted was good dramatic film and a good dramatic voice-over. He was even told he was not good on camera because his eye sockets were too deep and caused shadows. There were very few television guys who qualified, in my book, as serious journalists. There were a few, but damn few. It was show business."[25]

One of the earliest media controversies in Vietnam arose after a 1965 report by Morley Safer showing Marines igniting peasant huts with cigarette lighters. Visual media sought drama, and footage of a village on fire, or even a few burning huts, made the evening news more readily than the peaceful pro-regime village down the road. During Tet, television could show the guerrilla with an AK-47 darting down an alley but could not convey the failure of the VC to foment a mass uprising on which the guerrilla's success depended. Furthermore, the fact that enemy units conducted most of their operations at night while the U.S. made sweeps in the daytime limited coverage of the enemy to reporting on the aftermath of its attacks.

Political bias also sometimes played a role. John Roche described the difficulties of representing the Administration's policies on American television. "Just before going on the air, staffers would ask me how anyone can support an immoral war. On one news program I felt like a nun in a whorehouse. The producer was using a picture of Johnson for a dartboard. The whole atmosphere was of contempt for me and the views I accept."[26] But bias was introduced more frequently at the editorial level, through choices of which stories ran and how they were edited. Roche noted that a journalist friend of his used to file stories with "contrapuntal paragraphs: the first would set out U.S. strengths, the second our failures, and so on. When his stories appeared, alternate paragraphs were omitted; guess which ones."[27]

Peter Braestrup's *The Big Story* (1977) is the definitive study of press failings in coverage of the Tet Offensive.[28] Braestrup was a former Marine lieutenant who had been seriously wounded in the Korean War. He covered the Algerian revolution and the Vietnam conflict for the *New York Times* and in 1968 became Saigon bureau chief for the *Washington Post*. Braestrup spent six years studying every aspect of press performance during Tet. His thesis was that early in the coverage of Tet the press adopted a story line, "Disaster in Vietnam!" and held onto it through March 1968. He concluded that "the generalized effect of the news media's contemporary output in February-March 1968 was a distortion of reality—through sins of omission and commission—on a scale that helped shape Tet's political repercussions in Washington and the Administration's response." He rejected the "ideological" explanation for this failing, focusing instead on the structural aspects of news coverage that sought to promote drama, as well as the basic manpower limitations of news outlets, which could not cope with such a large-scale story. He also cited Lyndon Johnson's ambivalence about taking a definitive stand during the Tet crisis, noting that in general news managers look to the President "to define the new situation, at least initially, and to provide a coherent response to it." Johnson's failure to do this created a crisis for editors and producers, who are "ill-equipped psychologically to tolerate lingering uncertainty or ambiguity. They need a clear story line, an agenda, a framework, a plausible answer to that recurrent journalistic question: 'What next?'" Johnson's lack of response allowed his domestic opponents to insert their own story lines, and it also fed the natural impulse of journalists, especially on television, to yield to "a penchant for drama, controversy, and worst-case speculation."[29]

Tet was a watershed in the content of television coverage. Editorial comments on televised newscasts were rare, but they shifted markedly during and after Tet. Before Tet, 78.6% of editorial comments were positive toward the conduct of the war, and 21.4% were negative. After Tet, only 28.8% were positive, and 71.3% were negative. During Tet they were 100.0% negative. With respect to people quoted in television news coverage, critics of Administration policy were quoted in stories about the Vietnam War 4.5% of the time pre-Tet and 26.1% afterward. American officers and troops had been quoted 49.1% of the time pre-Tet, but this fell to 17.3% after. This shift is due largely to the fact that coverage of the peace movement increased markedly after Tet, and particularly after the 1968 New Hampshire primary, when opposition to the war became "not only a respectable but an obligatory subject for news coverage."[30]

The television anchors were not uniform in their views of the war. NBC's David Brinkley, who served in the Army until 1943 and was afterward the first White House correspondent for NBC News, considered the Vietnam War "an atrocity" and was certain that his opinion came across in the way he read the news, if not in its content. His partner, Chet Huntley, was more supportive of the Administration and somewhat more open about it, although neither man ever made his views explicit on the air. Brinkley once asked President Johnson why he didn't just give up on Vietnam and "save American lives that were being needlessly lost." Johnson replied that he was "not going to be the first American president to lose a war."[31]

ABC's Howard K. Smith, a war correspondent in World War II and former "Murrow Boy" at CBS, was known to be an off-camera hawk. His son Jack Smith, later an Emmy award-winning correspondent, also at ABC News, was an Army Spec 5 who fought at Ia Drang. Wounded when his company was overrun, with 93% casualties, he had to play dead. The PAVN used him as a sandbag for a machine gun emplacement and he was later nicknamed "Sandbag" Smith. His father was in Vietnam at the time and interviewed him as he was being evacuated. Jack related vivid scenes of North Vietnamese troops systematically seeking out wounded Americans on the battlefield, turning them over and shooting them. ABC later produced a special based on the story called "A Father, a Son and War." Later in the war Smith said, "The networks have never given a complete picture of the war." With respect to Khe Sanh, Americans were never told about the bravery of South Vietnamese fighting by America's side, or that the "Viet Cong's casualties were 100 times ours. We just showed pictures day after day of Americans getting the hell kicked out of them. That was enough to tear America apart."[32]

Walter Cronkite's "moment" was noteworthy because he seemed to switch sides, from being something of a supporter of the war to being a skeptic. Cronkite began his career as a UPI wire reporter, a punishing job, but one that gave him the opportunity to volunteer for combat reporting in World War II. After the war he got into TV, and his big break was as the standout talent covering the 1952 Party conventions. CBS News producer Don Hewitt coined the term "anchorman" to describe Cronkite during the 1952 Democratic convention, based on a relay-race analogy. In the mid-1950s Cronkite hosted the "You Are There" series, in which historical events were recreated as breaking-news stories.[33] Several episodes of the series were directed by Sidney Lumet, who said that Cronkite "seemed to me incorruptible, in a profession that was easily corrupted."[34]

Cronkite's stint as full-time news anchor came in 1962, when he succeeded the now forgotten Douglas Edwards, who had read CBS news since 1948. In 1963 Cronkite emotionally broke the news of the death of President Kennedy. William F. Buckley said that the gesture where Cronkite took off and put on his glasses to read the clock was the "consummation of an entire new age . . . there was a lot of poetry in it."[35] Cronkite was also a fervent booster of the space program; he described Alan Shepard's first U.S. manned space flight as a "Free World victory."

Cronkite was not the number one watched anchor at the time of Tet. His broadcast was second in the ratings behind NBC News through most of the war. But he was well liked by his peers and Americans generally. Dan Rather said in 1972 that "television, above all other mediums, gives you the quality of the man. . . . Take a look at Walter Cronkite, who I think the record will show has the highest believability quotient in the country." This opinion was borne out in a 1972 survey by *Broadcasting* magazine of personalities in media and politics. Rather also noted that "it simply is not true that it takes a slick Hollywood guy" to come across as credible on television. "If it did, Ronald Reagan would be President."[36]

Cronkite was more willing than others to couch events in Cold War terms, and he described the enemy in Vietnam as "Communists" more than any other newsman.[37] "While most of us knew little about Ho Chi Minh or the nature of his North Vietnamese government, we did realize that it was Communist," he wrote in his memoir, "and our interest, our policy since World War II and our young President's pledge all agreed that we would defend democracy wherever the Red menace threatened."[38] Cronkite went to Vietnam early in the conflict and flew on air missions, as he had in the Second World War, including a helicopter mission with the 173rd Airborne Brigade. In an August 27, 1965, on-air commentary he expressed skepticism that the United States should seek negotiations with the North Vietnamese or Viet Cong. He noted that recognition of the NLF as a legitimate political force would be "tantamount to an American defeat. The purpose of the American commitment is to demonstrate in Vietnam to the Communists everywhere, in this first showdown test, that the United States will not let them shoot their way into free governments."[39]

Cronkite returned to Vietnam in the latter stages of Tet and filed a number of reports from the scene. He had proposed to CBS News president, Dick Salant, that he "try to present an assessment of the situation as one who had not previously taken a public position on the war."[40] He had the advantage of being acquainted with General Abrams, whom he had met during the Ardennes Offensive in 1944, when Abrams was one of General Patton's most acclaimed battalion commanders. This connection gave Cronkite virtually unlimited access. He saw fighting in Saigon and toured the ruins of Cholon. He began to editorialize by way of analysis on February 14, 1968, when he stated that the enemy had been defeated militarily but not politically and that the "real meaning" of the Tet Offensive was that the South Vietnamese government had lost its credibility and must negotiate for peace.

Five days later Cronkite trucked into Hue as the house-to-house fighting continued. He said on the air that the fighting reminded "this World War Two correspondent of the battle for Bastogne."[41] While he was in Hue, an increase in the number of ambushes closed the land route into the city, and Cronkite flew out in a chopper carrying 12 body bags of Marines killed in action. Cronkite then spent an evening with General Abrams and his staff at his headquarters at Phu Bai, discussing the Tet Offensive and Abrams's view that with a few more reinforcements they could "finish the job." Cronkite listened but did not agree. "My decision was not difficult to reach," he wrote years later:

> It had been taking shape, I realized, since Cam Ranh Bay.
> There was no way that this war could be justified any longer—
> a war whose purpose had never been adequately explained to
> the American people, to a people whose conscience burned
> because of the terribly, the fatally unequal sacrifice of the
> troops and the home front.[42]

On February 27, 1968, CBS aired Cronkite's hour-long special, "A Report from Vietnam," which he later described as his "proudest moment." The special told the story of the Tet Offensive, using stories that had run on CBS News and new footage from Cronkite's trip. It included interviews with Westmoreland, Thieu, and Ky. The special showed Cronkite's tour of Hue, which he described as "obviously a setback." He asserted that because of Tet the nature of the war had changed. It would no longer be a guerrilla struggle but one featuring "large armies locked in combat moving towards decision on the battlefield."

In his concluding monologue Cronkite gave what he said was a "speculative, personal, subjective," analysis. "It seems now more certain than ever that the bloody experience of Vietnam is to end in a stalemate," he said. The Tet Offensive was a draw. The contest near the DMZ was a deadlock. The Saigon government would hold on but with no legitimacy. "This summer's almost certain standoff will either end in real give-and-take negotiations or terrible escalation," he said, "and for every means we have to escalate, the enemy can match us, and that applies to invasion of the North, the use of nuclear weapons, or the mere commitment of one hundred, or two hundred, or three hundred thousand more American troops to the battle. And with each escalation, the world comes closer to the brink of cosmic disaster.

"To say that we are closer to victory today," he continued, "is to believe, in the face of the evidence, the optimists who have been wrong in the past. To suggest we are on the edge of defeat is to yield to unreasonable pessimism. To say that we are mired in stalemate seems the only realistic, yet unsatisfactory, conclusion. On the off chance that military and political analysts are right, in the next few months we must test the enemy's intentions, in case this is indeed his last big gasp before negotiations. But it is increasingly clear to this reporter that the only rational way out then will be to negotiate, not as victors, but as an honorable people who lived up to their pledge to defend democracy, and did the best they could."

In retrospect, Cronkite's analysis was significantly flawed. The future was not one of land armies moving toward decision on the battlefield, and if it had been it would have been the kind of warfare at which the United States excelled. As the 1972 Easter Offensive demonstrated, even the much-maligned South Vietnamese forces could defeat a major North Vietnamese invasion, given adequate U.S. air and materiel support. The enemy did not have escalation parity with the United States, and the Johnson Administration had avoided large-scale escalatory moves. And ironically Johnson did not have to be told to seek negotiations; he had been pleading for peace talks since 1965. It was the North Vietnamese who were preventing them. But with this special Cronkite came out squarely against Johnson's war policies and the Vietnam War generally. His performance was so impressive that after the Tet special Robert Kennedy tried to enlist him to run for the Senate in New York.[43]

Bernard Kalb of CBS also voiced pessimism about the war. NBC News declared Vietnam a lost cause during a special one-hour broadcast March 10, 1968. Respected commentator Frank McGee delivered this verdict "as a conclusion to be drawn inescapably from the facts of the success of the January offensive of the North Vietnamese and the National Liberation Front . . . .The war, as the administration has defined it, is being lost." Both NBC and CBS maintained that such commentary was not editorializing but "reportorial candor." Jack Gould wrote in the *New York Times* that "if the mass media continue to raise doubts about national objectives and military strategy, it is believed in television circles that the home screen could be a new and unpredictable factor in influencing critical decisions, not only in Saigon but also in domestic Presidential politics."[44]

It is said that after watching Cronkite's documentary President Johnson said to his aides, "If I've lost Cronkite, I've lost Middle America."[45] Five weeks later Johnson decided not to run for reelection based on this belief. So the legend goes. This is the Holy Grail for a reporter, that a documentary, newscast, article, picture, or other product shapes history on a grand scale. This is also why Tet is an inspiration to America's enemies and has become a staple for critics of the use of force abroad by the United States. Raising the specter of Tet is a way for enemies to seek victory on the cheap.

But did Johnson lose Middle America? Did sensationalistic or misleading press coverage turn the country against the President and against the war? In a word, no.

Tet was not a definitive public turning point against the war, and the media's influence was less than generally believed. As noted in Chapter 3, "The War and Public Opinion," support for President Johnson's conduct of the war had collapsed much earlier; it bottomed out in the summer of 1967. The August 28, 1967, Gallup poll showed 60% disapproval of Johnson's war policies and a mere 27% approval, the lowest Gallup approval rating for his entire term of office. This approval low point was one of the reasons the Administration launched the "Good News" campaign in the fall of 1967, and even this effort raised public approval only to around 40% by November, where it flatlined until Tet. This was not a remarkable vote of confidence, and since Johnson did not go into the battle with broad public support, he could not lose what he did not have to begin with.

More important, the American people's response to Tet was not defeatist. In fact, the Tet attacks made the country more belligerent. A Harris survey taken February 3–4 showed that 61% of the public believed the Tet Offensive justified continued bombing of the North, compared to 15% that didn't. By 48% to 29% the public believed the Tet attacks were useful because they brought the enemy out into the open, where they could be engaged, which if nothing else demonstrated that the public had a better grasp of the basic problem of counterinsurgency warfare than much of the press. And 43% believed allied forces would win the battle, as opposed to 3% who felt the enemy would win.[46]

A Gallup poll released February 6 showed similar results. According to this survey, 69% wanted to continue the bombing campaign in the North, up from 63% in October 1967. The number calling for a bombing halt dropped from 27% to 16%. The poll also showed that the Tet attacks had made America more hawkish: the percentage self-identifying as "hawks" climbed from 52% in December 1967 to 56% in early January 1968 to 60% in the week after the start of Tet. The respective percentage of doves dropped from 35% to 28% to 23%. The only decline in public opinion in the first week of Tet was recorded in Gallup's reporting that Johnson's approval rating in handling the war had dropped slightly, from an already low 39% to 35%, which was still above the August 1967 low point of 27%.[47] And it is reasonable to assume that the decline had less to do with more people wanting to pull out of Vietnam, since the number of "doves" had been dropping since December, than it did with the increase in the number wanting to escalate the war.

On February 18, 1968, the New York Times illustrated the increasing public bellicosity with a graphic entitled "Johnson and the Hawks," showing side by side line graphs of Gallup poll numbers from December, with the "Hawks" line tilting upward and Johnson's war conduct line bending downward. The Times did not offer an analysis of the data other than to say that the hawks "evidently do not regard President Johnson as one of them."[48] Indeed, they never had. But it was a clear illustration of the true dynamic of public opinion, which demanded more action from the President than he was willing to give. A majority-hawkish country dropped support for Johnson not because it was discouraged that the enemy was winning but because it wanted him to strike back hard. Tet did not generate a sense of defeatism but of frustration with a government that refused to act decisively.

A Gallup poll released February 27 showed another slight drop in Johnson's war approval rating, down three points to 32%, with 57% disapproving. Hawkishness dropped a within-error two points to 58%, with dovishness increasing by the same number to 26%, although the number of doves was still two points below the 28% of Americans who thought the U.S. should "win a military victory in Vietnam using atom bombs." Thus three weeks into the Tet Offensive the percentage of doves in the country was less than half the number of hawks, and even lower than the percentage of "nuclear hawks," which destroys the argument that Tet generated a sense of defeatism.

But this poll also showed a measure of frustration. When asked how the war was going, 21% said the U.S. and its allies were losing, up from only 8% on November 21, 1967. This was a significant jump, though below the 27% who believed the U.S. was losing on August 18, 1966. The number thinking the war effort was standing still rose from 33% to 42%, and the number thinking the U.S. was making progress dropped from 51% to 31%. This was a significant decline, and, coupled with the sustained rate of hawkishness in the population, it signaled that President Johnson still retained a window of opportunity to act decisively to end the war with a win, but the window was about to close.

The day after the Gallup poll numbers were published John Roche wrote a personal memo to President Johnson, arguing that the best justification for remaining in Vietnam was presenting to the American people a combination of substance and success. "I may have a peculiar reading of the American character," he wrote, "but for what it is worth I think that you . . . might keep in mind

LBJ on media on casualties

the historical fact that Americans really don't give a damn about treaties, congressional resolutions, and other legalisms. . . . By and large, the American tradition assumes that when one is weak on facts, one talks about law. . . . [O]ur task is to convince the American people on *substantive* grounds that our commitment in Southeast Asia is vital to the national interest. Nobody cares about the Tonkin Gulf Resolution and the parade of other legal precedents if he is convinced:

1. That we are *right* in being there.
   and
2. That we are going to *win*."[49]

Roche knew that in the end the American people will rally behind a winning cause and will abandon an effort if the leadership appears unmotivated, confused, incompetent, or lacking focus. But the victory and its pursuit had to be defined in a way that the people could understand. The time had passed when attrition warfare and the pursuit of the "crossover point" adequately defined progress for the American people, whether those goals satisfied the Johnson Administration's strategists or not. In the wake of Tet, Americans wanted the war to be pursued with vigor, or not at all.

LBJ

THE QUESTION OF CASUALTIES

On casualties turn ans off

Another theory is that the public turned against the war around the time of Tet because of the increase in the number of casualties. Americans have become accustomed to wars with low casualty rates; General Petraeus wrote in 1987 that "the military are keenly aware of, and troubled by, the ambiguity in the American desire for what might be termed 'cost-free omnipotence.'"[59]

One problem with this thesis is that the public had highly inaccurate notions of the price being paid in lives during the war. A Gallup poll in December 1965 asking how many men had been killed in Vietnam showed that only 10% gave the correct answer in the range of 2,000–2,499 (the actual number being 2,264 at the

Didn't really know

end of the year); 21% thought the total was higher; 23% thought it was 1,000–2,000; 18% thought it was under 1,000; and 28% had no idea.[51] A survey asking the same question in June 1967 showed only 5% answering in the correct range of 14,050–15,050 (14,125 had been killed by the end of that month); 18% thought more than 15,050 had been killed; 33% thought the number was between 7,051 and 14,050; and a full 44% thought the number was under 7,050, less than half the actual total killed.[52]

In fact, there is no certain relationship between public opinion and casualties. The overall distribution of yearly casualty totals for the Vietnam War is an oddly uniform steeply shaped bell curve that peaked in 1968. But public opinion rose and fell without clear correlation to the casualty figures, which the public greatly underestimated anyway. May 1968 was the bloodiest month of the Vietnam War for the United States, with 2,412 American deaths, and February 1968 was the second worst at 2,255. Yet during this peak period Johnson's approval rating for conduct of the war increased. Another example is that percentages of Americans saying it was a mistake to get involved in Vietnam rose the same percentage between July and October 1967 (41% to 47%) as it did in the much bloodier period from October 1967 to August 1968 (47% to 53%).

In addition to being the bloodiest month, May 1968 was also the halfway point in terms of the overall number of Americans killed in the entire Vietnam War. In other words, slightly more troops died in the years following the Tet Offensive than died in the years leading up to it. The war ground on for seven years after Tet, and while U.S. involvement steadily declined, the United States could not be said to be driven from Vietnam by mounting casualties. Combat and other deaths dropped 96% in President Nixon's first term, most of the decline coming in 1969–1970. By the time Nixon's second term began in 1973, U.S. deaths in Vietnam had dropped to below 200 per year, and South Vietnamese forces were successfully holding their own against the North until the Democratic Congress cut military aid to Saigon in 1974.

A more important measure of the overall public mood is the sense of "buyer's remorse" that develops when wars drag on for years without resolution. Every long-duration limited conflict since the end of World War II has seen persistent erosion of public support on the question of whether the war was worth fighting. This makes sense intuitively; the longer a war continues, the more it costs and the less the original reasons for fighting it seem to matter.

Victory can be defined in limited terms in wars that do not last long, such as Operation Desert Storm in 1991. But in a protracted limited war, public frustration sets in as troops continue to fight and die with no clear progress on the ground. As General Maxwell D. Taylor said of the Korean War, it "illustrated the difficulty of convincing the American people and keeping them convinced for the long pull of the necessity and justification of exposing the lives of a small segment of our manhood for a stake far from home with little visible relation to the national security."[53] The same could be said of the wars in Vietnam, Iraq, and Afghanistan.[54]

Public belief in the value of fighting the Korean conflict dropped slowly but steadily after the first 18 months of war. The same was true of Vietnam. Johnson's war approval ratings rose and fell, but the number of Americans who believed that military intervention in Indochina was a mistake slowly increased. In September 1965, only 24% responded in the affirmative to the statement "the United States made a mistake sending troops to fight in Vietnam." A year later the number was 35%. In October of 1967, 47% regretted the war, and by the first week of April 1968, Gallup reported that 48% said it was a mistake, 40% said it was not a mistake, and 12% had no opinion.[55] These numbers not only illustrate the long-term trend but also show that the Tet Offensive had no particular impact on the buyer's remorse level.

Tracking poll data from the Iraq war shows a similar dynamic. ABC News/*Washington Post* numbers on whether the war is worth fighting showed the American people saying it was worth it from April 2003 (70%) to January 2004 (56%). In the seven months from February to September 2004 there was an interregnum in which the numbers of those who thought the war was worth fighting and those who believed it wasn't oscillated around the 50% mark, with no clear trend either way. This wait-and-see period ended in late September 2004, when the number believing the war was not worth fighting went over 50% and stayed there, remaining in the high 50s to mid 60s through the summer of 2009. Those who thought the war was worth fighting correspondingly sagged into the 40s and 30s.

Data from the Pew Center tracked with the ABC poll. Asked the question whether the decision to use military force in Iraq was right or wrong, the public said it was the right decision from the war's inception (with 72% support) in another uneven decline down to February 2005, when the "right" and "wrong" responses tied at 47%. The interregnum in the Pew data lasted until the summer of 2006, when the lines diverged, and by February 2008 54% believed the use of forces was the wrong decision, compared with 38% who backed it.[56]

The assessment of the value of a war is not affected by opinions about how well the war is going. In June 2007, only 32% of Americans thought the United States was making significant progress toward restoring civil order in Iraq, while 64% did not. After the successful implementation of the surge counterinsurgency strategy, the numbers reversed, with 61% believing progress was being made and 34% thinking otherwise as of July 2009. But the "not worth it" number barely budged; it stood at 61% at the beginning of the surge and was at 62% two years later. Similarly, in August 2009 President Obama's Afghanistan policies were rated positively by 60% of the population, even though 51% of Americans had concluded the war was not worth fighting. And although the American public's sense of the value of the wars in Korea, Vietnam, Iraq, and Afghanistan followed similar curves, the four conflicts came to different outcomes. In Korea, an armistice was reached after a change in the American Administration and President Eisenhower's veiled threat to use nuclear weapons. In Vietnam, the U.S. suffered a defeat after abandoning its ally. In Iraq, the U.S. has so far achieved an apparent victory because President Bush, though weakened politically, stayed the course and President Obama did not abruptly abandon the war effort even though he opposed President Bush's Iraq war policies. The matter of Afghanistan has yet to be decided.

In sum, although the media did misrepresent key aspects of the Tet Offensive, its influence on public opinion was much less than has been assumed. And the public itself was not driven to despair by Tet but felt ready to strike back by escalating the conflict and taking the war to the North. This decision, however, required decisive leadership, and as the weeks dragged on it became clear that Johnson was not up to the task. "It was 'rally round the tribal chief,'" Peter Braestrup said. "The press was saying all was lost. But the tribal chief did nothing."[57] Presidential historian Theodore White wrote that at that point "the facts were less important than the psychology, and the psychology left the enemy in command. Of their 'psychological victory,' Mr. Johnson was to be the chief victim within two months."[58]

Lyndon Johnson had not lost Middle America. Middle America lost Lyndon Johnson.

XV.

JOHNSON SURRENDERS

On Sunday evening, March 31, President Johnson made a televised address to the nation. He seemed weary on camera. One writer observed years later that Johnson "gazed into the television camera, looking as though he were tired of wearing his own head."[1] In his lengthy speech he reviewed the course of the Tet Offensive, repeating the key talking points of the preceding months and reiterating the Communists' failure. Next he offered a deal to Hanoi, that the United States would cease its bombing campaign against the North if the government would agree to start peace talks. Then Johnson made the biggest surprise move of the war. He

I've never been so heartsick in my life as I was that night.

—JOHN P. ROCHE, SPECIAL ADVISER TO LYNDON JOHNSON

announced that because of the divisiveness in the United States over Vietnam he would not seek the Democratic nomination for President.

Johnson's announcement was the first political surprise of a dramatic week. On April 2 Eugene McCarthy won the Wisconsin primary with 56% of the vote to 35% for Johnson, who by then was not a candidate. Robert Kennedy had entered the race too late to be on the Wisconsin ballot. On April 3 Hanoi finally accepted Johnson's proposal for peace talks. And the next day civil rights leader Martin Luther King was shot down while standing on the balcony of the Lorraine Motel in Memphis, Tennessee. Riots broke out in over 100 cities; 39 people were killed and over 2,500 injured.

The Tet Offensive either directly or indirectly spelled the end of Johnson's Administration. No single battle in American military history has had such an impact on the high office. But Johnson's announcement, timed as it was and being made in the context of reviewing the events of Tet, amounted to a personal act of unilateral surrender. It was an unprecedented abrogation of leadership. Johnson had lost faith in himself, and his announcement negated any chance for resolving the conflict before the end of his presidency.

THE REINFORCEMENTS ISSUE

Johnson had begun planning a national address on Tet in the first week of the offensive. He wanted to present the facts to the American people and to counter various lines of criticism, such as American forces had been caught by surprise or that the battle had in essence been a defeat. He had also been pondering not seeking another term of office, but he had not made up his mind in February. He added that detail to the speech much later.

The critical question after the first week of the Tet Offensive was how to best exploit the situation in Vietnam. It was clear to both sides that the general uprising was not going to materialize in the South, and the situation on the ground was largely under allied control. The enemy had been severely wounded, forces in disarray. There was no notion at that time that the proper response would be to offer a bombing halt. For some the first impulse was to consider escalation, to exploit the enemy's state of disruption to press the matter in ways that had not previously been done, such as moving into Laos, Cambodia, and the southern part of North Vietnam to cut supply lines to the South and change the dynamic of the war. The bombing campaign could be widened to targets previously off limits. Polls showed that the public would back a show of strength. The time was ripe for a bold gesture that conveyed strength and determination.

General Wheeler sensed an opportunity for operations against the enemy's lines of communication in Cambodia and Laos. Quick action could move the war in the direction he and others had wanted since its inception. But not all of the President's advisers agreed. On February 6, Robert McNamara told the President that, with respect to a response, "there just isn't anything the Chiefs have come up with that is worth anything." McNamara believed in the ability of the United States to inflict heavy casualties on the enemy "as our proper response and as the message we give to our people."² Characteristically seeking message over substance, McNamara argued for more of the same.

In order to exploit the Tet victory and go on the offensive, the United States would need more troops in-country, which was the basis of what came to be known as the reinforcements issue. In July 1967 Johnson had raised the American troop ceiling in South Vietnam from 470,000 to 525,000. The ceiling was supposed to be reached by June 1968. In the fall of 1967 the reinforcement schedule was accelerated due to suspicions that the North was going to conduct an attack in the early months of 1968, and by the end of the year there were 500,000 troops in-country, 102 of the 106 maneuver battalions due Westmoreland by June. It would not be possible to reinforce success after Tet without a greater surge capacity than the four remaining battalions.

On February 7, the day the Special Forces camp at Lang Vei was overrun, National Security Adviser Walt Rostow suggested sending the 82nd Airborne Division to Vietnam, extending enlistments (what in later years would be called stop-loss), and calling up the reserves. On February 9 General Westmoreland sent word that he "would welcome reinforcements at any time they could be made available," particularly in the north. But General Wheeler thought this message did not convey a sense of urgency, and on February 12 Westmoreland sent word to the White House that he needed reinforcements right away. At the very least Westmoreland wanted the balance of the forces due him by June immediately. His reasoning was that there was "a situation of great opportunity as well as heightened risk." He said that he did not see "how the enemy can long sustain the heavy losses which his new strategy is enabling us to inflict on him. Therefore, adequate reinforcements should permit me not only to contain his I Corps offensive but also to capitalize on his losses by seizing the initiative in other areas. Exploiting this opportunity could materially shorten the war."[3]

Daniel Ellsberg, who at the time was facilitating the transition from McNamara to Clifford as Secretary of Defense, later wrote that he had suspected that Westmoreland had wanted a wider war all along and had hinted as much in his November 21, 1967, National Press Club speech. "Down this path," he wrote, "I thought, lay certain ruin." Ellsberg was not concerned that the United States would lose if it escalated the war against Hanoi, but that it would succeed in conquering the North and become a neocolonial occupier.[4] It was clear that General Wheeler was the motive force behind seeking the military buildup, and Westmoreland was less convinced it would be necessary, at least not to continue fighting the war in the same way it had been fought.

The troop buildup question percolated among policymakers, who began to examine the various means available to deploy more fighting forces to Vietnam and determine how to fund them. The Office of the Secretary of Defense presented reserve call-up options of 40,000 to 130,000 troops. The Joint Chiefs recommended higher figures, ultimately settling for an immediate call-up of 51,100, and a further 186,100 being brought to a state of readiness for future contingencies. Johnson told Westmoreland that the time had come for an "all-out effort," yet at the same time he slowed the process by insisting that he receive an on-the-spot report from the theater before any action was taken. After some discussion, Johnson selected General Wheeler to make the trip and on February 13 ordered him to depart for Vietnam as soon as possible.

But politics kept General Wheeler stateside. Senator J. William Fulbright of Arkansas, who as Chairman of the Senate Foreign Relations Committee had guided the Tonkin Gulf Resolution to easy passage in 1964, convened new hearings on the incident, which started February 20, 1968.[5] After a week of hearings, he said that if he had known in 1964 what he knew in 1968, he would not have supported the measure. The Tonkin Gulf attacks had been a matter of some debate since they happened, and there were allegations that the crisis had been manufactured to give Johnson a free hand in Vietnam. As support for Johnson's handling of the war effort ebbed, politicians who had backed the resolution in 1964 began to seek means of finding political cover against a possible backlash. Since Tonkin Gulf was the "original sin" of congressional support for the war effort, discrediting the incident would in effect absolve Congress of anything that followed. In this respect it was the functional equivalent of the "Weapons of Mass Destruction" issue in the Iraq war, a means of giving politicians a credible way not only to shift their positions on the war but also to claim that any previous support they had given should not count against them in the moral tally because they had been "deceived." In time, the argument that Congress had been continually lied to during the Vietnam War became the standard means of avoiding culpability for complicity in the war effort, even though Congress had been briefed extensively on every aspect of the conflict throughout.

Secretary McNamara was scheduled to testify before the Senate on February 21 and wanted Wheeler with him at the hearings. This appearance delayed Wheeler's departure an additional week. Yet the anticipated renewal of the attack at Khe Sanh, the "main event" Westmoreland had been predicting, had not yet kicked off, and intelligence reports indicated it might not take place at all, since North Vietnam was focusing on the battle at Hue. The less than expected effort at Khe Sanh diminished some of the urgency for the troop request, although a resurgence of violence the weekend of February 17–18 (the "second pulse" of the original Tet attack, now much diminished) did create brief concern. But congressional opposition was already in evidence. On February 25 on ABC's "Issues and Answers," Senator Fulbright said that dispatching more troops to Vietnam would be "a disastrous course."

Wheeler left for Vietnam after the hearings and sent his report to the White House on February 27. He gave the President a mixed assessment of the situation in South Vietnam. U.S. forces were combat-ready but faced logistics problems. The enemy had been bloodied but was still intent on further attacks. South Vietnamese forces had performed better than expected but were not ready to assume the burden of defending their country. The rural pacification program had been severely damaged. If the enemy pressed another countrywide attack, the need for more troops would be acute. The consensus among the officers he spoke to was that 1968 would be the pivotal year. Wheeler recommended a three-stage troop buildup, with 108,000 additional troops to be sent by May, 42,000 more by September 1, and a further 55,000 by the end of the year. This 205,000-troop increase was the largest proposal yet and would put total U.S. forces in South Vietnam at three quarters of a million men.

That day the President convened a meeting of his top advisers at the White House to discuss the troop issue and future courses of action. McNamara was skeptical of Wheeler's proposal, which he estimated would cost an additional $15 billion dollars. This cost would necessitate either a tax increase or cuts to domestic spending. McNamara was also doubtful that the increase in forces would put the United States in a better posture on the ground. Clifford asked rhetorically whether mobilizing up to a million more men might make a difference. "That and the status quo have the virtue of clarity," McNamara said. He favored declaring South Vietnam secure and finding a way to get out. Rostow countered that this idea was defeatism, when what was needed was spirit. He felt the United States should exploit the Communist failure in Tet to ramp up the pressure on the North, particularly with increased bombing. But McNamara objected strongly. "What then?" he snapped. "This goddamned bombing campaign, it's been worth nothing, it's done nothing, they've dropped more bombs than in all of Europe in all of World War Two and it hasn't done a fucking thing." McNamara then began weeping uncontrollably as the rest of the senior advisers looked on, stunned.[6]

This pitiable scene was among the last acts for Robert McNamara as Defense Secretary. His lame duck period had dragged on through three critical months of the war, forcing him to be involved in events he no doubt would rather have avoided. There remained only his farewell ceremony on February 29, which was planned as a tribute but became an ignominious sendoff. The event was planned to take place on the Pentagon's River Terrace overlooking the Potomac. Things began to go wrong from the start. The elevator carrying the President, McNamara, and 11 others jammed between floors, and they were stuck in the car for 15 minutes. "What's wrong with this thing" Johnson asked. "Don't ask me," McNamara replied, "I don't work here any more." The group eventually had to climb out through a pried-open door.

The ceremony was being held outdoors to accommodate the thousands of attendees, but the weather that day was cold and rainy. Johnson and McNamara stood closely under a single umbrella until another could be found. Johnson's remarks were brief and noncommittal, but the public address system had shorted out in the rain, so the soggy assembled could not hear most of them. Commercial jets flying to nearby National Airport drowned out the parts that were broadcast, and jet noise eclipsed the 19-gun salute. McNamara's remarks were perfunctory; he had no raincoat, and by the end of his speech his blue suit was soaked, his trademark rimless glasses rain-streaked, and his shoes covered with freshly mown grass.[7]

After the dramatic February 27 meeting President Johnson again chose not to make a decision. Still seeking consensus, he asked incoming Defense Secretary Clark Clifford to convene a study group to review the conduct of the war, examine the range of recommendations, and present options. The Clifford group included McNamara, Rostow, Dean Rusk, General Wheeler, Richard Helms, General Maxwell Taylor, Deputy Secretary of

Defense Paul H. Nitze, Treasury Secretary Henry Fowler, Assistant Secretary of State for Far Eastern Affairs William P. Bundy, his deputy Philip Habib, Undersecretary of State Nicholas Katzenbach, and Assistant Secretary of Defense for International Security Affairs Paul Warnke.

One issue the Administration had to consider before authorizing a troop increase was the perception problem. The President, plus his military and civilian leaders, had assured the American public and Congress that the Tet Offensive had been a major U.S. victory. However, the urgency of the troop request seemed to imply otherwise. The credibility gap yawned again. Clifford asked, "How do we avoid creating the feeling that we are pounding troops down a rathole?"[8] This sense was captured in a March 4, 1968, Top Secret four-page memo by Phil G. Goulding, Assistant Secretary of Defense for Public Affairs, who detailed every possible objection to the deployment decision from various perspectives. The memo sought to give guidance on ways to favorably shape public opinion but listed so many anticipated objections that it was a blueprint for paralysis. Tellingly, one of the projected objections to the troop buildup was, "We won the Tet Offensive. Now we haven't."

The opportunity for bold action was fading. The sense of crisis generated by Tet had ebbed, and Johnson was losing his chance to take advantage of it. The Clifford group reported back March 4 and counseled vastly smaller commitments than those originally suggested by Wheeler. The group wanted only 22,000 additional troops and three tactical fighter squadrons, which would essentially bring Westmoreland's force up to the previously established troop ceiling. It approved the idea of a reserve call-up, estimated to be 262,000, but no large-scale reinforcement in Vietnam until the situation clarified. It recommended instead gradually handing off responsibilities to the South. The group also proposed initiating a study of possible new strategies. The members were split on bombing, with Wheeler and others advocating expanded targeting in the Haiphong area, mining Haiphong harbor, and extending naval gunfire up the coast to a Chinese buffer zone. Opponents of expanded bombing supported the usual seasonal variations in the campaign that had been conducted for years. Dean Rusk proposed another partial bombing halt and an offer to negotiate, reasoning that bombing was less effective during the rainy season anyway, and if Hanoi again refused the offer it would put "the monkey firmly on Hanoi's back for what was to follow."

But this sort of political posturing was being overcome by events. Any hope of using Tet to expand the war effort died on March 10, when the *New York Times* published a front-page story by Neil Sheehan and Hedrick Smith detailing the proposal to send 206,000 more troops to Vietnam, which until then had not been publicly discussed. The story contained much of the February 27 Wheeler report and was clearly based on it. John Roche speculated that it had been leaked by Daniel Ellsberg to one of Robert Kennedy's staff, who then forwarded it to the *Times*. Ellsberg later admitted that he had handed the Wheeler report to Kennedy personally. He justified the security breach by his belief that Kennedy was "in a category of his own."[9] The impact of the *Times* report was magnified by the secrecy of the reinforcement debate. The fact that it had been kept under wraps seemed to confirm the idea that the United States had in fact not "won" the Tet Offensive and that the government was misrepresenting the course of the war. Senator Fulbright saw this development as annulling the Tonkin Gulf Resolution. And all of the arguments anticipated by Phil Goulding's March 4 public affairs memo exploded across newspapers and television.

The reinforcement issue was a self-inflicted crisis brought about by the original sin of establishing arbitrary troop ceilings. The Administration boxed itself in by setting caps that eventually had to be broken. The fact that troop levels kept rising beyond established and then revised troop thresholds had added to the credibility gap. The simple fact of the changing ceilings became the dominant media story line, obscuring the reasons behind the change or the ways additional troops would be employed.[10] And the March 1968 troop request looked even worse because it came on the heels of Tet. It was perceived as evidence of panic and defeat, of a government vainly seeking a strategy and holding back defeat by sending in greater numbers of men to execute the same failed policies. Had the troop increase been explicitly linked to a change in strategy or a dramatic military operation, it could have redefined the terms of the debate. But, as it was, the proposed increase seemed to show only a leadership flailing about in search of an answer.

The troop ceiling was set based not on battlefield needs but political considerations, particularly the belief that there was a limit to the number of troops the American people would accept being sent to South Vietnam. But, like the casualty figures, Americans had only a vague idea of how many troops were in-country. A poll taken June 22–27, 1967, showed that only 29% of Americans estimated there were 300,000 to 500,000 troops in Vietnam, which was roughly the correct answer. But 26% believed there were over 500,000 troops in the country; 8% believed there were 200,000–300,000; and the plurality, 37%, believed there were under 200,000 troops in South Vietnam.[11] So arguments over the predicted political impact of reinforcement proposals differing by the tens of thousands were something of an inside-the-beltway pastime, disconnected from reality. However, given that many Americans thought that there were far fewer troops in Vietnam than the actual 500,000, discussion of an increase to close to three quarters of a million came as a shock.

On March 15, in the wake of the controversy generated by the *New York Times* article, Secretary Clifford came up with a new set of numbers: a 30,000 man deployment, a 37,000 (later 50,000) phase I reserve call-up, with 48,000 more reserves to be called up later. A week later, on March 22, Johnson told Wheeler to "forget the 100,000 men." An even smaller proposal was being drawn up that would not even meet the original troop ceiling set for June 1968. Johnson announced this plan in his March 31 speech; 13,500 support troops would be sent to South Vietnam over five months to augment the 11,000 combat troops already sent "on an emergency basis" in the first 48 hours of the Tet Offensive. This number was only 12% of the force that General Wheeler thought necessary to take advantage of the opportunity presented by Tet, but by then the moment for decisive action had passed. Ironically, reinforcements, the critical requirement necessary to exploit victory, became seen as evidence of a covered-up defeat. President Johnson's inability to act boldly, his delay and repeated requests for proposals, sacrificed the critical element of time. By the time the *New York Times* broke the story the momentum was already gone. Concerted military action that could have redefined the Vietnam War gave way to retrenchment in pursuit of a negotiated settlement. The reinforcements debate proved that the attrition strategy cut both ways. The United States had reached its own "crossover point."

THE DOVES TAKE FLIGHT

The Tet attacks, the bungled issue of reinforcements, and the Tonkin Gulf hearings were a blizzard of blows to the Johnson Administration. The impact in the political realm was dramatic as Johnson's opponents sensed blood in the water.

Many in the Democratic Party rushed to renounce the war effort. Oriana Fallaci wrote that "the word 'peace' was a passport for anyone seeking power and hoping to take over from [Johnson]; it was a commodity sold for votes."[12] The first post-Tet Democratic referendum on Johnson's leadership was the March 12 New Hampshire primary. Eugene McCarthy's insurgency had been gathering steam since November 1967, and Johnson had not taken sufficient steps to counter it, in part because he did not take it seriously. Johnson was not even on the New Hampshire ballot because he had not felt it necessary, and his supporters had to mount a vigorous last-minute write-in campaign to stave off total humiliation. In the nonbinding part of the race, Johnson won 49% of the vote to McCarthy's 42%, not an impressive showing for a sitting president but a considerable achievement for a write-in effort. However, in the substantive part of the contest, the race for delegates, McCarthy won 20, to only four for Johnson, a tribute to the McCarthy campaign's superior organizational skills.

McCarthy's New Hampshire victory is generally believed to illustrate the rising power of the peace movement, but exit-poll analysis revealed that over half of the McCarthy voters had no idea what his stand on the Vietnam War was and that many of his votes came from "hawks" who were casting protest votes against Johnson. In fact, polling showed that the more New Hampshire voters in general knew about McCarthy's position on Vietnam, the less likely they were to vote for him.[13] Johnson noted the protest nature of the vote the night before the primary: "Every Democrat who's mad at his wife or her husband or thinks taxes are too high or whatever is going to get it out of his or her system by kicking Lyndon Johnson in the ass."[14]

Johnson's diffidence about the approaching political season was causing alarm among his supporters. On March 14, in the wake of the New Hampshire debacle, John Roche sent a memo to the President urging him firmly to declare his candidacy. This declaration would boost the morale of his supporters and end the rumor-mongering and opportunism that was rising in the Party. "The air would be cleared, the drums would sound, and your millions of supporters would get a great injection of hope and vigor," Roche wrote. "You are their leader, but they need you in the flesh."[15] But the candidacy that was announced two days later was Robert F. Kennedy's.

Tet had quickly framed the rivalry between Johnson and Kennedy. On February 2, while fighting still raged in cities across South Vietnam, Robert Kennedy's brother, Massachusetts Senator Edward Kennedy, joked about the tensions between them in a speech to New Jersey Democrats. He said he could report that everything was fine in Washington and that his brother and the President were "enjoying their annual lunar new year's truce." Edward denied reports that his brother Robert was going to seek the Democratic nomination, and as a reward President Johnson was going to give Robert an important diplomatic post "on the first floor of our embassy in Saigon."[16]

The joking stopped six days later, when Robert Kennedy made a major speech about Tet entitled "A Time for Truth." Kennedy explicitly challenged the veracity of the Administration's account of the offensive and declared it a defeat. "Our enemy, savagely striking at will across all of South Vietnam, has finally shattered the mask of official illusion with which we have concealed our true circumstances, even from ourselves," Kennedy said. "We must, first of all, rid ourselves of the illusion that the events of the past two weeks represent some sort of victory. That is simply not so." The enemy had demonstrated that "we are unable to secure even a single city" from its attacks. "Unable to defeat our enemy or break his will, at least without a huge, long, and ever more costly effort," Kennedy concluded, "we must actively seek a peaceful settlement."

Ironically, a peaceful settlement had been the Johnson Administration's strategic goal all along. The quest inside the White House for the appropriate subtle signal to the North that the U.S. was open to talks continued. On March 23, the day the expected final ground assault at Khe Sanh failed to materialize, Harry McPherson suggested ceasing bombing north of the 20th parallel and sending negotiators to Geneva and Rangoon as a mark of good faith. Dean Rusk had made similar proposals, and Clifford apparently concurred. A bombing halt was discussed at the March 25 meeting of the special Foreign Policy Advisory Group known colloquially as the "wise men," which included Dean Acheson, George Ball, McGeorge Bundy, Cyrus Vance, Omar Bradley, Matthew Ridgeway, Maxwell Taylor, Arthur H. Dean, Douglas Dillon, Associate Justice Abe Fortas, Henry Cabot Lodge, John J. McCloy, Robert D. Murphy, and Arthur J. Goldberg. Rusk, Wheeler, and Rostow were also on hand to voice their opinions. During their meeting in November 1967 the wise men had approved of Johnson's move toward escalation. But four months later they had shifted opinion. Most backed some version of the bombing halt, and they advised the President of this on March 26. A series of meetings were then held in which the final proposal was crafted for the President's speech. Everyone around Johnson seemed to be giving up on the war, and all that was left was for Johnson to give up on himself.

The United States had been trying to draw Hanoi to the negotiating table since 1965. Numerous means were tried—bombing, not bombing, escalation, de-escalation. Secret channels opened and closed. Offers were made and rebuffed. Nothing seemed to work. Over time Johnson began to believe that the problem was not the amount of force the United States employed or the details of the offers Hanoi had refused. As "sending a message" became more important, Johnson focused inwardly on the messenger. What was needed was an honest broker, and he saw only one way of proving his sincerity. Johnson wrote in his memoir, "By renouncing my candidacy, I expressed a fervent wish that the problems that had resisted solution would now yield to resolution. I wanted Hanoi to know that Lyndon Johnson was not using this new move toward peace as a bid for personal political gain. Maybe now, with this clearest possible evidence of our sincerity thrown into the balance, North Vietnam would come forward and agree to a dialogue—a genuine communication dedicated to peace."[17] It was one of the most naïve actions of a President toward a military adversary in American history.

"I honestly believe that the overpowering motive was his conviction that he, Lyndon Johnson, was almost single-handedly standing in the way of peace," John Roche said, "that if he got out of there, then we could have negotiations and they'd know he had no political objectives to gain, that he was sincere in looking for peace and that this was not a political ploy and so on. There's a kind of simplicity about the man in this respect that's quite surprising given his general level of political sophistication." Roche concluded that Johnson "genuinely believed when he in effect took the veil on March 31, 1968 that this would now convince Ho Chi Minh and Co., the Lao Dong to use a collective, that we were sincere. As if they gave a shit whether we were sincere or not! This assumption of symmetrical moral values, you see. He never to the day he died understood the impact of that resignation of his, because he thought genuinely that he had made it possible for negotiations—real negotiations, effective negotiations—to take place."[18]

On April 3 the North Vietnamese accepted Johnson's proposal. Hanoi radio announced that envoys would be sent to discuss "the unconditional cessation of bombing and all other acts of war against North Vietnam." Johnson named ambassador-at-large Averell Harriman as his personal representative, and meetings were held with a delegation from Hanoi to establish the framework for formal negotiations. This diplomatic opening seemed to vindicate Johnson's gamble; he had catalyzed the peace talks that the United States had been seeking since combat troops were sent to South Vietnam in 1965.

But in other respects there was little immediate change. Bombing continued in the North, and in the South the Communists continued to seek ways to shape events on the ground to their benefit. This effort became vividly clear a month later. On May 4 the Administration announced that an agreement had been reached to open peace talks in Paris six days later. The same day the agreement was announced, the Communists launched a new series of attacks in cities across South Vietnam, a campaign soon dubbed Little Tet, and also known as Mini-Tet or the May Offensive. The attack plan was adapted from the original concept for a follow-on phase two of the Tet Offensive. Unlike its namesake, the revised Little Tet was intended to be symbolic, to achieve positional advantages ahead of the impending Paris peace talks. A captured VC document stated that the attacks' objective was "to create pressure over peace talks between our representatives and American representatives in Paris."[19] The Communists felt that they would be in a much better bargaining position if they were able to seize a few provincial cities or even maintain control over parts of the capital. They also understood the beneficial effects of press coverage of their previous attacks in helping to shape international opinion.

The United States responded forcefully to the attacks but did not derail the talks because of this act of bad faith on the part of the enemy. The process had become too important, and Johnson had sacrificed his presidency to get the enemy to the table. Communist attacks intensified, and May 1968, the advent of the long awaited peace talks, became America's bloodiest month in Vietnam.

Hanoi's decision to enter negotiations with the Americans did not meet with universal acclaim. Chinese Premier Zhou Enlai thought the United States was on the ropes and it was a mistake to begin talks. "After the Tet Offensives, the U.S. tried to cover up its difficulties," he told Pham Van Dong on April 13. "Westmoreland then asked for an additional 200,000 troops but the U.S.

Congress and government refused . . . Primary elections in some states showed that the number of expected votes for Johnson had decreased to only 38%. It proved that Johnson's policy of aggression was a failure. All over the world, everyone was asking Johnson to stop bombing." He also noted that Martin Luther King's assassination on April 4 had further disrupted American politics.[20] "The proposals for more troops, tax increase, and an increase in expenditures for the Vietnam War were not accepted by the U.S. Congress. In these circumstances, Johnson was forced to release the March 31 statement," Zhou Enlai argued. But he thought the proposal was just a trick, that Johnson would never willingly relinquish power. "It was a wicked and deceitful scheme," he said. "In fact, he doesn't want to give up the war. The statement is only a means for them to overcome the difficult time. And Johnson even declared that he should not run for reelection. It is also a familiar means being used in the history of the U.S. presidential campaigns . . . But as it turned out, your April 3rd statement solved his difficulties. The whole situation has been changed. Its impacts may be temporary, but disadvantageous."[21] To the Chinese at least, Johnson had not proven his sincerity.

But the American people by and large approved. A Gallup poll taken during the week after Johnson's announcement showed that Johnson's approval rating for handling the war jumped ten points to 42%—not an objectively strong showing and still below the 47% who disapproved (down from 57%)—but about where it had been in the spring of 1967. 64% approved of the decision to stop the bombing of North Vietnam. A majority of Americans expressed support for Johnson's decision not to seek the Democratic nomination for President, and only about 20% either thought that it was a bad idea or that he was going to re-enter the race later.

The clearest indicator of the transformative nature of Johnson's speech was the shift in the numbers of hawks and doves. At the end of February the balance was 58% hawk to 26% dove, reflecting the increased hawkishness that the Tet Offensive had generated. But once Johnson publicly gave up on escalation, the numbers shifted dramatically. The Gallup survey released April 9 showed hawks and doves at parity for the first time ever, at 41%.

(As in previous polls, young people showed no greater dovish tendencies than any other age group.) Ultimately, the hawks gave up on the war effort once the Administration had abandoned any chances of winning.[22]

Johnson later said that Tet had nothing to do with his decision not to run for another term. Others supported this assertion. Rostow said that Johnson's decision not to run "was 95% made long before Tet."[23] However, by making the announcement at the end of a speech in which he reviewed the course of the battle, Johnson inextricably tied the two, whether intentionally or not. Johnson left the impression that Tet had played a major role in his decision-making. And while his decision not to run may not have been a reaction to Tet per se, it was conditioned by his desire to make a sincere gesture of outreach to the enemy. True, he might have done the same thing had Tet never happened, but because it did the linkage between the two events in the public mind was unavoidable.

The March 31 speech came as a severe blow to John Roche, who was one of Johnson's most ardent political supporters. "I've never been so sick in my life, heartsick, as I was that night," Roche said, "because I read [the speech] entirely differently. I read it as a capitulation and I knew that that's the way it would be read in North Vietnam." But even with Johnson's capitulation the war would last seven more hard years.

XVI.

LOAN AGONISTES

General Loan's life became much more difficult after Eddie Adams's photograph of him shooting Bay Lop was published. Rumors swirled that Loan was to be cashiered, but he had heard such ideas before. Loan had no time for rumors; he was busy defending his country. Loan commanded the defense of Saigon throughout the Tet Offensive and had operational control of the military forces in the city in addition to his police troops. As was his way, he led from the front—he rushed to neighborhoods where fighting erupted and was wounded three times in the course of the Saigon battle. The last pockets of diehard VC were cleared toward the end

I sent flowers when I heard that he had died.

—EDDIE ADAMS

of February, and Saigon returned to a state of relative stability. But the fighting surged again in May with Little Tet.

The Communists kicked off the attack on May 4 by detonating a car bomb near the U.S. embassy. Over the course of the next few days they struck 119 targets throughout the South. But signs of an impending offensive had been taken more seriously this time, and defending forces were ready. Troops in Saigon had been on full alert since April 21, and on the 22nd General Loan told the press that an attack was coming, either sometime that week or later. U.S. and South Vietnamese troops conducted operations in the Saigon suburbs and countryside that disrupted enemy troop concentrations and captured stockpiled weapons. The South Vietnamese government issued a warning on Friday, April 26, that the attack might occur that weekend, and the next day U.S. papers ran headlines announcing "Saigon Awaits Attack." The allies had learned the value of publicizing what otherwise would have been reported as another surprise.

The Little Tet attacks were mainly confined to the outskirts of Saigon. The hardest fighting was at Phu Lam on the west side of the city; at Tan Son Nhut, where the base commander was killed; and near the Y-shaped Phan Thanh Gian bridge.[1] The bridge connected the Gia Dinh district and Saigon, and was at the southeast edge of Cholon. The second day of the attack found the Y-bridge partially damaged and crowded with people fleeing the fighting. Enemy troops had raised a flag over the bridge and were dug in solidly in a nearby group of houses. Snipers commanded the bridge approaches and fired on the nearby Agriculture Ministry. South Vietnamese Marines and naval troops had been unable to dislodge the enemy.

General Loan appeared on the scene and, showing his usual impatience with stalled battles, led an assault across the bridge himself, followed by South Vietnamese and American troops. He led a group of men into an alley between some fishing shacks trying to root out the VC. The general was armed with an AR-15 and backed by police troops and a tank. Halfway up the alley Loan began to fire his weapon at some hidden VC, then fell, shot in the leg and chest. A grenade followed that tore his shoulder. His men took cover, and enemy fire kept rescuers at bay. Loan's flak jacket saved his life, but he was severely wounded, and he lay in the alley bleeding for 20 minutes.[2]

Specialist-4 Robert L. Scott, a tall, tough black soldier from Chicago with the 716th Military Police Battalion, finally raced out into the alley, grabbed General Loan, and pulled him to safety in a nearby house, aided by two staff assistants from the *Pacific Stars and Stripes*. Scott was wounded but returned to the fight, running outside and picking off a VC guerrilla on the top floor of the house who was about to throw a grenade. Specialist-4 Scott was awarded the Silver Star for his heroism.[3] Loan was taken from the house to waiting ambulances by burly Australian war correspondent Pat Burgess. A picture of the event ran on the front page of the *New York Times* and was printed worldwide. Loan's expression showed pain and surprise. His hair was matted on his head, his uniform rumpled and bloody. Both his legs were wounded, the right one severely, and his spine was damaged.

A few days later Little Tet was essentially over in Saigon. The general lack of concern about the Communist attack is reflected in this vignette from the May 8 *New York Times* as fighting was dying down, of downtown hotel patrons seeing the fighting more as a spectacle than a threat: "At the restaurant atop the Caravelle Hotel, customers clamored for window seats and then sat eating steak and lobster and watching planes and helicopters strafing the city's outskirts. Nearby, at the United States officers club atop the Rex Hotel, captains and majors munched hamburgers and leaned out the windows to catch a glimpse of the fighting."[4]

That day President Thieu and Vice President Ky visited Loan in the hospital and presented him with a medal for valor. A picture that ran in the *Times* showed Loan sitting up in bed with his arms crossed, looking dejected. He had good reason to be. The previous day Colonel Dam Van Quy, Loan's close aide and second in command of the national police, was killed in the Cholon district when a B-40 rocket hit his jeep.

More honors followed for Loan, but even more serious troubles. In June, a still convalescing Loan was promoted to Major General. But on the afternoon of June 2, six of Loan's supporters were killed in a friendly-fire incident in Cholon during operations against a few VC holdouts. The men were at a command post on the porch of the Thuong Phuoc High School coordinating fire with a circling U.S. helicopter gunship. The friendly position was marked with blue smoke, but the gunship sent three missiles at the school. One malfunctioned; two hit the target. Among those killed were the police chief of Saigon, Lieutenant Colonel Nguyen Van Luan; Lieutenant Colonel Pho Quoc Chu, port director of Saigon and Ky's brother-in-law; Nguyen Van Phuoc, the commander of the ARVN Fifth Ranger Group; and two other high-ranking national police officers. Loan's brother-in-law, who was mayor of Saigon, was seriously wounded, and two members of his staff were killed.[5] Vice President Ky was supposed to have been with the group as well, but chose not to go at the last minute. This friendly-fire accident led to rumors that it was actually a scheme by Thieu to assassinate Ky.[6] The VC later claimed credit for the killings as a "wonderful victory."

Whether the attack was accidental or not, Thieu gained an opportunity to consolidate his power and marginalize Ky. On June 8, 1968, General Loan was ousted from his position as Director of National Police and replaced by Tran Van Hai, the commander of the South Vietnamese Rangers. The official story was that Loan resigned because of ill health. His replacement had been in the American helicopter that fired the missiles, which fueled the view that the killings had been intentional. But Tran Van Hai was widely regarded for his bravery and incorruptibility, and the overwhelming consensus was that he would not have been involved in such a plot.[7]

Tran Van Hai had been chosen by newly appointed Premier Tran Van Huong, on Thieu's orders. Within a week, he fired or transferred seven of nine district police chiefs in Saigon. The former premier, Nguyen Van Loc, a Ky ally, had been let go on May 17 without warning. The wounded mayor of Saigon was also replaced, citing health reasons. And Lieutenant General Le Nguyen Khang, commander of South Vietnam's III Corps, another Ky ally, was pressured into resigning, allegedly because of feelings of responsibility for the June 2 deaths.[8] Other firings and personnel shifts cascaded throughout government and military ranks.

Severely wounded, his government position gone, his network of influence shattered, and some of his closest friends and associates dead, General Loan felt there was little left in Saigon for him. His military career was over. In late June 1968 he left South Vietnam and went to Australia for treatment of his stubborn wounds, returning home later that year. In May 1969 Loan flew at his own expense to Washington, D.C., with his wife, Chinh Mai, their four children, an aide, a nanny, and a chauffeur.[9] He was examined at Walter Reed Hospital on May 13 and left with a leg brace.[10]

General Loan's timing could not have been worse. He arrived in Washington the same week that Eddie Adams was awarded the Pulitzer Prize for spot news photography for his photo, which had been formally entitled "Saigon Execution." In other circumstances Loan might have been able to come to the United States without being noticed, but the coincidence of the publicity surrounding the Pulitzer put him in the spotlight. Antiwar Senator Stephen M. Young (D-OH) denounced Loan on the Senate floor, calling him a "brutal murderer" and saying his presence was a "disgraceful end to a disgraceful, murderous episode."[12] An investigation was launched into why Loan was allowed into Walter Reed, and at whose expense. Loan had been assigned as Air Attaché Designate at the South Vietnamese embassy, which gave him access to American military medical facilities. But the embassy said he was in the U.S. on his own, and the State Department said he was here as part of a Defense program to give medical treatment to allied officers.[13] The flap was eventually resolved, but it underscored Loan's unpopularity. He spent his tour in America living in Alexandria, Virginia, under constant surveillance. In December 1969 he returned to South Vietnam.

By that time there was little for Loan to do. His patron Ky had little influence, and Loan had lost his access to the central channels of power. In August 1970 he was granted an appointment as special assistant in the South Vietnamese Defense Ministry, a nominal position with no real influence.[14] He offered to retire to pursue a more lucrative career in the private sector, but instead was given another meaningless promotion. "It is a joke," he told interviewer Tom Buckley. "I have no troops and no duties. I am in charge of long-range planning, maybe for the next war."[15] Loan's leg became weaker over the years and his mood darker. But he fought his disaffection by working to help construct hospitals for the war wounded, and sought emotional succor in children.

A 1972 article on Loan noted that he "spends his days on visits to orphanages and children's hospitals with candy and ice cream bought from his own pocket."[16] Reverend Robert Crawford, a Philadelphia priest who ran a Saigon home for 85 children crippled with polio, noted that Loan visited frequently. "The kids never saw so much ice cream in their lives," he said. "Loan's face just lights up as he moves among them." Loan refused to talk to the press or publicize his charity work. A Defense Ministry colleague commented on Loan's outings, "If he sees a camera anywhere around, he turns the jeeps around and heads back to his house at Tan Son Nhut. Loan doesn't care a damn any more what the world thinks of him."[17]

Loan did not undertake charity work to improve his public image but to battle his private torment. AP reported that a Vietnamese nun with the Sisters of Charity, "who watched him pick out the most deformed child in her ward to spoon ice cream to, thought perhaps the general was 'lonely like that little girl. It's more than just the friendship of two crippled people; it's as if only they understand each other.'"[18]

Loan could have chosen to leave the country and emigrate to the safety of the United States or France, as others who had lost power in South Vietnam had done. But he stayed, hoping that he could be of some use to his embattled country. His wounds continued to plague him, and in September 1974 his right leg was amputated. In the spring of 1975, with South Vietnam near collapse, Loan sought help from the Americans to escape the wrath of the Communists. But he was rebuffed at the American embassy; with North Vietnamese troops closing in, he, his wife, and children were flown out of Vietnam in the cargo bay of a South

Vietnamese Air Force C-130. They had been given five minutes' warning and allowed to bring no baggage.[19]

Loan and his family resettled in northern Virginia with the help of friends in the Vietnamese émigré community. He opened a restaurant, Les Trois Continents, in Burke, Virginia, outside Washington D.C., serving French and Vietnamese cuisine, and pizza. "We don't have much," Loan said in a 1976 interview. "We have a simple life."[20] His relatively humble lifestyle underscored both his fall from power and his integrity while in office. John L. Hart, CIA Station Chief in Saigon, noted in 1978, "He was honest as far as I knew. He had more opportunity than most to stash away a fortune abroad, but he did not. That is why he now runs a restaurant for a living."[21] Then in his late forties, Loan tried to forget the past.

But Loan's troubles had not ended. In November 1978, in what was front-page news, the Immigration and Naturalization Service brought charges against Loan and sought his deportation. It was the first case of its type brought against a former South Vietnamese ally. The INS contended that Loan should have been tried in Vietnam for executing Bay Lop, which was in its view a war crime, and that his permanent resident status should be rescinded on the grounds of "moral turpitude." This was a charge usually reserved for Nazi war criminals. INS official Silas Jervis stated, "He should not have been given a [resident alien] card in the first place. He just slipped through our bureaucracy."[22] The INS brought charges under congressional pressure.[23] The issue had been brewing since 1975, when Congresswoman Elizabeth Holtzman (D-NY) began a personal crusade against South Vietnamese refugees alleged to have been involved in persecution, corruption, or criminal activity prior to their entry to the United States. Congressman Harold Sawyer (R-MI) commented, "We've got enough guys like [Loan] around here without importing them."[24]

Loan faced deportation, but because of the certainty that he would face persecution in Vietnam, the proposed penalty was that Loan lose permanent resident status and live in the U.S. as a stateless person, a man without a country. Loan's lawyer,

Robert Ackerman, a former Marine, argued that Loan should not be charged, because his actions were legal. "Vietnam was under martial law at the time, civilian rule had broken down, the law of the military commander prevailed," he said. Furthermore, Loan was under direct orders to summarily execute any civilian found with a gun. Thus he had not broken any Vietnamese laws "because it was a combat death, not a murder."[25]

The case generated a lively debate over the nature of Loan's actions at a level of thoughtfulness missing in 1968, when the event was fresh and the war was ongoing. Ironically, Loan benefited from the low regard the entire war was held in by that time. One human rights worker noted that deporting Loan would be a great act of hypocrisy since he was no guiltier than anyone else. "I'm sure he's a thoroughly reprehensible figure," he said, "but what he did is just not that morally distinguishable in my mind from the actions of Americans who were involved in perpetrating the same war."[26]

The *Washington Post* agreed, editorializing that "the uncomfortable but critical fact was that Mr. Loan fought *on the American side*" [emphasis in original] and the United States had a tacit if not explicit agreement to support its erstwhile allies in defeat: "Now some Americans pretend that the United States did not dirty its own hands in Vietnam and had no responsibility for what our allies did there. Or is it that they think our own participation in a war about which they still feel guilty can be expiated by offering up Mr. Loan as a suitable public sacrifice?" The *Post* argued that far from "slipping through the cracks," as the INS averred, Loan was given sanctuary fully in the knowledge of what he had done, and should not now be handed over to Hanoi for a show trial. "A more pathetic confusion of values and laying off of blame is hard to recall. Moral turpitude, indeed."[27]

The *New York Times* took a harder line, running the Adams photo in a small box, seemingly to make its point inarguable. The *Times* noted that some people contended that Loan was simply being punished for having the bad luck of being photographed in the act. "Yes, Mr. Loan was 'unlucky.' So too were the Nuremberg defendants 'unlucky' in that they could not, like others, conceal their responsibility. And when Lieutenant Calley was awaiting court martial for his role in My Lai, the same point was made." The *Times* argued that simply because many more people were guilty of war crimes that was no reason not to punish those available. "Because Mr. Loan is guilty does not mean that others are not . . . To technically 'deport' Mr. Loan would not be to clear anyone else. It would be to declare that such acts as his—no matter who commits them—are morally indefensible."[28]

General Westmoreland stated that the shooting "was an imprudent act, but an act performed under stress. . . . [T]here was great stress in Saigon at that time and great anger at the acts of the communist terrorists."[29] Former Vice President Ky, then running a liquor store in Los Angeles, said that Loan "was just doing his job. At that time during the Tet Offensive any street was the front line."[30] Former Saigon CIA Station Chief John Hart also weighed in. "It is ironic," he wrote,

> that some Americans have singled out Mr. Loan as a war criminal for shooting a single civilian who had himself just finished slaughtering a number of South Vietnamese soldiers and policemen. There is a fine line between Mr. Loan's intentional action against a civilian combatant and the unintentional but nonetheless inevitable toll of Vietnamese civilian non-combatants that resulted from our modern military technology's emphasis on massive firepower. Given the circumstances of the Vietnamese war, one must indeed have acute ethical perception to distinguish between villains and heroes. . . . We would do well to recognize that "war" is a euphemism for killing the enemy, and thus generates many events that do not fall within the bounds of easy moral or legal judgment.[31]

Hart added that those in the U.S. who slashed Loan's tires "do not strike me as moral exemplars." Some of the people who only knew Loan as the proprietor of Les Trois Continents voiced support. "A man's trying to rebuild his life and people are not giving him a chance," one said. "I suppose that anybody that's involved in a war that did what they were supposed to do is a war criminal."[32]

Eventually President Carter and the Attorney General, Griffin Bell, overruled the INS, and the government dropped Loan's case. A Carter spokesman stated that "such historical revisionism was folly."[33] Representative Holtzman and the *Times* protested, but the matter was ended.

One of Loan's most ardent defenders throughout the controversy was Eddie Adams. The INS asked Adams to testify against Loan, but Adams said he would stand for the defense instead. Adams had spent time covering Loan after "Saigon Execution" was published, and he wrote a sympathetic profile of the general on the eve of Little Tet. "I had been up staying with him for a few weeks, actually just gone with him throughout Vietnam, and found out the guy was very well loved by the Vietnamese," Adams said. "He was a hero to them, you know. So he wasn't the idiot that he was taken to be . . . and it just saddens me that none of this has really come out."[34] Adams, who over his career photographed 13 wars, understood the ambiguous moral context that Loan had been in when he took the photo. "I'm not saying what Loan did was right," Adams said, "but this was in the middle of a war and he was shooting an enemy, a real bad guy. People tend to forget what that guy and his buddies did to a lot of innocent citizens."[35]

Adams visited Loan in Washington in 1969 after he won the Pulitzer, and tried to apologize for the photograph. Loan stayed him. "What is past is past," he said. "To be alive or dead, to be liked or not liked, it doesn't matter. Life belongs to Buddha, to God, to whatever it is that is higher than me."[36] Adams said he would donate his prize money, and an article published at the time of the INS debate stated that if Adams could change the past, he would not have taken the picture for which he was so famous. "I was getting money for showing one man killing another. Two lives were destroyed, and I was getting paid for it." He added, with evident sarcasm, "I was a hero."[37]

"Saigon Execution" haunted Loan, but it shadowed Adams as well. He was conflicted over winning the Pulitzer, saying, "It takes no talent to take that picture, it really doesn't, it was just a question of being there." He did not think he had used any of his special skills or capabilities. "I had nothing to do with that picture," he said. Over time he grew annoyed at the way the picture defined him professionally. Over his career Adams published hundreds of photos of men at war. He took portraits of Pope John Paul II, Deng Xiaoping, Mikhail Gorbachev, Fidel Castro, Anwar Sadat, and U.S. presidents from Richard Nixon to George W. Bush. For *Parade* magazine, he took pictures of celebrities, movie stars, musicians, politicians, the rich and the poor. But nothing he did was as influential as "Saigon Execution," and he became as much a captive of it as Loan. "I'm identified for that picture and nothing else," Adams said in 1982.[38] Hal Buell, his former boss in Saigon, said that the picture "became—often to his annoyance—his signature picture," and that it "haunted Eddie for decades afterward."[39]

Adams had continued to photograph the Vietnam War and its aftermath. He was at Hue and Khe Sanh and many other battles, although none of his later photos gained the notoriety of the execution picture. But some of his work had positive impact. On Thanksgiving Day 1977 Adams joined a group of boat people fleeing Vietnam. The conditions among the refugees were critical; in one case 50 adults and children were crammed onto a craft that was barely seaworthy. Food and water were in short supply. The U.S. Navy rendered humanitarian assistance, but undertook rescue operations only when boats were actually sinking. The photos Adams shot of the boat people and their dilemma were widely printed and helped influence Congress to allow 200,000 South Vietnamese refugees to come to the U.S. "It's probably the only thing I did in my whole life that was worthwhile," he said 20 years later.[40]

Once he was back stateside Adams sought out Loan again, and found him at his restaurant. By then the publicity of the INS case had begun to take a toll as the curious and ill-intentioned came to Loan's restaurant to gawk. "He was like a freak show," Adams said. "People had figured out who he was." Adams noticed that someone had scrawled "We know who you are, you f*****" on the bathroom wall.[41] But Loan was philosophical about the situation. "I got to know him very well," Adams says. "He never blamed me personally. He said, 'If it wasn't you, somebody else would have taken it.'"[42]

In 1988, with the support of Kodak and Nikon, Adams started an annual free workshop at his farm in Jeffersonville, New York, an hour north of New York City. It was known as Barnstorm, and 100 young photographers attended every year. Veteran editors and photojournalists came to give the young people the benefit of their experience in the profession. Famous Vietnam War-related personalities would also show up, like Mary Ann Vecchio, who was photographed kneeling next to the body of a student at Kent State in 1970, and Kim Phuc from "Vietnam Napalm."[43] Adams began each workshop with a memorial service at a stone marker he had erected in a stand of pine trees in tribute to five of his friends who died covering the war. "Except for the wind that whispers through their branches," Hal Buell said, "they are mute sentinels and memorials to the many other photographers who fell in Vietnam."[44] Adams discussed the Vietnam War in detail at Barnstorm, but he did not have a print of "Saigon Execution" on display and did not discuss it in other professional venues if he could help it. "I'm not going to talk about it," Adams said in a 1994 address to the National Press Photographers Association. "It's just a thing we don't talk about. We don't use it in my shows. We don't use it anywhere."[45]

"I feel pressured to find another picture I'd rather be remembered for," Adams said in 1982.[46] General Loan would have liked to have been remembered for something else as well, but that was impossible. His country was gone, and there was no nostalgia in the United States for the lost cause of the Vietnam War. The residual bitterness of the conflict and the persistence of the Adams photograph prevented General Loan from achieving any public redemption. "Photographs, they're half truths," Adams said, "that's only one side. It's just a sad statement, you know, I think, of America. He was fighting our war, not their war, our war, and every—all the blame is on this guy."[47] When periodically contacted for interviews about the incident, Loan declined. "That time," he said, "I hold to myself."[48]

Loan closed his restaurant in 1991 and retired to spend time with his family. Adams called Loan in early 1998 after hearing he was very sick. "I talked to him on the phone and I wanted to try to do something, explaining everything and how the photograph destroyed his life and he just wanted to try to forget it," Adams said. "He said let it go. And I just didn't want him to go out this way."[49] It seemed as though Adams was having a more difficult time than Loan in dealing with the impact of the photograph. But Loan was a deeply philosophical man who accepted the role that history had chosen for him. Thirty years earlier, shortly before Tet, Oriana Fallaci had asked Loan if he was a Buddhist.

"That's like asking me if I believe in God," Loan said.

"Do you, General?"

"No."

"What do you believe in, General?"

"In destiny."[50]

Nguyen Ngoc Loan died of cancer on July 14, 1998. The *New York Times* ran a six-column obituary along with the Adams photo and a picture of Loan in his restaurant in Virginia. Many papers ran only the shooting picture. Eddie Adams wrote an emotional eulogy in *Time* magazine, which read in part:

> I won a Pulitzer Prize in 1969 for a photograph of one man
> shooting another. Two people died in that photograph: the
> recipient of the bullet and GENERAL NGUYEN NGOC LOAN.
> The general killed the Viet Cong; I killed the general with my
> camera. Still photographs are the most powerful weapon in
> the world. People believe them, but photographs do lie, even
> without manipulation. They are only half-truths. . . . This
> picture really messed up his life. He never blamed me. He told
> me if I hadn't taken the picture, someone else would have, but
> I've felt bad for him and his family for a long time. . . . I sent
> flowers when I heard that he had died and wrote, "I'm sorry.
> There are tears in my eyes."[51]

Time ran Adams's eulogy next to "Saigon Execution."

Eddie Adams died in Manhattan of amyotrophic lateral sclerosis, or Lou Gehrig's disease, on September 19, 2004.[52] He was 71. "Saigon Execution" appeared with most of the obituaries. It was a moment in time Adams could never escape, and the photograph remains the most reprinted, most immediately familiar image of the war, and perhaps the most misunderstood. The clarity of Adams's photo obscures the ambiguity of the event. "I ask a lot of people," Adams once said, "If you were the general at that time, and your people were being killed all around you, how do you know that you wouldn't have pulled that trigger?"[53] The photo may be black and white, but life seldom is.

XVII.

TET'S LEGACY

" **I** told you the Tet offensive was a victory for our side," a Hawk said. "Hanoi is on its knees and that is why it agreed."

"Balderdash," a Dove said angrily. "The Tet offensive proved once and for all that we could never win the war in Vietnam and we'd have to go to the table whether we wanted to or not."

So wrote Art Buchwald in his column April 11, 1968. The debate over Tet was joined.

The speed with which the country went from a growing sense of progress in Vietnam to frustration and despair was breathtaking. The political landscape shifted dramatically over six

Tet was established in the public mind as a defeat, and therefore it was an American defeat.

—ROBERT NORTHSHIELD, NBC NEWS

months. Allied arms had achieved major victories on the battle-field, and the United States had a historic opportunity to escalate the conflict and impose its will on Hanoi. But President Johnson was not up to the task. His fading resolve allowed the opportunity to slip away. Johnson created a leadership vacuum that was exploited by America's adversaries and his own domestic political opponents. The notion that the enemy was using Tet to send a message, to achieve psychological or symbolic victories, arose from within. The Johnson Administration concluded that the enemy could not have been seeking victory and invented other, more realistic objectives for the Communists. Officials chose not to take the enemy's words at face value, not even from captured documents or interrogation reports, and instead invented what they thought to be a more plausible story line. Because it seemed reasonable, it gained traction with the press. After a few weeks of indecision, the damage was done and could not be reversed. In late 1968, Jack Fern, an NBC field producer, suggested that the network produce a program "showing that Tet had indeed been a decisive victory for America." Senior producer Robert Northshield vetoed the idea, explaining that Tet was "established in the public's mind as a defeat, and therefore it was an American defeat."[1]

Hanoi has always claimed the Tet Offensive as a major victory. In 2008 Vietnam held a series of commemorative celebrations, and one 40th-anniversary article claimed that the Communists not only decisively influenced the 1968 election but also attempted to affect American elections in 1964 and 1972 as well.[2] On occasion, however, more objective assessments have slipped through the wall of official congratulation. As noted, in 2005 General Giap wrote that "the flawed application of the idea of revolutionary offense during the war was yet another costly lesson paid for in blood and bone."[3] In 1982, General Tran Van Tra published an assessment of Tet in which he said the planners "did not correctly evaluate the specific balance of forces between ourselves and the enemy, did not fully realize that the enemy still had considerable capabilities and that our capabilities were limited, and set requirements that were beyond our actual strength." The Tet plan was not based on "scientific calculation or a careful weighing of all factors" but "on an illusion based on our subjective desires." In the course of the battle the Communists "suffered large sacrifices and losses with regard to manpower and materiel, especially cadres at the various echelons, which clearly weakened us. Afterwards, we were not only unable to retain the gains we had made but had to overcome a myriad of difficulties in 1969 and 1970 so that the revolution could stand firm in the storm." Tran Van Tra's blunt assessment was quickly banned in Vietnam.

"The Tet Offensive proved catastrophic to our plans," Truong Nhu Tang, Minister of Justice for the Viet Cong Provisional Revolutionary Government, said in 1982. "It is a major irony of the Vietnam War that our propaganda transformed this debacle into a brilliant victory. The truth was that Tet cost us half our forces. Our losses were so immense that we were unable to replace them with new recruits." Bui Tin, who became disillusioned with the Hanoi government and defected from Vietnam in 1990, was able to speak freely about the negative impact of Tet on the Communist war effort:

> Our losses were staggering and a complete surprise; Giap later told me that Tet had been a military defeat, though we had gained the planned political advantages when Johnson agreed to negotiate and did not run for re-election. The second and third waves in May and September were, in retrospect, mistakes. Our forces in the South were nearly wiped out by all the fighting in 1968. It took us until 1971 to re-establish our presence, but we had to use North Vietnamese troops as local guerrillas. If the American forces had not begun to withdraw under Nixon in 1969, they could have punished us severely. We suffered badly in 1969 and 1970 as it was.[6]

The Communist forces lost approximately 45,000 of the 84,000 attackers in 1968. Viet Cong losses were especially high among the covert leadership cadres. The VC was not completely destroyed after Tet, but badly hurt. Little Tet was even more damaging. The ARVN had left the villages during Tet to fight in the cities, and the NLF filled the vacuum, but when the ARVN returned, the Communist secret networks were exposed. The damage to the VC infrastructure was so great that some concluded it had been done on purpose, that Tet was a means of weakening the VC, seen as competitors to Hanoi for power. John Roche said that he and Australian counterinsurgency expert Ted Serong concluded that Tet was a rerun, Vietnamese-style, of Stalin's handling of the Warsaw Uprising in 1944, when the Soviets delayed entry into the city until the Polish resistance was annihilated by the Germans after more than two months of fighting. "What Tet did was get rid of the whole cadre of the southern, possibly independent, Communists," Roche said. "From that point on in the South it was a Northern operation entirely."[7]

The South Vietnamese government was not weakened after Tet, contrary to what many assumed in the United States. Viet Cong conduct during Tet, and particularly the Hue Massacre, convinced many in the South that the flawed Saigon government was preferable to rule by Hanoi. ARVN recruitment went up after Tet, and Rostow noted that the collective response to Tet galvanized the people of South Vietnam and left "a much stronger regime and . . . a more competent people" than before the offensive.[8]

Those who invoke the Tet analogy rarely get the facts right. The enemy did not seek a symbolic victory. The public was not turned against the war. The press did misrepresent or dramatize key aspects of the attacks, but the press never has had the ability to influence the public to the degree attributed to it. The media are easily influenced and geared toward the sensational, and terrorism seeks to exploit this to its own ends. But public opinion through the course of the Vietnam War demonstrated that at base the people had a sounder understanding of the use of force than did the press or policymakers in Washington. The majority of the public wanted to win in Vietnam, and use the means necessary to do so. They understood that the war could not be concluded favorably without taking the fight to Hanoi. The limitations that President Johnson placed on the conduct of the war in 1965 created inherent contradictions that Tet brought to the forefront. As long as the ground war was limited to the South, the United States would be on the strategic defensive. And even though the war was being won on the battlefield, it was taking too long and costing too much. Tet presented the United States with an opportunity to do what most in the country wanted done—win the war and come home.

The critical vulnerability was in Washington, not Vietnam. Tet demonstrated that at the strategic level the Vietnam War was an insider's game, being played out among the political power centers in the United States. It is ironic that Johnson, thought to be the consummate Washington pol, was paralyzed by this crisis. Johnson's instincts for deal-making and compromise ill served him when what was required was dynamism and decisiveness. Tet handed him the opportunity to respond forcefully, to reset the dynamics of the war, to respond to Communist aggression in a way that Hanoi would understand as serious. The North's all-out use of force in pursuit of victory demanded a response that was proportionate in intent. But Johnson clung to his limited war premises, oblivious to the facts on the ground, and assumed that the enemy shared his view of war as a complex means of diplomatic communication.

Johnson's successor showed a keener understanding of how to send a message. In 1972 the North Vietnamese mounted the Easter Offensive, a conventional invasion of the South in flagrant violation of the spirit of the ongoing peace talks, intended to seize control of the country and deliver the United States a *fait accompli*. Richard Nixon, facing an election year and a hostile Congress, weighed his options and understood that he had to demonstrate that the United States would stand by its ally and not allow the war to be lost. Nixon also knew that once the decision to respond with force was made, the response should be decisive. "The surgical operation theory is all right," he told National Security Adviser Henry Kissinger, "but I want that place, whenever the planes are available, bombed to smithereens during the blockade. If we draw the sword out, we're going to bomb those bastards all over the place. . . . And let it fly. Let it fly."[9] ARVN troops, with U.S. air support, stalled the Easter Offensive, and eventually the North Vietnamese were driven back.

The Iraq war also has demonstrated the value in staying the course. By 2007 the situation in the country had deteriorated, and President Bush's approval ratings had sagged to historic lows. Democrats sensed blood in the water and were increasingly calling for a U.S. withdrawal, a declaration of defeat that would have caused incalculable damage to American national security and to the military establishment. But President Bush did not bow to political pressure. He successfully pushed for the implementation of a new strategy, achieved authorization for a troop surge, and in the course of a year the situation in Iraq improved dramatically. The United States avoided what would have been a historic defeat of American arms because President Bush had committed himself to victory. He faced greater challenges than Johnson did, but he was determined not to give up. His action demonstrated that even a weakened president can lead, if he so chooses.

Tet is remembered as a turning point that seems to lead inexorably to a war's conclusion. Nothing that followed Tet seemed to reach the same level of drama or public importance. But the war in Vietnam ground on. The United States suffered more deaths in the war after Tet than before. And Tet did not make defeat inevitable. Creighton Abrams's shift in strategy on the ground, U.S. interdiction against Communist safe havens in Cambodia and Laos, more effective bombing in the North, and the successful Vietnamization strategy, shifting more responsibilities to South Vietnamese forces, all improved the situation in the Republic of Vietnam. In some regards, the war could be said to have been won by the end of 1970.[10]

In the end, Vietnam became a casualty of other events—Watergate, the 1973 oil embargo, and a general crisis of confidence. The 1973 Paris Peace Agreement was a flawed deal forced on Saigon with promises of future U.S. support that were soon broken. The 1974 mid-term congressional elections demonstrated the power of the left wing of the Democratic Party as antiwar congressional candidates swept into office. The Democrats, already in the majority, took 43 Republican seats, some of them in solid GOP districts. One of the last acts of the emboldened 93rd Congress was the Foreign Assistance Act of 1974, which cut aid to South Vietnam and left the Paris Peace Agreement unenforceable. The House passed the bill after Senate action on December 11, 1974.

Exactly one week later, North Vietnamese leaders convened in Hanoi to formulate their final attack plan. By the end of April 1975 South Vietnam was in its death throes. The United States broke its agreement to support its ally and allowed this defeat to happen. We lost the Vietnam War by choice.

The legacy of Tet from the point of view of our adversaries is that it is possible to defeat the United States by targeting its political will. Tet became perceived as a defeat because the United States did not behave as though it had won. In unconventional wars, these perceptions can lead to long-term failure, and in the long run the Tet Offensive left an enduring sense of American political weakness. But an enemy cannot achieve the same type of impact when our country has strong leadership, particularly a president willing to take the steps necessary to secure victory. We may yet again see Americans being choppered to safety as another former ally is abandoned, to insurgents, to foreign intervention, or a combination of both. Or perhaps not. The choice will be ours.

ENDNOTES

CHAPTER I

1. Osama bin Laden, "Declaration of War against the Americans Occupying the Land of the Two Holy Places," *Al Quds al Arabi*, Aug. 1996.

2. In *On War* Clausewitz defines the components of the trinity as: primordial violence, hatred, and enmity; the play of chance and probability; and war's element of subordination to rational policy. These have been interpreted in contemporary terms to relate to the national will, the fighting forces, and the political leadership. The view was popularized by Harry Summers in *On Strategy* (Novato, CA: Presidio Press, 1982). Whether or not it represents a strictly doctrinaire reading of Clausewitz, it is a salient model for purposes of this discussion. For a more in-depth discussion of the issue see Christopher Bassford and Edward J. Villacres, "Reclaiming the Clausewitzian Trinity," *Parameters*, Autumn 1995.

3. Osama bin Laden audio tape released Feb. 12, 2003.

4. Osama bin Laden video tape released Nov. 9, 2001.

5. Aired on CNN, May 10, 1997.

6. Al-Jazeera TV, Oct. 31, 2006. Translation by MEMRI.

7. Quoted in Neil Munro, "Real or Fake?" *National Journal*, Apr. 10, 2006.

8. This discussion is based on the author's "Baghdad Tet: How the Bad Guys Can Win," *National Review Online*, Mar. 15, 2006.

9. "Grisly video of U.S. pilot is real, officials say: Footage shows pilot, on fire, being dragged after helicopter downing in Iraq," NBC News Services, Apr. 7, 2006.

10. "The Mujahideen Shura Council in Iraq Issues a Video of the Mutilated Corpses of the Two Captured American Soldiers in al-Ysefiya," SITE Institute, July 10, 2006.

11. "'In Memory of the Sunnah of Our Ancestors in Mutilating the Infidels'—A Video from the Mujahideen Shura Council in Iraq Featuring the Revenge Attack Upon Two Captured American Soldiers in al-Yusufiyah," SITE Institute, Sept. 22, 2006.

12. "Iraq war may have same psychological effect as Tet offensive," *U.S.A Today*, June 30, 2004, p. 10A.

13. One possible point of comparison is that the attacks occurred during a holiday, although this is not significant since there was no "Ramadan ceasefire" to exploit in order to gain the element of surprise.

14. Arthur Schlesinger, Jr., "This is Bush's Vietnam: The Wrong War, at the Wrong Time, in the Wrong Place, *The Independent*, Apr. 15, 2004. The gratuitous reference to LBJ's choosing not to seek another term as President was no doubt a well-considered comment in an election year.

15. "Press, political pressure helped 'lose' Fallujah, report says," *The Washington Times*, Jan. 2, 2008.

16. Patrick Cockburn: "The Crushing of Al-Fallujah Will Not End the War in Iraq," *The Independent*, Nov. 9, 2004. In Apr. 2007 Sgt. Maj. Kent was selected as Sergeant Major of the Marine Corps, the highest enlisted rank in the service.

17. Editorial: "Insecurity," Paris *Liberation*, June 25, 2004.

18. Rory Carroll, "Iraq Insurgents Snatch Victory from Defeat," *The Guardian*, June 24, 2005. A similar massed attack in April 2005 on Abu Ghraib prison was defeated in the same manner. See the author's "Going for Broke: Seeking Martyrdom in an Indifferent World," *National Review Online*, Apr. 6, 2005.

19. Thomas Friedman, "Barney and Baghdad," *New York Times*, Oct. 18, 2006. In his piece Friedman noted the August 2006 Global Islamic Media Front working paper (mentioned above) that stated he was the type of person the Islamists would seek to influence. Ironically

and unintentionally his article had exactly the kind of effect the GIMF would have wanted.

20. Tony Snow had said, "I think Friedman may be right, but we'll have to see."

21. The support given to the insurgency by Iran notwithstanding.

22. Ironically, the highest monthly total was in May 1968 during the so-called "Little Tet."

23. "McCain fears 'Tet-style' offensive in Iraq," Associated Press [hereafter cited as AP], Feb. 12, 2007.

24. Frederick W. Kagan and William Kristol, "Like Vietnam, New Al Qaeda Offensive Aimed At Sapping Americans' Morale," *Weekly Standard*, June 17, 2007.

25. Robert H. Reid, "Top Commander Expects Big Iraq Strikes," AP, July 7, 2007.

CHAPTER II

1. John P. Roche (1923–1994) was a political scientist, writer, and political activist who served as an adviser to John F. Kennedy, Hubert Humphrey, and Lyndon Johnson. Roche's role in the Johnson White House was to serve as an honest broker, a person without a constituency or external vested interests. He was someone the president could rely on for advice, knowing that it would be plainspoken and objective. Roche was born in Brooklyn and attended Hofstra College and Cornell. He served in the Army Air Force during World War II as a staff sergeant. Roche was a liberal Social Democrat and anti-Communist, whose scholarship focused on American political thought and foreign policy. His groundbreaking article, "The Founding Fathers: A Reform Caucus in Action," was the most reprinted article from the prestigious *American Political Science Review*. Roche taught at Haverford College, founded the government department and served as academic dean at Brandeis University, and headed the program in Civilization and Foreign Affairs at the Fletcher School of Law and Diplomacy. In the mid-1960s he was the chairman of Americans for Democratic Action, and he held impeccable liberal credentials. Roche never let his access to power go to his head. He was skilled in the ways of Washington without being a power seeker. He

saw government service the same way the Roman general Cincinnatus did, as something to be done well and then to be done with. He was frequently "inside" but would never brag about being an "insider." He knew all of the custodial and kitchen staff of the White House on a first-name basis, and while on long trips on Air Force One he would occupy his time playing poker with the Secret Service agents.

2.   "Can a Free Society Fight a Limited War?" in John P. Roche, *Sentenced to Life* (New York: Macmillan Publishing Co., 1974), p. 67.

3.   For a comprehensive review of the Diem period and the circumstances of his overthrow, see Mark Moyar, *Triumph Forsaken: The Vietnam War, 1954–1965* (Cambridge: Cambridge University Press, 2006).

4.   A second attack reported on August 4 was later found not to have taken place, but the report did have an impact on the Tonkin Gulf Resolution debate.

5.   One notes the similarity to the strategic objectives in Operation Iraqi Freedom.

6.   For an interesting study of Vietnam-era decision-making see Leslie H. Gelb and Richard K. Betts, *The Irony of Vietnam: The System Worked* (Washington, D.C.: Brookings Institution Press, 1979).

7.   The premise embedded in Johnson's speech—that the American people will be more willing to fight long-term struggles for principle rather than for some measurable objective—is curious and unsupported by history. If anything, such abstract wars will garner less support since they incur costs of blood and treasure yet give nothing tangible in return.

8.   Roche: "It was sort of like Roosevelt's attitude toward Stalin. In fact, it's an interesting parallel because Roosevelt was Johnson's idol. Roosevelt viewed Stalin as being [Jersey City Boss] Mayor [Frank] Hague with an overactive police force." John P. Roche, Fletcher School of Law and Diplomacy Oral History Project transcript, March 31, 1986, hereafter cited as Roche, OHP interview.

9.   The expression is often attributed to Lenin, although the imagery was used by Montesquieu to describe the support given by financiers to the governments to which they lend money. Lenin used it in his 1920 tract, *Left Wing Communism: An Infantile Disorder*, with reference to British Labour Party leader Arthur Henderson, whom Lenin regarded as a dupe. In 1957 Nikita Khrushchev said with respect to U.S. support

(or lack thereof) for the failed 1956 Hungarian revolution, "Support by United States rulers is rather in the nature of the support that the rope gives to a hanged man." Perhaps not coincidentally, Imre Nagy, who led the uprising, was executed the following year by hanging.

10. General Maxwell D. Taylor, "Peace and Stability for Vietnam is Constant U.S. Objective," undated text, Maxwell Taylor Papers, National Defense University, Washington, D.C.

11. Roche, *Sentenced to Life*, p. 67. Emphasis in original.

12. Herman Kahn, *On Escalation* (New York: Praeger, 1965), p. 39.

13. For a discussion of the sometimes irrational nature of crisis and strategic decision-making, see Graham Allison, *Essence of Decision: Explaining the Cuban Missile Crisis* (Boston: Little Brown, 1971).

14. Quoted in Barbara W. Tuchman, *The Guns of August* (New York: Macmillan, 1962), p. 91.

15. Gallup survey Oct. 6–11, 1967.

16. While by the mid-1960s escalation had become something to be avoided, for the reasons noted above, a decade earlier the threat of nuclear escalation helped force an end to the Korean War. See David Rees, *Korea: The Limited War* (Baltimore: Penguin Books, 1970), chap. 22, "The Atomic Threat."

17. Quoted in "Riding the Tiger," *Time*, Oct. 27, 1967.

18. Only 8% suggested that large-scale Chinese intervention would be a reason to withdraw.

19. Roche, OHP interview.

20. Quoted in Fox Butterfield, "The New Vietnam Scholarship," *The New York Times*, Feb. 13, 1983, p. 26. Colonel Summers also noted the following passages from the Hague Convention of 1907: "A neutral country has the obligation not to allow its territory to be used by a belligerent. If the neutral country is unwilling or unable to prevent this, the other belligerent has the right to take appropriate counteraction."

21. The sanctuaries and supply routes could effectively be interdicted only by ground action, as was demonstrated by the 1970 incursion into Cambodia. But while the operation was supported by a majority of Americans, there was substantial domestic and international political fallout over the incursion because the United States had ceded ground on the "neutrality" issue for years. The same was true about revelations of the CIA's "Air America" missions in Laos.

22. This is unusual, given the emphasis placed on the enemy order of battle as an indicant of progress in the war.

23. Bruce Palmer, *The 25 Year War: America's Military Role in Vietnam* (Lexington: University Press of Kentucky, 1984), pp. 177, 183. The amphibious feint during Operation Desert Storm is another example. Not using this method to keep Communist troops tied down is especially puzzling, given the Administration's fixation on diminishing the North Vietnamese order of battle as a metric of progress.

24. On Lee's strategy, see James A. Kegel, *North with Lee and Jackson: The Lost Story of Gettysburg* (Mechanicsburg, PA: Stackpole Books, 1996).

25. Summary of Joy's view from David H. Petraeus, "The American Military and the Lessons of Vietnam: A Study of Military Influence and the Use of Force in the Post-Vietnam Era" (Ph.D. diss., Princeton University, 1987), pp. 38–9.

26. Quoted in Paul Hendrickson, *The Living and the Dead: Robert McNamara and Five Lives of a Lost War* (New York: Alfred A. Knopf, 1996), p. 163. The story originated with Bill Moyers.

27. See Lyndon Baines Johnson, *The Vantage Point: Perspectives of the Presidency, 1963–1969* (New York: Holt, Rinehart and Winston, 1971), pp. 133–4.

28. C.f. H. R. McMaster, *Dereliction of Duty: Johnson, McNamara, the Joint Chiefs of Staff, and the Lies That Led to Vietnam* (New York: Harper Collins, 1997), *passim*, and Lt. Gen. Phillip B. Davidson, U.S.A (ret.), *Vietnam at War: The History: 1946–1975* (Novato, CA: Presidio Press, 1988), chap. 16. The parallels to Iraq are too noteworthy to ignore.

29. Interview with General Andrew Goodpaster, June 6, 1996, as part of CNN "Cold War" series.

30. Lieutenant General Charles G. Cooper, USMC (ret.), *Cheers and Tears: A Marine's Story of Combat in Peace and War* (Reno, NV: Wesley Press, 2002), pp. 3–5. "I almost dropped the map," Cooper recalled.

31. Palmer, *25 Year War*, p. 37.

32. Quoted in Petraeus, "Lessons of Vietnam," p. 120.

33. James C. Thomson, Jr., "How Could Vietnam Happen—An Autopsy," *Atlantic Monthly*, Apr. 1968, p. 51.

34. Roche, OHP interview.

35. Petraeus, "Lessons of Vietnam," p. 119.

36. Gallup survey Dec. 31, 1965–Jan. 5, 1966. Of all the insults for a Washington heavyweight, public anonymity is the worst. The poll supports the old adage that "Washington is full of famous people that no one ever heard of."

37. The inability of the U.S. to "fine-tune" the bombing instrument is covered in Wallace J. Thies, *When Governments Collide: Coercion and Diplomacy in the Vietnam Conflict, 1964–1968* (Berkeley: University of California Press, 1980). See also James Clay Thompson, *Rolling Thunder: Understanding Policy and Program Failure* (Chapel Hill: University of North Carolina Press, 1980).

38. Gallup survey Dec. 11–16, 1965.

39. Palmer, *25 Year War*, p. 177; Johnson, *The Vantage Point*, Appendix A.

40. Quoted in Petraeus, "Lessons of Vietnam," p. 125.

41. Bui Tin, *Following Ho Chi Minh: The Memoirs of a North Vietnamese Colonel* (Honolulu: University of Hawaii Press, 1995), pp. 63–4.

42. Quoted in Lewis Sorley, *A Better War: The Unexamined Victories and Final Tragedy of America's Last Years in Vietnam* (New York: Harcourt Brace & Co., 1999), p. 2.

43. Quoted in George Arthur Bailey, "The Vietnam War According to Chet, David, Walter, Harry, Peter, Bob, Howard and Frank: A Content Analysis of Journalistic Performance by the Network Television News Anchormen 1965–1970" (thesis, University of Wisconsin, 1973), p. 186.

44. Roche, OHP interview. Roche continued, "If you go back and look at the contingency plans that were worked out by John McNaughton and Bill Bundy in 1965 in which they lay out odds—60-40, 75-25, this, that, and the other thing—it's really interesting to say the least."

45. See the National Intelligence Council's *Estimative Products on Vietnam 1948–1975* (Pittsburgh, PA: Government Printing Office, Apr. 2005), document 29, pp. 427–56. Also Palmer, *25 Year War*, p. 78.

46. The 2007 NIE on Iranian nuclear intentions and capabilities is another example of a fundamentally political intelligence document. See Jay Solomon and Siobhan Gorman, "In Iran Reversal, Bureaucrats Triumphed Over Cheney Team; Rivalries Behind Iraq War Play Out in Risk Report; Bush Issues New Warning," *Wall Street Journal*, Jan. 14, 2008, p. 1.

47. Palmer, *25 Year War*, p. 43.

48. Col. Hang Ngoc Lung, *The General Offensives of 1968–69* (Washington, D.C.: U.S. Army Center of Military History, 1981), pp. 38 ff.

49. AP wire Apr. 20, 1967.

50. AP wire June 29, 1967.

51. New York Times News Service, October 31, 1967.

52. *Washington Post*, Apr. 6, 1969. The legacy of the data question was the "Order of Battle" controversy over the conflicting views on data regarding enemy troop strength just prior to Tet. Since the Communist offensive seemed to expose the lower MACV numbers as erroneous, some claimed they had been purposefully deflated. In 1982 CBS News produced a documentary entitled "The Uncounted Enemy: A Vietnam Deception," which claimed to demonstrate "a conspiracy at the highest levels of American military intelligence" and seemed to suggest that General Westmoreland had purposefully manipulated estimates of enemy presence in the South to give the impression the war was being won. Westmoreland sued the network for libel but dropped the case before it went to trial. See Bob Brewin and Sydney Shaw, *Vietnam on Trial: Westmoreland vs. CBS* (New York: Atheneum, 1987). Details on the political and methodological problems with counting the enemy can be found in Sam Adams, *War of Numbers: An Intelligence Memoir* (South Royalton, VT: Steerforth Press, 1994).

CHAPTER III

1. The term "Vietnam syndrome" was popularized by Ronald Reagan in an Aug. 18, 1980, speech entitled "Peace: Restoring the Margin of Safety," given at the Veterans of Foreign Wars convention in Chicago. But it had been used earlier, even before Tet—for example, here in 1967, on the reticence of members of Congress to discuss U.S. intervention in a crisis in the Congo: "Of overriding concern was the possibility that once the first step toward intervention was taken other steps would be inevitable. This feeling—what might be called the Vietnam syndrome—has been increasingly evident lately. It was visible during the recent Middle East crisis, when members of Congress almost unanimously urged no unilateral intervention. The evident danger of the Vietnam syndrome is that it could lead to a paralysis of will and action in cases where unilat-

eral U.S. efforts might indeed be necessary to protect American lives or vital American interests." See "U.S. Intervention in the Congo," *Fresno Bee,* July 13, 1967, p. 16C, reprinted from the *Los Angeles Times.*

2. Gallup survey Apr. 24–29, 1964.

3. Gallup survey Aug. 6–11, 1964.

4. Gallup survey Nov. 6–11, 1964.

5. For example, Aug. 10, 1965, as U.S. involvement escalated, 40% identified Vietnam as the most important issue. Civil rights was second at 21%.

6. Gallup survey July 16–21, 1965.

7. Gallup survey June 24–29, 1965.

8. Gallup survey June 24–29, 1965.

9. Gallup survey June 16–21, 1966.

10. Gallup survey Aug. 18–23, 1966.

11. Harris poll data Sept. and Dec. 1965, Feb. and June 1966.

12. Gallup survey Apr. 19–24, 1967. For Rusk response, see AP wire Apr. 20, 1967.

13. Sept. 18, 1967, confidential memo to the President from Fred Panzer, p. 12, The Vietnam Archive, Texas Tech University.

14. Gallup survey May 11–16, 1967.

15. Harris survey Dec. 1967, released Jan. 29, 1968.

16. Gallup survey June 16–21, 1966.

17. C.f. Mitchell Lerner, "Vietnam and the 1964 Election: A Defense of Lyndon Johnson," *Presidential Studies Quarterly,* fall 1995, pp. 751–66.

18. Terry Dietz, *Republicans and Vietnam, 1961–1968* (New York: Greenwood Press, 1986), p. 149.

19. "Reagan Urges U.S. to Declare North Viet War," *Fresno Bee,* Oct. 10, 1965, pp. 1A, 4A.

20. "Extremist Wreckers," *Fresno Bee,* Oct. 18, 1965, p. 16B.

21. Gallup survey Dec. 7–12, 1967.

22. This review ran in the *Van Nuys Valley News,* July 5, 1968, p. 23.

23. Roche, OHP interview. See, for example, Henry Cathcart's syndicated "Inside Washington" column, noting this as "Roche's Law," May 10, 1967.

24. Gallup survey Dec. 7–12, 1967.

25. Gallup survey Apr. 19–24, 1967.

26. C.f. Palmer, *25 Year War*, p. 81

27. Poll results in a Sept. 18, 1967, confidential memo to the President from Fred Panzer, p. 12, The Vietnam Archive, Texas Tech University.

28. "A Strong Party-line on the Riots and Vietnam," memo to the Vice President from William Connell, Aug. 30, 1967, p. 5, The Vietnam Archive, Texas Tech University.

29. George Horace Gallup, *The Gallup Poll: Public Opinion 1935–1971* (New York: Random House, 1972), p. 2065.

30. "A Strong Party-line" memo to the Vice President from William Connell, Aug. 30, 1967, pp. 3–4, The Vietnam Archive, Texas Tech University.

31. Gallup poll taken Oct. 29–Nov. 2, 1965.

32. Gallup survey Sept. 1–6, 1968.

33. Bui Tin in an interview with Stephen Young, *Wall Street Journal*, Aug. 3, 1995. Hereafter cited as Bui Tin/Young interview, 1995. Bui Tin was the highest ranking officer with the first North Vietnamese troops entering Saigon in 1975 and accepted the surrender of the South Vietnamese.

CHAPTER IV

1. Bui Tin/Young interview, 1995.

2. The Soviet Union might have used its veto power on the Security Council to halt the intervention but was boycotting the U.N. at the time to protest the U.N.'s refusal to seat representatives of the People's Republic of China as the legitimate Chinese government. When the decision to intervene was taken without them, the Soviets protested that the vote had been illegal.

3. There was a similar debate during the Iraq war. Fomenting civil war was an explicit objective of al Qaeda. See the author's "Civil War in Iraq?" *National Review Online*, Nov. 30, 2006.

4. Telephone Conversation between President Johnson and Senator J. William Fulbright, Washington, D.C., Jan. 20, 1967, 5:30 p.m. *Foreign Relations, 1964–1968*, vol. V, Vietnam 1967, document 23.

5. Bui Tin/Young interview, 1995. On Giap, see Peter Macdonald, *Giap: The Victor in Vietnam* (New York: W.W. Norton & Co., 1993) and

Cecil B. Currey, *Victory at Any Cost: The Genius of Vietnam's General Vo Nguyen Giap* (Washington, D.C.: Brassey's, 1997).

6. For the periodization of the North Vietnamese strategies, c.f. Douglas Pike, *War, Peace and the Viet Cong* (Cambridge: MIT Press, 1969), chapter 4.

7. Ang Cheng Guan, "Decision-making Leading to the Tet Offensive (1968)—The Vietnamese Communist Perspective," *Journal of Contemporary History*, vol. 33 (3), pp. 341–53.

8. Palmer, *25 Year War*, p. 60. Shelby Stanton argues that the VC benefitted from being driven into Cambodia because it placed the combatants beyond reach of U.S. attacks. Shelby L. Stanton, *The Rise and Fall of an American Army: U.S. Ground Forces in Vietnam, 1965–1973* (Novato, CA: Presidio Press, 1985), p. 133. However, clearly the enemy would have preferred to have maintained and expanded its presence closer to Saigon, so it is difficult to declare American operations a failure on that basis. The true failure in this regard was the strategic decision to allow the Communists to maintain safe havens in Cambodia, which ultimately was Johnson's fault and that of his senior strategists. Stanton's assertion is an example of the type of argument that tried to turn an obvious enemy setback into some form of victory.

9. Guan, "Decision-making," p. 344.

10. C.f. Richard H. Shultz, Jr., *The Secret War Against Hanoi: The Untold Story of Spies, Saboteurs, and Covert Warriors in North Vietnam* (New York: Harper Collins, 2000). This program was a remarkable example of the use of unconventional tactics and psychological warfare, and should be a model for other such efforts in America's unconventional wars. The program was so effective that the Johnson Administration shut it down for fear it would seriously destabilize the Hanoi government.

11. Davidson, *Vietnam at War*, p. 438, notes a former NLF member in 1982 stating that because of this sense of mistrust Tet was actually intended to wipe out the VC leadership.

12. 1990 interview with NVA General Tran Van Tra by John M. Carland, published in *Vietnam* magazine, Dec. 2002.

13. Discussion between Zhou Enlai and Pham Van Dong, Apr. 10, 1967, Cold War International History Project, document 5034C9A7–96B6–175C-9171AB983FB3D783, Woodrow Wilson International Center for Scholars, Washington, D.C.

14. C.f. Pike, *War, Peace and the Viet Cong*, pp.165–6, for a useful breakdown of the strategies and arguments for and against.

15. See, for example, Bui Tin, *Following Ho Chi Minh*, p. 61. He says Tet was "largely the brainchild" of Thanh. Pike believed that Thanh wanted to phase back, à la Mao, to the initial stages of Revolutionary War and negotiate. Understanding Thanh's role in planning Tet is made problematic by the fact that he died in the summer of 1967, and also that since Tet was a failure it was sensible to shift responsibility for it to the deceased Thanh, who could not argue otherwise and in any case was beyond punishment.

16. Bui Tin/Young interview, 1995.

17. Note that Osama bin Laden had a similarly poor assessment of the United States not being able to mount a long-term fight against terrorism.

18. Davidson, *Vietnam at War*, p. 499.

19. Al Qaeda also frequently cites sources in the U.S. press to justify its conclusions.

20. Note that this is the American assessment of the plan, which more closely tracks what was actually implemented.

21. Bui Tin/Young interview, 1995.

22. C.f. John M. Gates, "Philippine Guerrillas, American Anti-Imperialists, and the Election of 1900," *The Pacific Historical Review*, Vol. 46, No. 1 (Feb. 1977), pp. 51–64.

23. Davidson, *Vietnam at War*, p. 446.

24. Bui Tin/Young interview, 1995.

25. Guan, "Decision-making," p. 347.

26. Transcript of meeting between Mao Zedong, Pham Van Dong, and Vo Nguyen Giap, Apr. 11,1967, Cold War International History Project, document 5034C9C6–96B6–175C-96D86CF8502CADDD.

27. Bui Tin/Young interview, 1995.

28. Cheng Guan An, *The Vietnam War from the Other Side: the Vietnamese Communists' Perspective* (London: Routledge Curzon, 2002), p. 123.

29. James F. Dunnigan, and Albert A. Nofi, *Dirty Little Secrets of the Vietnam War* (New York: Thomas Dunne Books, 1999), p. 284. Soviet anti-aircraft gunners may have been responsible for the first downing of

American planes in the war. C.f. also Ilya Gaiduk, *The Soviet Union and the Vietnam War* (Chicago: I.R. Dee, 1996).

30. Record of the President's Debriefing, Glassboro, New Jersey, June 23, 1967, *Foreign Relations of the United States, 1964–1968*, vol. XIV, Soviet Union.

31. Major Nicholas P.Vaslef, "Some Politico-Military Aspects of the Sino-Soviet Rift," *Air University Review*, May-June 1967.

32. Don Oberdorfer, *Tet!* (Garden City, N.Y.: Doubleday, 1971), p. 83.

33. Davidson, *Vietnam at War*, p. 419.

34. "The Death of General Thanh," Radio Free Europe Research, July 10, 1967, has a good biography and analysis, without going into his cause of death.

35. Bui Tin, *Following Ho Chi Minh*, p. 61.

36. CMIC 02–040–68 23 Feb 68. Note that citations marked CMIC are interrogation reports from the Combined Military Interrogation Center, followed by the report number and date.

37. CMIC US 1478–68 4 Jun 68.

38. Giap, "Big Victory/Great Task," in Patrick J. McGarvey, ed., *Visions of Victory; Selected Vietnamese Communist Military Writings, 1964–1968* (Stanford, CA: Hoover Institution on War, Revolution and Peace, 1969), pp. 199–251.

39. Essay by Vo Nguyen Giap, Hanoi VNA News Service, Apr. 29, 2005.

40. Ibid.

CHAPTER V

1. "The U.S. is supporting and promoting a cruel and nasty war that has no visible end," Lippmann wrote in his May 21, 1964, column. "There is no light at the end of the tunnel." Lippmann later called for a "pull back from the Vietnamese mainland to continental islands inhabited by Western white men." Quoted in "Riding the Tiger," *Time*, Oct. 27, 1967.

2. Truong Dinh Dzu was eventually arrested, charged with "actions which weakened the will of the people to fight against the Communists," and on July 26, 1968, was sentenced to five years in prison.

3.   Quoted in Alex Abella, *Soldiers of Reason: The RAND Corporation and the Rise of the American Empire* (Orlando, FL: Harcourt Trade, 2008), p. 180.

4.   At the village level there was an 88-question survey filled out every quarter.

5.   Roche, OHP interview.

6.   Palmer, *25 Year War*, p. 56.

7.   Davidson, *Vietnam at War*, p. 391.

8.   Roche, OHP interview.

9.   Ibid.

10.   Palmer, *25 Year War*, p. 74.

11.   John Roche wrote, "An adequate one-sentence review would state: 'While occasionally interesting and enlightening, the *Pentagon Papers* is fundamentally a historical junkpile which provides neither proof nor disproof for any hypotheses about the origins and character of the war in Vietnam.'" Roche believed it was a mistake for the government to challenge the publication of the collection, since it reinforced the idea that there were secrets, and that perception only gave stature to the documents and lionized those who leaked them. C.f. George McGovern and John P. Roche, "The Pentagon Papers—A Discussion," *Political Science Quarterly*, vol. 87, no. 2, June 1972, pp. 173–91.

12.   "LBJ denies any rift over Viet bombing," UPI, Sept. 2, 1967.

13.   Roche, OHP interview.

14.   Quoted by AP in wire copy Jan. 20, 1968. The quote was so noteworthy it was included in Clifford's official brief Defense Department biography.

15.   *The Pentagon Papers* (Boston: Beacon Press, 1971), vol. 4, chap. 2, "U.S. Ground Strategy and Force Deployments, 1965–1968," Section 4. For information on the covert war waged against the North, see Shultz, *The Secret War Against Hanoi*.

16.   Gallup survey Oct. 6–11, 1967. 49% opposed what was presented as "Plan X."

17.   Song Be had been the site of a major NVA attack in the spring of 1965, meant to deter the United States from intervening in Vietnam, but its troops were defeated after two days by surprisingly resilient South Vietnamese forces.

18. Lieutenant General John H. Hay, Jr., *Vietnam Studies: Tactical and Materiel Innovations* (Washington, D.C.: Department of the Army, 1989), chap. 4, "Loc Ninh."

19. C.f. Edward F. Murphy, *Dak To* (New York: Presidio Press, 2002).

20. Davidson, *Vietnam at War*, p. 469.

21. "Sen. Keating: Cuba Affair Not yet Over," AP wire report, Dec. 10, 1962. A May 28, 1965, David Wise column on the Dominican Republic did not use the expression, but several headline writers derived it from his column. See for example, "Caught in Credibility Gap," *The Valley Independent* (Monessen, PA), May 28, 1965, p. 4.

22. Murrey Marder, "Credibility Gap: Greater Skepticism Greets Official Declarations," *Washington Post*, Dec. 6, 1965, p. A21.

23. Jack Wilson, "Potomac Fever," *Washington Post*, Dec. 31, 1966, p. A9.

24. Gallup survey Mar. 9–14, 1967. It is worth noting that the question and answer as reported are unclear—not telling the public all it should know does not equal not telling the truth.

25. Gallup survey Oct. 6–11, 1967.

26. Daniel Ellsberg, *Secrets: A Memoir of Vietnam and the Pentagon Papers* (New York: Viking Press, 2002), p. 199.

27. "Bunker Optimistic About Vietnam War," UPI, Nov. 14, 1967. The same article reported a Harris poll showing Johnson's approval rating for handling the war at an "all time low" of 23%.

28. Gallup polls taken July 13–18 and Nov. 16–12, 1967.

29. *The Pentagon Papers*, Gravel ed. (Boston: Beacon Press, 1971), vol. 4, p. 538.

30. Quoted in Davidson, *Vietnam at War*, p. 483.

31. Tom Buckley, "Portrait of an Aging Despot," *Harpers*, Apr. 1972, p. 69.

CHAPTER VI

1. "Seized Vietcong Aide Is Identified in Saigon," *New York Times*, Dec. 3, 1967, p. 2.

2. John L. Hart, "The Attempt to Deport Gen. Loan," *Washington Post*, Nov. 12, 1978, p. B6.

3. Nguyen Cao Ky, *Buddha's Child: My Fight to Save Vietnam* (New York: St. Martin's Press, 2002), pp. 176, 265.

4. Ky, *Buddha's Child*, p. 265.

5. Ibid., pp. 175–6.

6. CIA Intelligence Information Cable, Feb. 9, 1966.

7. The South Vietnam Political Scene, 1968, folder 01, box 16, pp. 15–16, Douglas Pike Collection: Unit 06—Democratic Republic of Vietnam, The Vietnam Archive, Texas Tech University.

8. Neil Sheehan, "Renewed Fighting Flares in Danang Outside Pagodas," *New York Times*, May 19, 1966, p. 1.

9. Ky, *Buddha's Child*, pp. 222–3.

10. Brice Miller, "Police Raid Viet Pagoda," UPI wire service, June 19, 1966.

11. Buckley, "Despot," *Harpers*, Apr. 1972, p. 69.

12. R.W. Apple, Jr., "Saigon Assembly Upholds Election by a Narrow Vote," *New York Times*, Oct. 3, 1967, p. 1.

13. Thich is an honorific meaning "venerable."

14. R.W. Apple, Jr., "Vietnamese Assembly Will Decide the Election Today," Warren (PA) *Times Mirror and Observer*, Oct. 2, 1967, p. 3.

15. Oriana Fallaci, *Nothing, and So Be It* (Garden City, NY: Doubleday and Co. Inc., 1972), pp. 90, 92.

16. John L. Hart, "The Attempt to Deport Gen. Loan," *Washington Post*, Nov. 12, 1978, p. B6.

17. Fallaci, *Nothing*, p. 88. Fallaci was in Vietnam prior to Tet and returned as the battle was still raging. Encounters with General Loan form the fascinating sub-text to this very interesting memoir.

18. Philip Goodhart, MP, *Vietnam—Autumn Reflections*, a pamphlet of newspaper articles reprinted in late 1967. The Vietnam Archive, Texas Tech University.

19. Ibid. Presciently, Goodhart wrote: "An all-out effort to increase terrorism in Saigon is possibly the only military threat left in Viet Cong hands." Ibid., p. 7.

20. "Saigon Gets Suggestion Box," *New York Times*, Oct. 30, 1966, p. 5.

21. R.W. Apple, Jr., "New Phase for Thieu," *New York Times*, Oct. 30, 1967, p. 6.

22. Peter Arnett, "To War with Eddie Adams," *The Digital Journalist,* Oct. 2004.

23. Hanson W. Baldwin, "2 Year Drive in Saigon Cuts Terrorism Sharply," *New York Times,* Jan. 19, 1968, p. 12.

24. "The Creation of Uncle Nguyen," *Time,* June 21, 1968.

25. Horst Faas, "The Saigon Execution," *The Digital Journalist,* Oct. 2004.

26. Fallaci, *Nothing,* pp. 87–8.

27. In this sense Loan faced the same problem as Diem or any other person of influence in a regime supported by the United States— the U.S. tends to prefer officials in independent sovereign states to do what they are told.

28. "Saigon Forbids the Arrest of Vietnamese by the U.S.," *New York Times,* Dec. 9, 1966, p. 11.

29. Interview with Harry McPherson by David Culbert, undated, Douglas Pike Collection, The Vietnam Archive, Texas Tech University.

30. John L. Hart, "The Attempt to Deport Gen. Loan," *Washington Post,* Nov. 12, 1978, p. B6.

31. "Vietcong Threaten to Kill G.I. Captives," *New York Times,* June 17, 1967, p. 11; "3 Terrorists Get Reprieve in S. Vietnam," *Washington Post,* Nov. 17, 1967, p. A1.

32. "Viet Cong Execute U.S. Army Sergeant in Reprisal For Terrorists' Deaths," AP, June 25, 1965.

33. Versace was a 1959 graduate of the U.S. Military Academy. His father Colonel Humbert Joseph Versace was in the class of 1933.

34. See memo for Ambassador Bunker, "Release of the Three Sergeants by the Viet Cong in Phnom Penh Should be Publicly Reciprocated by the Release of Three VC PW's by the GVN," Nov. 24, 1967, The Vietnam Archive, Texas Tech University.

35. Quoted in William Tuohy, *Dangerous Company: Inside the World's Hottest Trouble Spots with a Pulitzer Prize-winning War Correspondent* (New York: Morrow, 1987), pp. 116–17.

36. Harriman memo, Nov. 3, 1967, The Vietnam Archive, Texas Tech University. The fact that Hanoi continued to hold out could, of course, have been taken as the evidence that Harriman said did not exist, and it was a more compelling argument than the belief that Hanoi in

fact sought peace on any terms other than total victory, for which there really was no evidence whatever.

37. See Rostow memo to Johnson, Nov. 8, 1967, 0900, The Vietnam Archive, Texas Tech University.

38. Ibid.

39. See Rostow memo to Johnson, Nov. 3, 1967, The Vietnam Archive, Texas Tech University. The U.S. Ambassador in Pakistan made it a point to get clarification on whether the offer for negotiations was that a bombing halt "could" lead to talks or "would" lead to them. The word came back through channels that the offer was "could." It was almost two months later when North Vietnamese Foreign Minister Nguyen Duy Trinh created a diplomatic flurry by saying that a bombing halt "would" lead to negotiations. Note also that the North's claim that it did not seek to take over the South was a transparent lie.

40. Fallaci, *Nothing*, pp. 86–7.

41. Cable from Bunker to Rostow *et al.*, Nov. 7, 1967, The Vietnam Archive, Texas Tech University.

42. R.W. Apple, Jr., "Amnesty Granted to 6,270 Prisoners by Saigon," *New York Times*, Nov. 4, 1967, p. 6.

43. "Saigon Cabinet Rift Ends, But Rivalry Continues," *Washington Post*, Dec. 1, 1967, p. A12.

44. Cable from Bunker to Rostow *et al.* Dec. 1, 1967, The Vietnam Archive, Texas Tech University; R.W. Apple, Jr., "A Vietcong Envoy Reported Seized," *New York Times*, Dec. 2, 1967, p. 1; James Pringle, "Arrest of Viet Cong Official Stirs Storm," Reuters, Dec. 3, 1967.

45. Lee Lescaze, "VC's Arrest Stirs Saigon's Rumor Mill," *Washington Post*, Dec. 10, 1967, p. A1.

46. See Peter R. Kann, "Saigon Snafu," *Wall Street Journal*, Dec. 12, 1967, p. 20.

47. Saigon Embassy to Secretary of State, Dec. 27, 1967, The Vietnam Archive, Texas Tech University.

48. "Saigon Politico Declares U.S. '2nd Enemy,'" *Stars and Stripes*, Jan. 5, 1968, p. 24.

CHAPTER VII

1. The seminal works on the topic of intelligence failure and the Tet Offensive include James J. Wirtz, *The Tet Offensive: Intelligence Failure*

in War (Ithaca, NY: Cornell University Press, 1994), and Ronnie E. Ford, *Tet 1968: Understanding the Surprise* (London: Frank Cass, 1995).

2. Ward Just, "McNamara Says VC Suffered Big Losses, Warns of New Raids," *Washington Post*, Feb. 2, 1968, p. A12.

3. "Hanoi Offensive Fails: McNamara," AP, Feb. 2, 1968.

4. Arnold Abrams, "Turning Point," *Newsday*, Feb. 2, 1998, p. B3.

5. Quoted in Davidson, *Vietnam at War*, pp. 483–4. Johnson was in Australia for a memorial for Prime Minister Harold Holt, who had drowned December 17. It was his first stop on a round-the-world good will tour and peace mission.

6. "Cong Terrorists Double Toll," AP, Jan. 5, 1968.

7. Quoted in the Aiken (SC) *Standard and Review*, Jan. 3, 1968, p. 4.

8. Guan, "Decision-making," p. 351.

9. Don North, "V.C. Assault on the U.S. Embassy," *Vietnam* magazine, Feb. 2001.

10. For example: "an August 1964 National Intelligence Estimate of the chances of a Chinese nuclear detonation noted that a test site was being prepared at Lop Nor, and would be ready in two months. However, the CIA stated that the Chinese would not have the necessary fissionable material to finish a bomb, so they doubted anything would happen for the rest of the year. Sure enough, two months later, on October 16, 1964, the Chinese successfully tested a nuclear weapon." James S. Robbins, "Time Bomb: The poor track record of atomic predictions," *National Review Online*, May 16, 2006.

11. Palmer, *25 Year War*, p. 78.

12. Davidson, *Vietnam at War*, p. 45.

13. Chalmers M. Roberts, "East-West Semantics Sticky as Vietnam Mud," *Washington Post* column reprinted in the Charleston *Gazette-Mail*, Jan. 28, 1968.

14. Hedrick Smith, "A New U.S. Offer of Peace Terms is Sent to Hanoi," *New York Times*, Jan. 30, 1968, p. 1.

15. Robert J. Hanyok, *Spartans in Darkness: American SIGINT and the Indochina War, 1945–1975* (Ft. Meade, MD: Center for Cryptologic History, National Security Agency, 2002), chapter 7. In general, the NSA provided vast, detailed information on enemy troop movements and communications that far exceeded anything available to earlier generations of military

leaders and policymakers. Yet the analyses based on this information were only as good as the premises that underlay them, and in any case could serve only to advise, not direct, the intelligence consumers.

16. "Marines Bolster Strength in Crucial Border Areas," AP, Jan. 12, 1968.

17. Westmoreland to Wheeler, Feb. 1, 1968, The Vietnam Archive, Texas Tech University.

18. There was a statue of the emperor in Westmoreland's official residence in Saigon.

19. American Embassy Saigon, "Periodic Report on Tet Truce," Feb. 10, 1967.

20. CMIC 02-043-68 12 Mar 68.

21. "Foe Begins Truce but Allies Report Attack on a Post," *New York Times*, Jan. 27, 1968, p. 1.

22. Helmer Aslaksen, "The Mathematics of the Chinese Calendar," Department of Mathematics, National University of Singapore, http://www.math.nus.edu.sg/aslaksen/calendar/cal.pdf, Feb. 6, 2009.

23. Quoted in United States Army, *II Field Force Press Briefing on VC Tet Offensive*, II Field Force Record, Mar. 20, 1968, p. 7.

24. As the Communists swept through the countryside, they captured six American missionaries working in a nearby Montagnard village and summarily killed them.

25. HIESS Briefing, 1968 Tet Offensive TS II CTZ, Apr. 17, 1968.

26. See, for example, the pamphlet "Chaos in Saigon" published by the International Committee of Conscience on Vietnam of the Fellowship of Reconciliation, Feb. 25, 1968.

27. Arnold Abrams, "Turning Point," *Newsday*, Feb. 2, 1998, p. B3.

28. LTC Edward C. Peter, "The Press and the War in Vietnam," Industrial College of the Armed Forces, Ft. Lersley J. McNair, Washington, D.C., 1969, pp. 13–14.

CHAPTER VIII

1. Ba Van's story is taken from CMIC U.S. 538–68 12 Mar 68, his interrogation report. Chuc's is from CMIC U.S. 382–68 26 Feb 68.

2. In Chuc's account he refers to Ba Dan, presumably Ba Van.

3. Chuc's account has seven men in the truck, with "Ba Dan" driving.

4. Chuc said the team stayed at the house, and that eight VC arrived later and also stayed there.

5. Dang Van Son's interrogation report. CMIC U.S. 1571–68 11 Jun 68.

6. Other names mentioned in interrogation reports as being on the team were Sau, Mang, Chinh, Tai, Bay Quyen, Duong, and Thanh.

7. Eight years later to the day, Mar. 29, 1973, the last American combat troops left Vietnam.

8. Jackson Bosley, liaison officer between MACV-CIA and the embassy, later noted "That big door was later cut up and made into paperweights for the staff."

9. Peter, "The Press and the War in Vietnam," p. 48.

10. See, for example, Edwin Q. White, "Cong Invaders Wiped Out In Raid on U.S. Embassy," *Charleston Gazette*, Jan. 31, 1968, p. 1. On Arnett's belief that the VC were inside the chancery, see Don North, "V.C. Assault on the U.S. Embassy," *Vietnam* magazine, Feb. 2001.

11. Roche, OHP interview.

12. Quoted in James H. Willbanks, *The Tet Offensive: A Concise History* (New York: Columbia University Press, 2007), p. 37.

13. On the golf course fighting, see Peter Arnett, *Live From the Battlefield: from Vietnam to Baghdad: 35 Years in the World's War Zones* (New York: Simon & Schuster, 1994), p. 246.

14. CMIC 02–005–68 9 Feb 68.

15. Oberdorfer, *Tet!*, pp. 144–5.

16. See "Order for a General Attack in Sub-Region 1," captured enemy document from December 1967/January 1968, translated and distributed by COMUSMACV (CDEC), ISC number 708.100, report dated May 1, 1968. The lengthy planning document goes into minute detail on the targets in and around the air base.

17. CMIC 02–022–68 12 Feb 68. The report has many details on the attack plan.

18. CMIC 02–017–68 12 Feb 68.

19. Arnold Abrams, "Turning Point," *Newsday*, Feb. 2, 1998, p. B3.

20. Oberdorfer, *Tet!*, pp. 147–8.

21. The technique is used on a smaller scale in contemporary urban warfighting. It is easier to take a house down than to assault it, and results in fewer friendly casualties.

22. Roche, OHP Interview.

23. Fallaci, *Nothing*, p. 115.

CHAPTER IX

1. Fox Butterfield with Karl Haskell, "Getting It Wrong in a Photo," *New York Times*, Apr. 23, 2000, and Hubert Van Es, "Thirty Years at 300 Millimeters," *New York Times*, Apr. 29, 2005. People were, however, being choppered from the embassy; this just wasn't a picture of that.

2. The most compelling claim that the man in the picture is Bay Lop comes from his wife, Nguyen Thi Lop. See Greg Torode, "War secret dies with killer of Saigon," *South China Morning Post*, July 23, 1998, p. 16. He has also been identified as Viet Cong political officer Le Cong Na, and as Nguyen Tan Dat, alias Han Son. All accounts of his identity agree that he was part of a sapper unit.

3. This drawn from captured VC pay records. C.f. Captured Documents (CDEC): Notebook and Record (Military Intelligence of Military Region IV) 23 Jan 1967.

4. Fallaci, *Nothing*, p. 92.

5. See, for example, study of the use of terror tactics by the VC, "The Mariah Project—A Study of the Use of Terror by the Viet Cong," prepared by HQ 5th Special Forces Group, May 1966.

6. "Viet Cong Terror Tactics in South Viet-Nam," Viet-Nam Information Notes #7, Office of Media Services, Bureau of Public Affairs, U.S. Department of State, July 1967, p. 3.

7. "Viet Cong Terrorism Continues as Elections Near," USIA Report, Aug. 29, 1967. This report notes that "captured enemy documents spell out plans for harassment, assassination and terror countrywide" in the lead-up to the election. Teams were going to attempt to infiltrate Saigon "disguised as bamboo basket sellers."

8. "Dragon Lady Held; Killed 5," *Oakland Tribune*, Sept. 22, 1967, p. 4.

9. Department of Defense Intelligence Information Report 6–027–0738–68, 25 Jan 68.

10. On this last in particular, see "Seduce and Destroy: Pretty Girls Could Have Kiss of Death," *Stars and Stripes*, May 31, 1968. The article noted that the VC was using "seduce and destroy" squads of attractive women near a Marine base to entice men to their death. Apparently several Marines had fallen victim to this technique. See also "Vietcong Use Girls as Bait for Marines," *Washington Post*, May 2, 1968, p. A1.

11. Report of Security Poss Section of Saigon Giadinh Region, Feb. 27, 1968, CDEC Doc Log No. 03–2497–68.

12. CMIC U.S. 1297–68 22 May 68.

13. "Order for a General Attack in Sub-Region 1," captured enemy document from December 1967/January 1968, translated and distributed by COMUSMACV (CDEC), ISC number 708.100, report dated May 1, 1968, p. 25. General Loan's residence was also mentioned as a target, p. 26.

14. Davidson, *Vietnam at War*, p. 482.

15. Report of Security Poss Section of Saigon Giadinh Region, Feb. 27, 1968, CDEC Doc Log No. 03–2497–68.

16. Buckley, "Despot," p. 72.

17. Arthur McCafferty to LBJ, Feb. 1, 1968, The Vietnam Archive, Texas Tech University.

18. Quoted in Daniel C. Hallin, *The Uncensored War* (New York: Oxford University Press, 1986), p. 172.

19. George Esper, "Remembering Eddie Adams," *The Digital Journalist*, Oct. 2004.

20. Hal Buell, "On 'Easy Ed' Adams," *The Digital Journalist*, Oct. 2004.

21. Wally McNamee, "Remembering Eddie Adams," *The Digital Journalist*, Oct. 2004.

22. Peter Arnett, "To War with Eddie Adams," *The Digital Journalist*, Oct. 2004.

23. Ibid.

24. Tuckner's account quoted in Robert J. Donovan and Raymond L. Scherer, *Unsilent Revolution: Television News and American Public Life, 1948 to 1991* (Cambridge: Cambridge University Press, 1992), p. 100.

25. Ibid.

26. Horst Faas, "The Saigon Execution," *The Digital Journalist*, Oct. 2004. Like the Rosenthal photo on Iwo Jima, Adams took the photo on reflex.

27. Donovan, *Unsilent Revolution*, p. 100.

28. "Obituary: Nguyen Ngog Loan," *New York Times*, July 16, 1998.

29. Buckley, "Despot," p. 72.

30. Colonel Tran Minh Cong, personal interview with the author, May 23, 2010. Colonel Cong was later the head of the South Vietnamese Police Academy.

31. Ky, *Buddha's Child*, p. 265.

32. "Ho Chi Minh Memories," *Time*, Mar. 15, 1993.

33. Nguyen Truong Toai, "We Died," in Larry Engelmann, *Tears Before the Rain* (New York: Oxford University Press, 1990), pp. 233–4.

34. Susan Herendeen, "Area restaurateur recalls another lifetime: Cameraman's images of Vietnam influenced nation," Annapolis *Capital*, Nov. 24, 1997, p. A1.

35. Colonel Tran Minh Cong, personal interview with the author, May 23, 2010.

36. "S. Viets' killer-cop has become gentle as a kitten," AP, Dec. 26, 1972.

37. Quoted in Kevin Jackson, "To hell and back—Susan Sontag in the wars," *Weekend Australian*, Nov. 22, 2003, p. B1.

38. Colonel Tran Minh Cong, personal interview with the author, May 23, 2010.

39. Horst Faas, "The Saigon Execution," *The Digital Journalist*, Oct. 2004.

40. Ibid.

41. Ibid.

42. Ibid.

43. Quoted in George A. Bailey and Lawrence W. Lichty, "Rough Justice on a Saigon Street: A Gatekeeper Study of NBC's Tet Execution Film," *Journalism Quarterly*, summer 1972, pp. 221–2.

44. Harry McPherson interview with David Culbert, undated, Douglas Pike Collection, The Vietnam Archive, Texas Tech University.

45. William F. Buckley, Jr., "European Reports Illustrate U.S. Foreign Policy Chaos," *Ogden Standard-Examiner*, Feb. 9, 1968, p. 6A. Buckley had seen the photographs in the Paris edition of the *Herald Tribune*.

46. Greg Torode, "War secret dies with killer of Saigon," *South China Morning Post*, July 23, 1998, p. 16.

47. Horst Faas, "The Saigon Execution," *The Digital Journalist*, Oct. 2004.

48. Ibid.

49. Quoted in George A. Bailey and Lawrence W. Lichty, "Rough Justice," p. 224.

50. Ibid., p. 225.

51. Tom Buckley, "Portrait of an Aging Despot," *Harpers*, Apr. 1972, p.71; also Tim Page, "The Shots Seen Round the World," *Washington Post*, May 21, 2001, p. C1.

52. David D. Perlmutter, "Wisdom from Images of War," *Chronicle of Higher Education*, Apr. 25, 2003, p. 11.

53. "Jurists Say Viet Brutality Gets Worse," *Washington Post*, Mar. 8, 1968, p. A19.

54. Buckley, "Despot," p. 71.

55. "U.S. Cautions Saigon on Captives' Treatment," *New York Times*, Feb. 5, 1968, p. 14.

56. Tom Buckley, "Ky Says Regime Will Arm Public," *New York Times*, Feb. 6, 1968, p. 1.

57. Quoted in Willbanks, *Tet Concise History*, p. 37.

58. Colonel Tran Minh Cong, personal interview with the author, May 23, 2010.

59. Bailey and Lichty, "Rough Justice," p. 227.

60. Quoted in Carol K. Winkler, *In the Name of Terrorism: Presidents on Political Violence in the Post World War II Era* (Albany: State University Of New York Press, 2006), pp. 34–5.

61. Eddie Adams interview, undated, Item #1770101001, The Vietnam Archive, Texas Tech University.

62. Harry McPherson interview with David Culbert, undated, Douglas Pike Collection, The Vietnam Archive, Texas Tech University.

63. Ibid. McPherson also said the event seemed to "demonstrate the Oriental's lack of concern for human life, which we hear a lot about when there were mass deaths in Vietnam."

64. Ky, *Buddha's Child*, p. 265.

CHAPTER X

1. White House, Memorandum for the Record of 583rd NSC meeting, Mar. 27, 1968.

2. Quoted in Peter Arnett, "The Only Way To 'Save' City Was To Destroy It," AP, Feb. 7, 1968.

3. Ibid.

4. Michael D. Miller, "Saving Ben Tre," Oct. 25, 2006. http://www.nhe.net/BenTreVietnam/

5. Ibid.

6. Hanoi NVA International Service in English, Feb. 8, 1968, 0545 GMT.

7. Orr Kelly, "U.S. Caught Off Guard by Intensity of Attacks," *Washington Evening Star*, Jan. 31, p. A6.

8. AP report, "Painstaking Organization," Feb. 3, 1968.

9. "Circular from Central Office of South Vietnam (COSVN) Current Affairs Committee and Military Affairs Committee of South Vietnam Liberation Army (SVNLA) Headquarters Concerning a Preliminary Assessment of the Situation," Feb. 1, 1968.

10. Ibid.

11. Ibid.

12. "After Tet: Three Viet Cong Assessments," Viet-Nam Documents and Research Notes, United State Mission in Vietnam, Apr. 1968.

13. Samuel L. Popkin quoted in Fox Butterfield, "The New Vietnam Scholarship," *New York Times*, Feb. 13, 1983, p. 26.

14. Statement by Col. R.D. Sonstelle, former senior adviser, 5th ARVN Division, Washington D.C., Feb. 13, 1969. Quoted in Peter, "The Press and the War in Vietnam."

15. Fallaci, *Nothing*, pp. 105–6.

16. Douglas Pike, *Tet 1968: U.S. Embassy Attack*, monograph, Saigon, South Vietnam, Feb. 14, 1968.

17. Don North, "V.C. Assault on the U.S. Embassy," *Vietnam* magazine, Feb. 2001.

18. Murrey Marder, "U.S. Experts Concede Gain by VC," *Washington Post*, Feb. 3, 1968, p. A1.

19. Memorandum for Honorable Walt W. Rostow, "The Situation in South Vietnam," Jan. 30, 1968, The Vietnam Archive, Texas Tech University.

20. "The Communist Tet Offensive," Intelligence Memorandum, CIA Directorate of Intelligence, Jan. 31, 1968, The Vietnam Archive, Texas Tech University.

21. "Hanoi Offensive Fails: McNamara," AP, Feb. 2, 1968.

22. Quoted in Peter, "The Press and the War in Vietnam," p. 42.

23. Ward Just, "U.S. Voices Confidence, Raids Were Expected," *Washington Post*, Feb. 1, 1968, p. A4.

24. "President Johnson's Notes on Conversation with Secretary McNamara, Feb. 6, 1968."

CHAPTER XI

1. See generally Keith William Nolan, *Battle for Hue: Tet 1968* (Novato, CA: Presidio Press, 1996), and "Victory at Hue," *Army Journal*, Feb. 1969, pp. 3–20.

2. MCO P5060.20, *Marine Corps Drill and Ceremonies Manual*, Appendix D, p. 25.

3. From Tran Van Trug, *Les Hommes d'au-dela du Sud* (Neuchâtel: la Baconnière, 1957), quoted in J. R. Bullington, "Religion and Romance in Wartime Vietnam," *American Diplomacy*, vol. III, no. 3, 1998.

4. Joe Vargo, "A Hero Looks Back," Riverside *Press-Enterprise*, Feb. 3, 2000.

5. Renita Foster, "Hell years: Ex-prisoner of war recounts horrors of North Vietnamese capture," Public Affairs Office, Fort Monmouth, NJ (undated). See also accounts at http://www.pownetwork. org and the AFVN website at http://webspace.webring.com/people/rr/ rmorecook/index.html.

6. Quoted in William Tuohy, *Dangerous Company*, p. 118. For a good analysis of urban combat in Hue, see Maj. Jonathan P. Hull, "Hue, The Mirror on the Pole View Around the Corner to the Future Urban

Combat," Marine Corps University Command and Staff College, Quantico, VA, 1997.

7. G. R. Christmas, "A Company Commander Reflects on Operation Hue City," *Marine Corps. Gazette*, Apr. 1971, pp. 34–9. Quoted in Earle Rice, Jr., *The Tet Offensive* (San Diego: Lucent Books, 1997).

8. Ibid.

9. Alje Vennema, *The Viet Cong Massacre at Hue* (New York: Vantage Press, 1976), p. 115.

10. Quoted in Tuohy, *Dangerous Company*, p. 119.

11. In fact, the two-hour delay preserved the pagoda in question; since the enemy left, it could be occupied peacefully.

12. Quoted in Tuohy, *Dangerous Company*, p. 120.

13. Ibid., p. 119.

14. James S. Robbins, "Insurgent Seizure of an Urban Area: Grozny 1996," in James J. F. Forest (ed.), *Countering Terrorism and Insurgency in the 21st Century*, vol. 3 (Westport, CT: Praeger, 2007), pp. 88–102.

15. Fallaci, *Nothing*, p. 167. Fallaci arrived in Hue on February 27.

16. "Grim Death Grips Ancient City of Hue," *Arizona Republic*, Mar. 1, 1968, p. 2.

CHAPTER XII

1. "Third Annual Veterans' Day Weekend Festival," 1990, Folder 6, Box 37, Douglas Pike Collection: Unit 03—Veterans, The Vietnam Archive, Texas Tech University. Dr. Truong added, "I will never forget how the Viet Cong killed thousands of civilians who were fleeing toward Hue on Highway 1 in 1975. I remember my parents' concern that antiwar demonstrations would undermine U.S. support for the war at a time when Russian and Chinese support for North Vietnam was stronger than ever."

2. Bui Tin, *Following Ho Chi Minh*, p. 63.

3. Quoted in Jack Anderson, "Hanoi, VC Kill Civilians Regularly," *Washington Post*, Dec. 6, 1969, p. C15.

4. "Plans for the Offensive and Uprising of MUI A," Jan. 26, 1968, document captured Aug. 28, 1968, p. 1, The Vietnam Archive, Texas Tech University. This 12-page document contains detailed instructions for the assault on and occupation of Hue.

5. Vennema, *Viet Cong Massacre*, p. iv.

6. Ibid., p. 1.

7. "Plans for the Offensive and Uprising," p. 12.

8. Vennema, *Viet Cong Massacre*, p. 95.

9. Ibid., p. 94.

10. "Plans for the Offensive and Uprising," p. 7.

11. Vennema, *Viet Cong Massacre*, p. 94.

12. Bui Tin, *Following Ho Chi Minh*, p. 63.

13. Fallaci, *Nothing*, pp. 168–9.

14. Douglas Pike, "The Viet Cong Strategy of Terror" (Saigon: U.S. Mission, Feb. 1970), p. 57.

15. "Plans for the Offensive and Uprising," p. 8.

16. Fallaci, *Nothing*, pp. 168–9.

17. Bui Tin, *Following Ho Chi Minh*, p. 63.

18. Truong Nhu Trang, *A Viet Cong Memoir* (San Diego: Harcourt Brace Jovanovich, 1985), pp. 153–4.

19. J. V. Stalin, "Dizzy with Success: Concerning Questions of the Collective-Farm Movement," *Pravda*, no. 60, Mar. 2, 1930, in J. V. Stalin, *Works*, vol. 12, pp. 197–205 (Moscow: Foreign Languages Publishing House, 1955).

20. Recapitulative Report, Phase of Attack on Hue from 31 January to 25 February 1968, report March 30, 1968, CDEC Doc Log No. 05–2470–68, p. 28.

21. Note that by southern armed forces and people they meant the Viet Cong and NLF. On April 27, 1969, Radio Hanoi denounced as a "farce" the search by the South for the burial place of "the hooligan lackeys who had owed blood debts to the Tri Thien Hue compatriots and who were annihilated by the southern armed forces and people in early Mau Than spring."

22. "Execution of Captured VC," telegram from the Secretary of State to the U.S. Ambassador in Saigon, Apr. 19, 1968.

23. "Plans for the Offensive and Uprising," p. 10.

24. Vennema, *Viet Cong Massacre*, pp. 98–9.

25. Pike, *Strategy of Terror*, p. 48.

26. See Vennema, *Viet Cong Massacre*, p. 140. As well, three Communist defectors stated that they had witnessed the killings. Pike, *Strategy of Terror*, p. 49.

27. C.f. Seymour M. Hersh, *My Lai 4: A Report on the Massacre and Its Aftermath* (New York: Random House, 1970).

28. "U.S. Says Enemy Report Put Hue Toll at 2,900," *New York Times*, Nov. 25, 1969.

29. *Congressional Record*, Dec. 3, 1969, pp. H11667–8.

30. The briefing materials and after-action review are available at the U.S. Army Center of Military History, Ft. Lesley J. McNair, Washington, D.C.

31. Richard Homan, "Pentagon Briefs Lawmakers on Hue Massacre," *Washington Post*, Dec. 9, 1969, p. A8.

32. Roche, OHP Interview.

33. James Jones, "In the Shadow of Peace," *New York Times Sunday Magazine*, June 10, 1973, p. 17.

34. Pike, *Strategy of Terror*, p. 43.

35. "Peace and Violence," *New York Times*, Sept. 15, 1973, p. 31. Solzhenitsyn's real crime from the liberal point of view was pointing out the "hypocritical, clamorous rage" displayed by Democrats over Watergate when such activities were obviously part of the political system all along and had previously remained "happily undiscovered."

36. Jones, "In the Shadow of Peace," p, 17.

37. D. Gareth Porter and Len E. Ackland, "Vietnam: The Bloodbath Argument," *Christian Century*, Nov. 9, 1969.

38. *Congressional Record*, Feb. 19, 1975, pp. S2189–94. See also Edward Herman and D. Gareth Porter, "The Myth of the Hue Massacre," *Ramparts*, May-June 1975, pp. 1–4.

39. Fallaci, *Nothing*, p. 191.

> Sant' Anna di Stazzema—On August 12, 1944, 560 Italian villagers were killed by retreating SS troops.
>
> Marzabotto—Over 750 Italian civilians were killed by the SS in the fall of 1944 in reprisal for alleged support of anti-Nazi guerrillas.
>
> Lidice—a town northwest of Prague in which 192 men and boys were killed on June 10, 1942, and the women and children were sent to concentration camps as reprisal for the assassination of Nazi leader Richard Heydrich.

Babi Yar—a location near Kiev that was the site of 100,000 killings of civilians by the Nazis, notably 33,771 Jewish civilians over the course of September 29–30, 1941.

Ardeatine ditches or caves—355 Italian civilians were gunned down by the SS outside Rome on March 24, 1944.

40. On those incidents:

Katyn—In 1940 on Stalin's order the NKVD murdered over 22,000 people, mostly Polish POWs and several thousand Ukrainians and Byelorussians. Over half the Polish officer corps was wiped out.

Malmedy—Around 500 American POWs and Belgian civilians, most famously 120 soldiers of the American 285th Field Artillery Observation Battalion, were killed by Kampfgruppe Peiper of the 6th SS Panzer Army near Malmedy, Belgium, in several incidents in mid-December 1944, during the Battle of the Bulge.

41. Neil Sheehan review of Mark Lane's *Conversations with Americans*, in *New York Times Book Review*, Dec. 27, 1970, pp. 5, 19.

42. "Anti-War YouTube 'Vet' Admits He Is Faker," ABC News "The Blotter," Sept. 21, 2007.

43. Charles J. Hanley, "No Gun Ri source wasn't there, records show," *Charleston Gazette*, May 26, 2000.

44. C.f. Scott Thomas (pseudo.), "Shock Troops," *The New Republic*, July 23, 2007, p. 56. See also James S. Robbins, "Shattered Diarist," *National Review Online*, Oct. 25, 2007.

45. Arthur Koestler, "On Disbelieving Atrocities," *New York Times Magazine*, Jan. 1944.

46. Solzhenitsyn, "Peace and Violence," p. 31.

CHAPTER XIII

1. See John Prados and Ray W Stubbe, *Valley of Decision: The Siege of Khe Sanh* (Boston: Houghton Mifflin, 1991).

2. Clark Dougan and Stephen Weiss, et al., *Nineteen Sixty-Eight* (Boston: Boston Publishing Company, 1983), p. 42.

3. William C. Westmoreland, *A Soldier Reports* (New York: Doubleday, 1976), p. 236.

4. C.f. Jacob Van Staaveren, *Interdiction in Southern Laos, 1961–1968* (Washington, D.C.: Center of Air Force History, 1993).

5. The Hill Fights took place Apr. 28–May 11, 1967.

6. Michael MacLear, *The 10,000 Day War: Vietnam* (New York: St. Martin's Press, 1981), p. 192.

7. Westmoreland, *A Soldier Reports*, p. 317.

8. Giap was not present at the battle, but Khe Sanh may have been his contribution to the Tet plan. The battle as it was executed does not integrate well with the rest of the plan and may have been Giap's attempt to recreate a Dien Bien Phu, to prove the value of the conventional assault. If so, the proponents of the Dien Bien Phu analogy were on the right track, although they may not have known why.

9. MacLear, *10,000 Day War*, p. 197. A small study group convened by Westmoreland at the suggestion of General Wheeler briefly examined the possibility of using tactical nuclear weapons as a contingency matter, but the suggestion was dropped out of concern that even discussing it might become a political issue.

10. Quoted in MacLear, *10,000 Day War*, p. 191.

11. MacLear, *10,000 Day War*, p. 190.

12. Ibid.

13. Hugh Sidey, "The Presidency: A Long Way from Spring," *Time*, Feb. 9, 1968, p. 16.

14. Fall was killed on February 21, 1967, by a mine while on a patrol with Marines 14 miles northwest of Hue.

15. Michael Herr, *Dispatches* (New York: Alfred A. Knopf, 1977), pp. 99–100.

16. Karl E. Meyer, "A Strangled Cry for Eternal Bums," *Washington Post*, Oct. 6, 1962, p. A8.

17. "U.S. Claims Victory at Conthien," *Washington Post*, Oct. 5, 1967, p. A1.

18. "The Analogy of Dienbienphu," *Washington Post*, Feb. 10, 1968, p. A6.

19. Quoted in MacLear, *10,000 Day War*, p. 193.

20. "Langvei," *Washington Post*, Feb. 9, 1968, p. A1.

21. The T-34 remained in production until 1958, and though obsolete as a main battle tank in the Soviet inventory, it was widely used in the developing world, especially in the Soviet bloc. The T-34 was still in the North Vietnamese inventory in the 1990s, primarily as a training platform.

22. William Beecher, "Latest Soviet Tanks Used by Enemy Near Khesanh," *New York Times*, Feb. 8, 1968, p. 1.

23. Don Sider, "Khe Sanh—Ready to Fight," *Time*, Feb. 16, 1968.

24. Eddie Adams interview, undated, Item #1770101001, The Vietnam Archive, Texas Tech University.

25. Tuohy, *Dangerous Company*, p. 129.

26. Ibid., p. 133.

27. Ibid., p. 132.

28. MacLear, *10,000 Day War*, p. 194.

29. USMC KC-130F BuNo 149813 crashed on February 10, 1968, when ground fire ignited an on-board fuel bladder. The scene was recorded on film in full color and appeared on network news.

30. In this respect the Khe Sanh coverage was similar to the ABC News "America Held Hostage" nightly updates in 1979–1980 about the American hostages being held in Iran, which made Ted Kopple's career and helped end Jimmy Carter's presidency. The updates morphed into "ABC News Nightline."

31. MacLear, *10,000 Day War*, p. 200.

32. Quoted in Westmoreland, *A Soldier Reports*, pp. 335–6.

33. Quoted in Clayton Fritchey, "Is Khe Sanh Battle Really Needed?" *The Yuma Daily Sun*, Mar. 13, 1968, p. 4.

34. "Soldiers Wanted to Attack," AP, May 27, 1968.

35. See Sorley, *A Better War*.

36. "U.S. Says Khe Sanh Abandonment Not Military Loss," AP, June 27, 1968.

37. "Hanoi Says Troops at Khe Sanh Base," AP, July 9, 1968.

38. "Khe Sanh Abandonment Boosts Red Propaganda," AP, July 13, 1968.

CHAPTER XIV

1. Bui Tin, *Following Ho Chi Minh*, p. 62.

2. Rupert Cornwell, "The War on Terror: Fourth of July Celebrations Dampened by the Mood Over the War in Iraq," *The Independent*, July 5, 2003, p. 2.

3. CNN Live, June 24, 2004. McGovern was a virulent critic of the Administration's use of intelligence in the lead-up to the war in Iraq, founder of Veteran Intelligence Professionals for Sanity (VIPS), and a spokesman for the antiwar group "Not in Our Name," for which he served war crimes indictments on the Bush White House from a "people's tribunal."

4. Susan Paynter, "Sowing Changes from a Texas Ditch," *Seattle Post-Intelligencer*, Aug. 10, 2005, p. D1.

5. Michael Wolff, "Survivor: The White House Edition," *Vanity Fair*, Dec. 2006, p. 194.

6. "Countdown," MSNBC, Nov. 27, 2006.

7. *Variety*, Nov. 27, 2006.

8. "Hannity & Colmes," Fox News Network, Nov. 27, 2006.

9. Michael Learmouth, "Couric Strafes Iraq War," *Daily Variety*, Sept. 26, 2007, p. 15. Couric had previously stated, "I think the situation [in Iraq] is so dangerous, and as a single parent with two children, that's something I won't be doing," which dampened her potential credibility as a military expert.

10. See Jeffery Alan Smith, *War and Press Freedom: The Problem of Prerogative Power* (New York: Oxford University Press, 1999). Sherman was famous for his dislike of reporters and had Thomas Knox of the *New York Herald* arrested for reporting a Union setback at the Battle of Chickasaw Bluffs.

11. Quoted in Page, "The Shots Seen Round the World," p. C01.

12. Browne's best known work is his award-winning photograph of the self-immolation of Buddhist monk Thich Quang Duc in Saigon, June 11, 1963.

13. Jennings was not an American in 1989. The Canadian-born reporter did not become a naturalized American citizen until 2003.

14. "Under Orders, Under Fire," PBS "Ethics in America" series, taped Oct. 31, 1987.

15. Quoted in Bailey, *The Vietnam War According to,* p. 191.

16. Joe Galloway, "The Military and the Media: One Man's Experience," address to the Air War College, Oct. 22, 1996.

17. Jonathan Alter, "In Bed with the Pentagon," *Newsweek*, Mar. 10, 2003, p. 45.

18. Goodhart, *Vietnam—Autumn Reflections*, p. 15.

19. Peter Braestrup, Lyndon Baines Johnson Library Oral History Collection, Mar. 1, 1982.

20. Quoted in Georgie Anne Geyer, "Vietnam Media Reality an Uncommon Wisdom," *Kerrville (TX) Times*, Nov. 20, 1990, p. 4.

21. Bailey, *The Vietnam War According to*, p. 398.

22. See, for example, the essay of the same name in Michael J. Arlen, *The Living Room War* (New York: Penguin, 1982).

23. See Bailey, *The Vietnam War According to*, p. 61.

24. Quoted in Davidson, *Vietnam at War*, p, 485.

25. Peter Braestrup, Lyndon Baines Johnson Library Oral History Collection, Mar. 1, 1982.

26. Lester Bernstein, "Does Agnew Tell It Straight?" *Newsweek*, Nov. 24, 1969, p. 92.

27. John P. Roche, "A Word Edgewise," King Features Syndicate, Oct. 17, 1977.

28. Peter Braestrup, *The Big Story: How the American Press and Television Reported and Interpreted the Crisis of Tet 1968 in Vietnam and Washington*, 2 vols. (Boulder, CO: Westview Press, 1977).

29. Ibid. Braestrup won the 1977 Society of Professional Journalists' Distinguished Service Award for *The Big Story*, but the overwhelming reaction from the media establishment was silence. Braestrup's opus was too detailed to rebut, so it was ignored. "If Braestrup had documented a massive media cover-up of Richard Nixon and his myrmidons, an enormous howl would have arisen, complete with demands for an investigation," John P. Roche wrote. "Two foundations would have rushed to sponsor private, non-partisan commissions loaded with eminent citizens to conduct an inquest. A 90-minute TV special would rush Bill Moyers to the scene of the crime. Instead the reaction has been—silence. The networks, which really got a pasting, haven't even bothered to react." "A Word Edgewise," King Features Syndicate, Oct. 17, 1977.

30. See content analysis in Daniel C. Hallin, "The Media, the War in Vietnam, and Political Support: A Critique of the Thesis of an Oppositional Media," *The Journal of Politics*, Feb. 1984, pp. 8, 10.

31. C.f. Lyle Johnston, *"Good Night, Chet": A Biography of Chet Huntley* (Jefferson, NC: McFarland & Co., 2003), pp. 86–94.

32. Quoted in Bailey, *The Vietnam War According to*, p. 182.

33. It would be interesting to see a new version of that 1950s series with coverage of World War II using the modern lens, particularly the segments where Nazis are given equal time to get their points across, strategic bombing is declared a war crime, and D-Day is reported as a major defeat after the first day's casualties.

34. Lumet later directed the 1976 feature *Network*, which not only sought to dramatize just how corruptible the news profession was, but also accurately predicted the descent of TV news from information to infotainment to undisguised entertainment mixed with occasional dramatic fiction.

35. One of the earliest uses of the expression "Walter Cronkite Moment" was in a 1997 article on British journalist Martyn Lewis's tearful reaction to the death of Princess Di. By this rendering, the original "moment" was in 1963, not 1968.

36. Dan Rather, "Covering the White House in Particular," *Quill*, Jan. 1972, p. 17.

37. Bailey, *The Vietnam War According to*, p. 217. Cronkite described the enemy as "Communists" in 28% of his stories. CBS in general used the word "Communist" to refer to the enemy in 29% of news stories, against 14% for ABC and 12% for NBC.

38. Walter Cronkite, *A Reporter's Life* (New York: Alfred A. Knopf, 1996), p. 242.

39. Quoted in Bailey, *The Vietnam War According to*, p. 298.

40. Cronkite, *A Reporter's Life*, p. 256.

41. Cronkite certainly did not mean to cast the North Vietnamese in the role of the U.S. 101st Airborne, who were defending Bastogne, and the Marines in the role of the attacking German Army. Also of note is that in April 1968 the 101st Airborne established Fire Support Base Bastogne 16 miles west-southwest of Hue to support Operation Delaware in the Au Shau valley.

42. Cronkite, *A Reporter's Life*, p. 257. The notion that the purpose of the conflict had never adequately been explained was developed toward the end of the war as a means of giving cover to members

of Congress and the media who sought to avoid culpability. It is now taken as a given that the Vietnam War was the product either of deception or stupidity.

43. Cronkite, *A Reporter's Life*, p. 259.

44. Jack Gould, "U.S. Is Losing War in Vietnam, NBC Declares," *New York Times*, Mar. 11, 1968, p. 82.

45. C.f. Cronkite, *A Reporter's Life*, pp. 258 ff. Bill Moyers is the main source for this story. Cronkite quotes Press Secretary George Christian saying, "It didn't quite happen that way." A less famous but more apt moment was on May 1, 1970, when Paul Harvey, another, perhaps more genuine voice of Middle America, began a broadcast on Vietnam by saying, "Mr. President, I love you... but you're wrong." He was critiquing Richard Nixon's expansion of the war to include Communist bases in Cambodia. Nixon was not apparently affected.

46. "Poll Finds Rise in War Support From 61% to 74% in 2 Months," *New York Times*, Feb. 13, 1968, p. 5.

47. "Johnson's Rating on Vietnam Drops," *New York Times*, Feb. 14, 1968, p. 4.

48. "Johnson and the Hawks," *New York Times*, Feb. 18, 1968, p. 161.

49. Roche memo to LBJ, secret/eyes only, Feb. 26, 1968, author's personal collection.

50. Petraeus, *Lessons of Vietnam*, p. 107.

51. Gallup survey Dec. 11–16, 1965.

52. Gallup survey June 22–27, 1967.

53. Quoted in Petraeus, *Lessons of Vietnam*, p. 87, fn. 113.

54. C.f. James S. Robbins, "Afghanistan is Worth the Fight," *Washington Times*, Aug. 24, 2009, from which this discussion has been drawn.

55. Gallup, *The Gallup Poll*, p. 2125.

56. "Public Attitudes Toward the War in Iraq: 2003–2008," Pew Research Center Publications, Mar. 19, 2008.

57. Georgie Anne Geyer, "We got what we wanted; why aren't we happy?" *Tucson Citizen*, Dec. 12, 1977.

58. Theodore H. White, *The Making of the President: 1968* (New York: Atheneum Publishers, 1969).

CHAPTER XV

1. Verlyn Klinkenborg, "The Tet Offensive and the Scent of Memory," *New York Times*, Mar. 22, 1998, p. 14.

2. President Johnson's Notes on Conversation with Secretary McNamara, Feb. 6, 1968, The Vietnam Archive, Texas Tech University. See also Larry Berman, *Lyndon Johnson's War: The Road to Stalemate in Vietnam* (New York: Norton, 1989), p. 155. McNamara probably would rather not have had Tet happen on his watch, given that he had already announced his departure from the Department of Defense. In his memoir he discusses the Tet Offensive in one sentence. He clearly felt no ownership of events by the spring of 1968. See Robert S. McNamara, *In Retrospect: The Tragedy and Lessons of Vietnam* (New York: Times Books, 1995), p. 315.

3. See Westmoreland, *A Soldier Reports*, p. 352.

4. Ellsberg, *Secrets*, p. 200.

5. See Gary Stone, *Elites for Peace: The Senate and the Vietnam War, 1964–1968* (Knoxville: University of Tennessee Press, 2007).

6. David Milne, *America's Rasputin: Walt Rostow and the Vietnam War* (New York: Hill and Wang, 2008).

7. See AP report on the events on Mar. 1, 1968; also LBJ comments Feb. 29, 1968, at the Governor's Dinner in Washington D.C., The Vietnam Archive, Texas Tech University.

8. Clark Clifford with Richard Holbrooke, *Counsel to the President* (New York: Random House, 1991), p. 485.

9. Ellsberg, *Secrets*, p. 202.

10. There were strong resonances of the Vietnam-era reinforcement debase during the discussion in the spring of 2007 of the new "Surge Strategy" in Iraq. Almost all attention focused on the numbers of troops to be sent, and little on the more significant and ultimately decisive question of the changes in U.S. counterinsurgency strategy.

11. Gallup survey June 22–27, 1967.

12. Fallaci, *Nothing*, p. 204.

13. "Poll of Democrats Finds Many Hawks Backed McCarthy," *New York Times*, Mar. 15, 1968.

14. Roche OHP interview. Johnson said this in a phone call to Roche the night before the primary.

15. Roche to LBJ, Mar. 14, 1968, author's personal collection. Roche noted that Johnson need not actively campaign at that point—"FDR in 1944 did not even go to the Convention."

16. UPI, Feb. 4, 1968.

17. Johnson, *Vantage Point*, p. 436.

18. Roche, OHP Interview.

19. "The Second Tet," *Time*, May 17, 1968.

20. Zhou curiously claimed that "Had [the North Vietnamese] statement been issued one or two days later, the murder [of King] might have been stopped," although it is unclear what he thought the linkage was, and he seems to be implying that King was killed intentionally by the government for some reason related to King's opposition to the war. This is another example of mirror-imaging, since any dissident of King's stature in Red China would have been quickly eliminated.

21. Discussion between Zhou Enlai and Pham Van Dong, Apr. 13, 1968, Cold War International History Project, document 5034CCB4–96B6–175C-9714D9C4E8278C7F.

22. Of note is that there was little difference between age cohorts. The youth, who are generally thought to have been more dovish, tracked with the national average. Those 30–49 years old were slightly more hawkish (44% to 38%); and the most dovish cohort were those 50 years and older, 43% doves and 38% hawks. There was also no partisan gap, as Republicans and Democrats tracked the national average. Gallup, *The Gallup Poll*, pp. 2124–5. By November 1969 the general number of doves outnumbered hawks 55% to 31%. Interestingly, the percentage of doves among those aged 21–29 and 50 years and older was almost identical (58%/57%). At the time, Richard Nixon enjoyed a 77% approval rating on handling the war, a higher rating than the highest of LBJ's ratings. Ibid., pp. 2222–3.

23. Rostow interview with Culbert, undated, The Vietnam Archive, Texas Tech University.

CHAPTER XVI

1. The bridge was named for Phan Thanh Gian (1796–1867), a Vietnamese diplomat who failed to prevent the French from invading his country and took his own life by poison.

2.   Joseph B. Treaster, "Vietcong Press Saigon Attacks," *New York Times*, May 6, 1968, p. 1; "The Second Tet," *Time*, May 17, 1968.

3.   Andy Watson, "Military Police Heroism," *Military Police*, spring 2007.

4.   Gene Roberts, "Fires Sweeping Saigon Outskirts as Fighting Eases," *New York Times*, May 8, 1968, p. 1.

5.   Joseph B. Treaster, "Investigators Confirm U.S. Rocket Killed Six Saigon Officials," *New York Times*, June 5, 1968, p. 15.

6.   See Ronald H. Spector, *After Tet* (New York: The Free Press, 1993), p. 164; Ky, *Buddha's Son*, p. 270.

7.   Tran Van Hai was a general commanding the 7th Division at the end of the war. On April 30, 1975, as Saigon fell to the Communists, he committed suicide by poison, perhaps emulating Phan Thanh Gian (see above).

8.   Bernard Weinraub, "Ousters in Saigon a Setback for Ky," *New York Times*, June 9, 1968, p. 3.

9.   In 1968 Loan told Adams, "My wife gave me hell for not taking the film from the photographer who took the picture. She thought that was all that was on my mind, taking film from a photographer." Eddie Adams interview, undated, Item #1770101001, The Vietnam Archive, Texas Tech University.

10.   Lloyd Shearer, "The Strange Treatment of General Loan," *Parade*, June 29, 1969, p. 7.

11.   "Mailer, 'White Hope' Win Pulitzer Prizes," *Washington Post*, May 6, 1969, p. A1. Norman Mailer won that year in nonfiction for *The Armies of the Night*, his account of the 1967 Pentagon antiwar demonstrations.

12.   "Surgery for Viet 'Murderer' Hit," *Oakland Tribune*, May 14, 1969, p. 6.

13.   Claudia Levy, "Viet General's Visit Scored," *Washington Post*, May 15, 1969, p. A8. In April 1969, Vu Ngoc Hoan, ARVN Surgeon General, had written to General Fred Hughes, the Commanding General of Walter Reed Hospital in Washington, stating that General Loan was "being assigned by the government of Vietnam to the Vietnamese embassy in Washington" and asked for medical help to be provided Loan during his stay.

14.   "Saigon's Gen. Loan Given Defense Post," *Washington Post*, Aug. 3, 1970, p. A13. Note that every newspaper article about General

Loan contextualized him by mentioning Eddie Adams's photograph. The photo had by this time completely defined him for the world.

15. Buckley, "Despot," p. 68.

16. "S. Viet's killer-cop has become gentle as a kitten," AP, Dec. 26, 1972.

17. Ibid.

18. Ibid.

19. Linda White, "One Picture Time Cannot Erase," *Baltimore Sun*, Feb. 1, 1998, p. 2A. By 1975 the Loans had five children.

20. Patricia Camp, "Saigon Police Chief Now Runs Burke Café," *Washington Post*, April 28, 1976, p. C1.

21. John L. Hart, "The Attempt to Deport Gen. Loan," *Washington Post*, Nov. 12, 1978, p. B6.

22. "The Executioner," *Newsweek*, Nov. 13, 1978, p. 70.

23. Christopher Dickey, "U.S. Acts to Deport Saigon Official Who Killed Bound Prisoner in 1968," *Washington Post*, Nov. 3, 1978, p. A1.

24. Christopher Dickey, "Sympathy Expressed for Ex-Gen. Loan," *Washington Post*, Nov. 4, 1978, p. C5. It is unclear to whom the Congressman was referring when he said "enough guys like that."

25. "Exiles Fight Ouster of Viet 'Criminal,'" AP, Nov. 2, 1978.

26. Dickey, "Sympathy Expressed," p. C5.

27. "Moral Turpitude," *Washington Post*, Nov. 5, 1978 p. D6. Emphasis in original.

28. "The Case of Nguyen Ngoc Loan," *New York Times*, Nov. 13, 1978, p. 22.

29. "Exiles Fight Ouster," AP, Nov. 2, 1978.

30. Dickey, "Sympathy Expressed," p. C5.

31. Hart, "The Attempt to Deport Gen. Loan," p. B6.

32. Dickey, "Sympathy Expressed," p. C5.

33. Martin Tolchin, "Carter Will Not Seek to Deport Former Vietnam General, Aide Says," *New York Times*, Dec. 2, 1978, p. 20.

34. Interviewed in Bob Edwards, "South Vietnam General Dies," NPR Morning Edition, July 16, 1998, Transcript # 98071612–210.

35. Adams quoted in Arnold Abrams, "Turning Point," *Newsday*, Feb. 2, 1998, p. B3.

36. Buckley, "Despot," p. 72.

37. "Ten Years Later a Photo Haunts Men and Nation," *Washington Post*, Dec. 17, 1978, p. SM5. Over the years Adams thought about whether he'd take that picture again, knowing the effect it would have on Loan, and later concluded he probably would, saying, "It's my job." Steve Fennessy, "A behind-the-lens vet of 13 wars to speak here," *Rochester Democrat and Chronicle*, Dec. 1, 1999, p. 1C.

38. Liz Nakahara, "Pulitzers: The Power and the Pressure," *Washington Post*, Sept. 12, 1982, p. G1.

39. Buell, "On 'Easy Ed' Adams," Oct. 2004.

40. Fennessy, "A behind-the-lens vet," p. 1C.

41. Dave Saltonstall, "War photographer tells of regret over picture," *South China Morning Post*, Oct. 15, 1993, p. 14.

42. Fennessy, "A behind-the-lens vet," p. 1C.

43. George Judson, "Stepping Out From the Lens Of History," *New York Times*, Oct. 11, 1995, p. B1. Kim Phuc was exploited by the victorious Communist Vietnamese for propaganda purposes until defecting to Canada in 1992.

44. Buell, "On 'Easy Ed' Adams," Oct. 2004. On Barnstorm, see Judson, " Stepping Out," Oct. 11, 1995, and Jay DeFoore and David Walker, "In Memoriam: Eddie Adams, 71" *Photo District News*, Nov. 2004, p. 20.

45. Quoted in White, "One picture time cannot erase," p. 2A.

46. Nakahara, "Pulitzers," p. G1.

47. Interviewed in Edwards, "South Vietnam General Dies," NPR, Transcript # 98071612–210.

48. *Washington Post*, Apr. 19, 1985, p. A15.

49. Interviewed in Edwards, "South Vietnam General Dies," NPR, Transcript # 98071612–210.

50. Fallaci, *Nothing*, p. 91. See also "An Interview with the Most Hated Man in Saigon," *Look*, June 25, 1968.

51. Eddie Adams, "Eulogy," *Time*, July 27, 1998, p. 19.

52. It had been a tradition at *Parade* for Adams to photograph the Labor Day cover each year, to promote awareness of the Jerry Lewis Muscular Dystrophy telethon; ALS was one of the deadliest of that class of disease.

53. Saltonstall, "War photographer tells of regret over picture," p. 14.

CHAPTER XVII

1. Edward J. Epstein, *TV Guide*, Oct. 6, 1973.

2. Considering that two of those were incumbent landslides, they did very poorly.

3. VNA: General Giap on American War and its Historical Lessons SEP20050429000082 Hanoi VNA (Internet Version-WWW) in English 29 Apr 05.

4. Tran Van Tra, *Vietnam: History of the Bulwark B2 Theater: Concluding the 30 Years War* (Ho Chi Minh City: Van Nghe Publishing House, 1982). An English language version of General Tra's essay on the Tet Offensive is found as "Tet: The 1968 General Offensive and General Uprising" in Jayne S. Werner and Luu Doan Huynh, eds., *The Vietnam War: Vietnamese and American Perspectives* (New York: M.E. Sharpe, 1993), pp. 37–65.

5. Quoted in *New York Review of Books*, Oct. 21, 1982.

6. Bui Tin/Young interview, 1995.

7. Roche, OHP interview.

8. Rostow interview with Culbert, undated, The Vietnam Archive, Texas Tech University.

9. Conversation Between President Nixon and his Assistant for National Security Affairs (Kissinger), U.S. Department of State, *Foreign Relations of the United States, 1969 to 1976*, vol. XIV, Soviet Union, Oct. 1971–May 1972, eds. David C. Geyer, Nina D. Howland, Kent Sieg (Washington, D.C.: U.S. GPO, 2006), p. 749.

10. C.f. Sorley, *A Better War*.

ACKNOWLEDGMENTS

The author would like to express gratitude to those who helped at various stages of this project, including Erik Villard at the U.S. Army Center of Military History, Dave Spencer at the Center for Hemispheric Defense Studies, John Williamson at the Congressional Research Service, Ambassador Bui Diem, Professor Nguyen Ngoc Bich, and Colonel Tranh Minh Cong. Also Sven Kraemer for his wisdom and guidance, and John P. Roche for hours of conversations setting the record straight.

INDEX